A Tra Course for TEFL

Peter Hubbard
Hywel Jones
Barbara Thornton
Rod Wheeler

Oxford University Press

Oxford University Press
Walton Street, Oxford OX2 6DP

Oxford New York Toronto Madrid
Delhi Bombay Calcutta Madras Karachi
Kuala Lumpur Singapore Hong Kong Tokyo
Nairobi Dar es Salaam Cape Town
Melbourne Auckland

and associated companies in
Berlin Ibadan

OXFORD and OXFORD ENGLISH are trade marks of
Oxford University Press

ISBN 0 19 432710 8

© Peter Hubbard, Hywel Jones, Barbara Thornton, and
Rod Wheeler 1983.

First published 1983
Eleventh impression 1993

Illustrations by Anne Morrow
Handwriting by Avril Taylor

The publishers would like to thank the following for permission
to reproduce photographs:

Bonar and Flotex Ltd.
Frank Gayton Advertising Ltd.
Habitat Designs Ltd.
Hoover Ltd.
The National Magazine Company Ltd.
Rolex Watch Co. Ltd.

While every effort was made, the publishers were unable to trace
and clear copyright on the photograph reproduced on page 96.

Printed in Hong Kong

Contents

Contents

Introduction

This book is for teachers of English as a second or foreign language teaching anywhere in the world, under any circumstances.

However, the book was written in response to a demand from teachers of EFL (particularly from non-native speakers) for an up-to-date and clear-cut statement on the principles and practice of TESL/TEFL. The majority of teachers of EFL in the world are not in fact native speakers. And, while their level of English is adequate to teach their classes, it may not be good enough to cope with standard books on the subject.

In any case such teachers all too often find these books academic and seemingly irrelevant. Then again, there are so many books on ESL/EFL at present, all presenting different points of view, that there is a need for a guide to the reading matter available. Otherwise there is a danger that teachers will extract sufficient practical ideas and suggestions to become adequate 'technicians', but never really grasp the principles that underlie modern practice. Among other things, this would prevent them from becoming innovators themselves or contributors to the technology, which would be a pity, because such teachers are in the best position to see how well new techniques and materials work in practice. The gap between the 'expert' and the practitioner would become wider.

In this book, then, we have attempted to set out the basic principles, simply and clearly; to provide a guide to key passages in the literature; and to offer a framework which links together the ideas contained in those passages. However, since many of these ideas are controversial, we have attempted, wherever possible, to encourage readers to arrive at their own conclusions by setting exercises, problems and questions for discussion.

It will also be seen that, while we have been primarily concerned with setting out the theoretical background, we have not neglected the practical side. Most of the theoretical points are illustrated with practical examples or suggestions. And some sections of the book are designed to provide a series of 'recipes' for successful teaching activities.

We believe the book is versatile enough to suit a wide range of needs. Here are some possible ways in which it could be used:

1 As a basic textbook for the non-native speaking teacher under-going in-service (or initial) training outside Britain;
2 As a starting-point for the teacher trainer faced with the prospect of designing a course;
3 As an introduction to the theoretical principles of ESL/EFL for the native speaker undergoing initial training;
4 As a source-book of practical suggestions for any teacher of ESL/EFL in any part of the world.

The chapters in the book are intended to follow a logical progression of ideas and may be read through in normal sequence. However, there is nothing to prevent teachers or teacher trainers from using sections of the book in any order which suits them. In this case, technical terms introduced earlier in the book can be found in the GLOSSARY at the end or the INDEX will provide reference to the passages where they first occur.

Note that throughout this book teachers are referred to as 'he', 'his', and 'him'. We do this to avoid the clumsy repetition of 'his or her' etc. and also because, from a linguistic point of view, 'he' is the neutral or 'unmarked' term. In other words, it refers to teachers in general, both male and female.

Footnote

The book is based on the experience of the authors in training non-native speakers for the *Royal Society of Arts Certificate for Overseas Teachers of English (COTE)*. Since this qualification is attracting increasing attention and centres for courses leading to the Certificate are being established in different parts of the world, we have included references to COTE exam questions. In our experience, the COTE scheme is an extremely promising development and we would recommend that overseas teacher training centres consider it as a possible means of establishing a worldwide standard in EFL teaching for non-native speakers.

Acknowledgments

The authors would like to thank all the people who helped in the development of this book. In particular, we are grateful to the RSA COTE course in Nicosia 1979-1981. Thanks are also due to Noel Brookes for his ideas on songs and reading games; to Ian Forth for ideas on making visuals move; and to Pat Charalambides for suggestions on early writing and copying activities.

1 First principles

A look at some common techniques

In this chapter we are going to be looking at a number of basic techniques used effectively in EFL classrooms all over the world. Teachers should know how to use these techniques, but it is also important that they should know something about their background: how they developed historically and what theoretical principles they are based on.

Each of the following fragments (A – D) of English classes in progress illustrates a different technique commonly used in the EFL classroom. After each fragment, there are a number of questions, exercises and discussion points.

FRAGMENT A
(Students have just read a text about Mrs Black and can see a picture in the book.)

Teacher:	Right! Now, Mrs Black is in the supermarket. She's shopping. She's got a trolley. What's in it? Lots of things. Listen! *She's got some butter. She hasn't got any sugar.* *She's got some butter. She hasn't got any sugar.* *Some butter... any sugar. Some butter... any sugar.* *Some... any. Some... any.* How do we use these words? Listen again! *She's got some bread. She hasn't got any tea.* *She's got some butter. She hasn't got any sugar.* Let's see if you can do it. Marios! *Butter.*
Marios:	She's got some butter.
Teacher:	Good! Theresa! *Tea.*
Theresa:	She hasn't got some tea.
Teacher:	Um... Is that right?

Anna: No!
            She hasn't got any tea.
Teacher: Good, Anna. Again, Theresa!
Theresa: She hasn't got any tea.
Teacher: Good! Now, when do we use *some* and when do we use *any*?
            Well, let's look at it like this.
            (*He writes sentences on the blackboard.*)

	not / n't
She's got <u>some</u> bread.	She hasn't got <u>any</u> tea.
She's got <u>some</u> butter.	She hasn't got <u>any</u> sugar.

            Do you understand this?
Students: Yes!
Teacher: Good! Well, let's try it with another word. Look at the picture.
            What's in the trolley?
            Antonis, *coffee.*
Antonis: She hasn't got any coffee.
Teacher: Good!
            Sofia, *ice-cream.*
Sofia: She's got some ice-cream.
Teacher: Very good, Sofia!
            Do you all understand now? I think you do.
            Let's try something else. Ask me a question, Anna. *Coffee.*
Anna: Has she got any coffee?
Teacher: Good! Did she say *some* or *any*? Ask it again, Anna.
Anna: Has she got any coffee?
Students: Any.
Teacher: Right! So we can now write up this...

	not / n't	?
She's got <u>some</u> bread.	She hasn't got <u>any</u> tea.	Has she got <u>any</u> coffee?
She's got <u>some</u> butter.	She hasn't got <u>any</u> sugar.	Has she got <u>any</u> flour?

In this fragment, the main technique used by the teacher was giving the students a *grammatical rule*: the rule about how to use *some* and *any* in English.

Points for discussion

1 How did the teacher actually give the students the rule? (Mark in pencil the part of the fragment where he started giving the rule.)

2 What did the teacher do before he gave the rule? Would it have been better to give the complete rule right at the beginning of the fragment? Give reasons for your answer.

3 In your own words, as briefly as possible, describe the rule for the use of *some* and *any* in English.

4 Now give a simple and clear rule which might help your students to do one of the following:

Use *in*, *on* and *at* correctly as prepositions of *place*.
Form the comparatives of adjectives.
Find the correct word order in sentences.
Use the past continuous tense (*was/were -ing*) correctly.
Form question-tags (*wasn't he? ..., did he?*) correctly.

Now that you have done this exercise, would you say that giving clear, simple rules of grammar is always easy?

Exercise

Consult the *University Grammar of English* (see Bibliography) Sections 7.35, 7.46 & 7.47 and make a list of exceptions to the rule about *some* and *any* you gave in answer to question 3 above. To what level of student would you give these exceptions, basic, intermediate or advanced?

FRAGMENT B

(Again the students have read a text and have a picture to look at.)

Teacher:	Right, everybody! Listen and repeat!
	She's got some bread.
Students:	She's got some bread.
Teacher:	Again. *She's got some bread.*
Students:	She's got some bread.
Teacher:	Good! Marios?
Marios:	She's got some bread.
Teacher:	Good! Anna?
	(Students repeat the pattern individually round the class.)
Teacher:	Everybody! *She's got some bread.*
Students:	She's got some bread.
Teacher:	*Butter...*
Students:	She's got some butter.
Teacher:	Good! *Flour.*
Students:	She's got some flour.
Teacher:	Very good!
	Now listen and repeat! *She hasn't got any tea.*
Students:	She hasn't got any tea.
Teacher:	Right! Theresa?
Theresa:	She hasn't got any tea.
Teacher:	Good! Antonis?
Antonis:	She hasn't got any tea.
Teacher:	Good! Now, Anna. *Sugar.*
Anna:	She hasn't got any sugar.

Teacher:	Very good!
	Now listen, everybody. Listen and repeat!
	She's got some bread, but she hasn't got any tea.
Students:	She's got some bread, but she hasn't got any tea.
Teacher:	Very good! Now, *butter... sugar.*
Students:	She's got some butter, but she hasn't got any sugar.
Teacher:	Good!
	(He continues in this way using different words – *butter, coffee,* etc. until everybody seems to be producing the pattern correctly.)

Activities

1 This technique really has two stages to it. Mark the place in the text where the teacher switches from the first stage to the second – i.e. where the activity changes slightly. (This happens more than once in the fragment.)

2 What exactly does this technique consist of? Describe the stages as they occur.

3 Comparing this technique to the one used in fragment A, could we say that each would be suited to a different type of student? If so, what type of student and why?

4 What are the advantages and disadvantages of using this technique with a large class (i.e. more than 30 students)?

5 Could the teacher have used a tape-recorder effectively to teach this lesson, using this technique? Describe ways in which a tape-recorder might help.

FRAGMENT C
(*The students have in front of them a large picture of Mrs Black in the supermarket. They are familiar with this character.*)

Teacher:	(*points*) Now, who's this?
Marios:	Mrs Black.
Teacher:	Yes. Where is she?
Theresa:	In the supermarket.
Teacher:	Good. What's she doing?
Anna:	She's shopping.
Teacher:	Yes, she's shopping. Look at her trolley. What's in it? (*points*)
Antonis:	Bread.
Teacher:	Yes. And ... (*points*)
Sofia:	Butter.
Teacher:	That's right. *She's got some butter.* Repeat, everybody!
Students:	She's got some butter.
	(*The teacher now does some choral and individual repetition of this model sentence.*)
Teacher:	Good! What about *bread?*

Marios:	She's got some bread.
Teacher:	Fine! *Soup?*
Anna:	She's got some soup.
Teacher:	Very good! What about sugar?
Theresa:	No.
Teacher:	No. *She hasn't got any sugar.* Repeat, everybody!
Students:	She hasn't got any sugar.
	(*More choral and individual repetition. The teacher then begins drilling by pointing at the picture or giving word cues.*)
Teacher:	(*points*)
Sofia:	She's got some bread.
Teacher:	Good. Coffee?
Antonis:	She hasn't got any coffee. (Etc., etc.)
	(*In the next stage, the teacher makes Anna empty her bag on to his desk. All students look at the objects on the desk.*)
Teacher:	Anna's got some books.
Students:	Yes.
Teacher:	What about sandwiches?
Theresa:	No, she hasn't got any sandwiches.
Teacher:	That's right. Tell me more, somebody.
Antonis:	She's got some pencils.
Teacher:	Very good, Antonis. Anything else?
Sofia:	She hasn't got any elephants.
	(*Laughter*)

Activities

1 The technique used here shows some similarities to that in fragment B. What are they?

2 In what respect(s) does this fragment differ from the two previous fragments?

3 In all three fragments so far, the teacher is aiming to get the students to produce correct examples of the pattern, but in fragment C he uses several slightly different methods to get the students to speak. What are these?

4 At the end of the fragment the teacher switches from practice on the picture to practice on a real situation in the classroom (when Anna empties her bag on the desk). What are the advantages of doing this? And what are the advantages of just changing to a different situation? (E.g. A different picture?)

5 At the end of the fragment Sofia says, 'She hasn't got any elephants.' Naturally the other students laugh. And yet her statement is both true and grammatically correct. The teacher should now say 'Good!'
What does this tell us about this kind of classroom practice?

FRAGMENT D
(The teacher shows the students a picture.)

Teacher:	Tell me about this picture.
Marios:	It's a shop.
Teacher:	Good!
Theresa:	She is a woman.
Teacher:	There's a woman, yes.
Anna:	Coffee... There's coffee.
Teacher:	Yes?
Antonis:	There's butter.
Teacher:	Yes, we can see coffee, butter, bread, sugar. Can we see books in the picture?
Students:	No.
Teacher:	No, it isn't a bookshop. It's a grocer's shop. Repeat, everybody! *Grocer's.*
Students:	Grocer's.
	(writes the word on the board)
Teacher:	In a grocer's shop we can buy *(shows them money)*... coffee, butter and things like that. What else can we buy?
Marios:	Tea?
Teacher:	Yes.
Anna:	Bread.
Teacher:	Yes.
	(Students go on giving examples using known vocabulary. When they run out of ideas, teacher shows flashcards of new items and teaches students the new words.)
Teacher:	Right! Now, listen everybody. We are in a grocer's shop. This *(indicates teacher's desk)* is a grocer's shop. Marios here is the shopkeeper. *(laughter – teacher installs Marios behind the desk)* Now, Marios. These are the things you've got in your shop *(Hands him a list)* OK? What have you got? Tell me one thing.
Marios:	I've got coffee.
Teacher:	Fine. Now, all the rest of you are buying things. Here are your shopping lists. *(Hands out cards to each student)* Right! Who wants to begin? Anna?
	(She comes up to the desk.)
Anna:	Hullo. I want tea.
Marios:	No. No, I haven't got tea. Sorry.
Anna:	Oh. Um ... Have you got butter?
Marios:	Yes. How many you want?
Anna:	Two. Yes. Thank you.
Teacher:	Good. Sit down now, both of you. Now let's listen to the tape. This lady is buying some things in the grocer's.

TAPE

Lady:	Oh, good morning.

Grocer:	Good morning. What can I do for you?
Lady:	Um... Have you got any coffee?
Grocer:	Yes, certainly. Here you are.
Lady:	Thank you. Um... What about butter?
Grocer:	Yes. We've got some butter. In the fridge over there.
Lady:	Good. Now, have you got any bread?
Grocer:	No, I'm sorry. We haven't got any bread today. Come tomorrow morning.

(Teacher plays the dialogue several times, checking for comprehension. Then he practises have got *and* some/any *with choral repetition and drilling from the picture.)*

Teacher:	Right! Now let's try buying things again. Have you got your shopping lists?
Marios:	Good morning.
Antonis:	Good morning. Have you got any sugar?
Marios:	Certainly. Here you are.

(Practice continues. Students take turns to be the shopkeeper and the teacher sorts out any problems which arise. Sometimes it is necessary to do some repetition and a little drilling.)

Activities

1 Mark the place in the fragment where the new language *(some/any)* was introduced for the first time.

2 What was happening before this? What was the purpose of these activities?

3 Suppose the tape-recording had been played near the beginning of the fragment. How do you think the lesson would have progressed? Describe the stages of practice that would have taken place.

4 What similarities does this fragment share with the previous one? What are the main differences?

5 Can you see any advantages in using this technique for introducing new language to your students?

These four fragments, A – D, are all examples of ways in which a teacher might introduce some new piece of language to the students. The term for this is *presentation;* and we talk about *presenting* a new language *item.* In this case, the new item was *some/any. Has/have got* was evidently an item already taught and familiar to the students – a *known item.*

We will now give a name to each of these techniques:

Technique A: Presentation by examples and grammatical explanation, plus drilling.
Technique B: Presentation of an oral model, plus drilling.

Technique C: Presentation of an oral model contextualized in a situation, plus drilling.
Technique D: Presentation through role-play, plus drilling.

In each fragment the teacher went on from presentation into practice – a practice activity we are all familiar with, the drill. We will be looking at *presentation* and *drilling* in more detail later on in this chapter.

Points for discussion

1 From your own experience in the classroom, which technique would you regard as most effective? (You will first have to agree on what you mean by 'effective'.)

2 Which of these techniques do you regularly use with your own classes? (Probably more than one.)

3 Are there any practical factors (e.g. large classes) which prevent you from using one or more of these techniques? Are there any practical reasons why you find one or more of these techniques particularly useful with your classes?

4 Putting yourself in the place of the student, which technique would you personally find most interesting? Satisfying? Effective? Explain why.

5 In fragment D, the new language was introduced in a tape-recording, not by the teacher himself, as in other fragments. Can you think of any advantages in introducing new language this way? Or disadvantages?

6 What other techniques do you sometimes use for presenting new items to your students? Explain exactly the procedure you follow.

7 In all these fragments, the model sentences containing the new items were presented as *sound* (either the teacher's voice or a tape-recording). Is there any reason why we should not present these in writing?

Language items

On page 10 we introduced the term language *item*. An item is a 'bit' of language we can teach our students. For example, the item being taught in fragments A -D was *some/any*.

What kinds of item are there? There are three obvious kinds: *structural* items; *lexical* items; and *phonological* items.

Structural items like *some/any, has/have got, there is/are*, are grammatical points about the language. We nearly always introduce these in the form of examples or model sentences. Textbook writers and teachers often call these *patterns;* and we hear terms like *pattern practice* or *pattern drilling.* Although a verb tense like the simple present tense is an important structural item, we would certainly not attempt to teach every form and usage of this tense in the same lesson; nor would they be likely to occur in the same unit of a textbook. So major items such as these are broken down into smaller items. For example we might teach first the *I,* *we,* and *they* statement forms:

I live, we go, they like, etc.

Then the *he, she* statement forms. Then possibly the *you* question form:

Do you like...? etc

This process of breaking down larger steps into smaller steps is called *structural grading.* The idea of large and small steps can be illustrated like this:

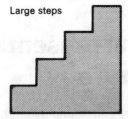
Large steps

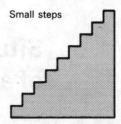
Small steps

Lexical item is simply another phrase for a new bit of vocabulary. If a word like *factory* comes up in the textbook for the first time, this is a new lexical item. Sometimes it is difficult to decide whether an item is structural or lexical. It is not just a question of whether the new item consists of more than one word. The preposition of place *in,* for example, is usually regarded as a structural item. On the other hand, the verb *look for* is clearly a lexical item.

Phonological items are new features of the sound system of the language. For example, the contrast between the vowel sounds in *sit* and *seat* is a phonological item. An intonation pattern, the way the voice rises and falls when we say a particular utterance, is another example. And so is the stress pattern of a word or utterance.

The teaching of lexical and phonological items will be considered in detail in later chapters. Here we are more concerned with structural items.

Points for discussion

Look at the textbook you use for beginners.

1 Is it structurally graded? If not, how is it organized?

2 If it is structurally graded, make a list of the structural items contained in the first five units (or 'lessons'). How many different

items are there in every unit? Which is/are the most important item(s) in each unit? In your experience, is there much new material in any of the first five units? (i.e. The steps are too large.)

3 How long would you spend teaching each important item? And how much time do you normally have to spend on a unit?

4 Does the same item come up again later in the book in any form, or is it assumed that once it has been taught it is known?

5 Could these items be taught in a different order from that which occurs in the book? Suggest a new order and discuss problems which this might cause.

6 When starting a new unit, do you follow exactly the order of the material in that unit of your book? Or do you follow a special order of your own? Give examples of the order you might follow, with reasons for this.

Situational presentation of a structure

When presenting a new structural item (or structure) we should be primarily trying to achieve two things:

1 to enable the students to recognize the new structure well enough to be able to produce it themselves (establish the *form*);
2 to make absolutely clear the usage of the patterns, so that when the students produce them, prompted by the teacher, they know what they are saying (establish the *meaning*).

The next stage, of course, which usually proceeds straight after the presentation, is for the students to produce the patterns themselves (drilling). But here we are concerned with this first stage of presenting the structure, in the form of an example or examples (models) to the students.

To achieve (1) above, the teacher must supply (either in his own voice or on tape) clear models of the structure. Not all teachers agree about the *amount* of exposure to the new patterns which should be given at this stage. Some believe that plenty of examples should be given or the same example repeated many times, often with the new forms spoken louder or with more emphasis. Others prefer to give less exposure to the patterns and force the students to work hard to pick them out. Another popular technique is for the teacher to slip the new forms into an earlier practice activity without focusing the students' attention on them or asking them to reproduce the patterns. Probably all these techniques work well in different circumstances and it is a good idea to experiment with all of them rather than choosing one and sticking to it.

An economical way of achieving (2) is for the teacher to present the models in a readily understandable *situation*, one which makes the meaning of the patterns clear. This situation might be live in the classroom *(Mario is sitting behind Anna)*; or it might be some true statement which is known by the students *(Mario has got two sisters. France is bigger than Spain)*; or it might be a fictional situation (such as events or a state of affairs in a picture or a text).

Practical exercise

Here is a list of structural items which are found in beginners' textbooks. Choose *one* and decide how you would present it to your students. Collect any materials you need (pictures, real objects, etc.) and demonstrate it in front of the other teachers. See if they agree that it is perfectly clear and the meaning unmistakable.

> *He, she* form of the simple present *(He goes,* etc.)
> *There is/are*
> *I, you, we, they* form of the present continuous
> *He's/she's got*
> *My, your, his, her*
> *Is it a...?*
> *Which (one)...?*
> *This is a pencil; that's a pen*

Do you have students who are coming up to a new structure in the book in a few days' time? If so, plan the presentation of that structure. Show it to other teachers to get their reaction.

Would you normally do your presentation at the beginning, in the middle or at the end of a lesson? Discuss this point with other teachers.

Reading assignment and exercises

Now read *Introduction to English Language Teaching* by John Haycraft, pages 31-35 (Section 4.2) on different methods of presentation.

1 Think of one structure which would be suitable for presenting in a dialogue (apart from the example in the book). Work out a suitable presentation for this. Give details of the stages you would follow in doing the presentation. (Section 4.2.3)

2 Do the same for a presentation through mime. (Section 4.2.5)

3 Do the same for a presentation through descriptions or narrative. (Section 4.2.6)

Repetition

In order to produce an utterance, the student must first hear it. Repetition is an activity which puts these two steps directly together. It is the simplest possible way of getting a student to produce foreign speech and, despite its limitations as a classroom technique, it is seldom a bad idea to resort to repetition when a practice exercise gets out of control or when the class as a whole show signs of getting into serious difficulties.

A Choral work

Points for discussion

Working in groups, try to answer these questions, if possible from your own teaching experience. You may get some ideas from the section on choral work on pages 32-33 of Donn Byrne's *Teaching Oral English.*

1 What difficulties would you anticipate in using choral drills with large classes?

2 Donn Byrne suggests that the class can be divided up into units for the purpose of choral work. How will doing this overcome any of the disadvantages you have mentioned above?

Give some examples of different ways of dividing your class. How well would these work in practice?

3 When doing choral repetition, what ways are there of making sure that the class starts speaking all together?

Try out the different ways on each other and list them in order of effectiveness.

4 Another problem teachers sometimes have is making sure students keep together while speaking. Possible ways of doing this are by conducting the class as if you were the conductor of an orchestra or by beating out the time. If you were beating time, where would you put the beats in the following sentences?

There's a post office next to the bank.
You should have come to the party.
Mr Brown and Jim can swim.
Mr Brown and Jim can't swim.
If it rains, he'll wear his raincoat.

Make up five more sentences which have the same structure as the sentences above and which also have the same beat or rhythm.

5 Donn Byrne (page 33) states that 'sentences for repetition must not be too long or too complicated, or have a rhythm which makes it difficult to say them in unison.'

Which of the following would you reject as being unsuitable for repetition by your students?

If he had gone in, he would have seen his wife cleaning the windows.
He oughtn't to have come to work late.
She usually drinks tea, but today she's drinking champagne.
Rod arranged to meet Megan outside the photographer's.
She sells shoes in Smith Street.

Activity

Which of the following points do you agree with?
Give reasons for your answers.

1 If asked to speak in chorus, the shy students will just say nothing.

2 When repeating chorally, it is very easy for a student to open and close his mouth without actually saying anything.

3 It is impossible for the teacher to hear if anyone is making a mistake even if fewer than twenty students are repeating chorally.

4 With a group smaller than twenty, it is much better for the teacher to say the sentence and then for each student to repeat it once, rather than for all students to repeat the sentence twenty times.

5 Choral work is only suitable for small children. Adults and adolescents find it silly.

6 Time spent doing choral work means that *all* the class are actively doing something and not merely listening to other students doing things.

B Individual repetition

Teachers often follow up choral work by getting students to repeat patterns or words individually. Often they intersperse choral repetition with individual repetition.

The practical considerations for individual repetition are the same as for choral repetition, but the teacher has more opportunity to pay attention to individual pronunciation problems and structural errors.

In a sense, repetition is a drill – the simplest possible kind of drill. But when we talk about drilling we usually mean something more elaborate. And that is the subject of the next section.

The anatomy of a drill

The time has come to look closely at the process of drilling. The drill is important because it is a technique used by almost every foreign language teacher at one time or another; and in some cases, rightly or wrongly, it constitutes the basis of their method.

So what are we doing when we drill?

The drill in the language classsroom derives directly from behaviourist theories of learning. The behaviourist movement in psychology became extremely influential in the 1950's and behaviourist learning theory was one of their most convincing developments. Mostly this was based on experimental research on animals (such as rats and pigeons) and is still strongly associated with the theories of Professor B.F. Skinner of Harvard University.

The principles behind behaviourist learning theory are relatively simple and correspond to a commonsense view of how we learn to do things.

Look at this diagram of a rat in a simple T-shaped maze.

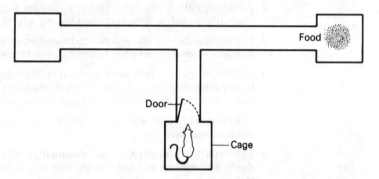

It is not hard to see that, if food is always placed in the right-hand side of the maze, the rat will learn after a series of runs (or 'trials') to turn *right* when it is released from its cage. We could say here that a *habit* is being formed. *Habit formation* is the basis of behaviourist learning theory.

The process of habit formation, according to the behaviourist, is developed as follows:

> *A habit is formed when a correct response to a stimulus is consistently rewarded.*

The habit therefore is the result of *stimulus, correct response* and *reward* occurring together again and again. The more frequently this happens, the stronger the habit becomes. Once the habit is established, the subject (animal or human) will continue to respond correctly to the stimulus, even if the reward is not present.

For the behaviourists, both *reward* and *punishment* can have an effect on habit formation. Reward has a positive effect; punishment, a negative effect. Both were covered by the term *reinforcement*. Reward was *positive reinforcement;* punishment, *negative reinforcement*.

According to Skinner, reward was much more effective than punishment in a teaching situation. He concluded that the students' task should be so arranged that they had a very good chance of getting the answer right – of responding correctly. In other words, a teaching programme should be split up into a series of very simple steps. Once the student had succeeded in getting one step right, he could go on to the next.

Question

Does this remind you of anything you have already read in this chapter? (If you are uncertain, read page 11 again.)

Now let us look at behaviourist learning theory applied to English teaching.

Consider this episode in a very early English lesson:

STAGE 1

Teacher: (Holds up a book) *Book. Book.* Repeat!
Students: Book.
Teacher: Good!
(Teacher does the same with about four other objects).

STAGE 2

Teacher: (Holds up a book)
Students: Book.
Teacher: Good!

In stage 1 the teacher is showing the students an object and giving them the sound at the same time. All the pupils have to do is to repeat the sound.

In stage 2, the students have to produce the appropriate sound (in this case, one word) in response to the teacher's holding up an object. We can analyse this as follows:

	stimulus	*correct response*	*reward*
Stage 1	Object and sound	Correctly repeated sound	Teacher says 'Good!'
Stage 2	Object	Correct sound	Teacher says 'Good!'

Exactly the same kind of procedure can be applied to sentence patterns. The stimulus (or 'cue', as we generally call it) can be a question, a statement, a single word, a mime and so on. E.g.:

Teacher: Can you play football?
Student: Yes, I can.
Teacher: Good!

or

Teacher:	The table's in the corner.
Student:	No, it's near the door.
Teacher:	Good!

or

Teacher:	Door.
Student:	The door's green.
Teacher:	Good! Table.
Student:	The table's brown.
Teacher:	Good!

We have already pointed out (page 15) that repetition (stage 1 above) is the simplest possible form of drill. The other examples (stage 2 and the examples on page 17 and this page) are closer to what we normally call a drill. In every case they conform to behaviourist learning theory's process of habit formation, consisting of *stimulus* (cue or prompt), *response* (student's response) and *reward* (teacher's approval).

This type of learning procedure was at one stage laid down as the basis of language learning according to a method known as the audio-lingual method, which became very fashionable in the 1950's. The advent of the tape-recorder as a language teaching device combined with a belief in habit formation as a fundamental process of language learning led to the development of the *language laboratory*. Typical language laboratory drills took the form of four-phase drills. Here are some examples:

REPETITION DRILL

Tape:	Johnny's English. (1)
Student:	Johnny's English. (2)
Tape:	Johnny's English. (3)
Student:	Johnny's English. (4)

Here (1) is the stimulus; (2) is the response; (3) is the reinforcement; (4) is the second response. In theory, if the student repeated correctly in (2), when he heard phase (3) and recognized this as being the same as his response (2), he was rewarded by knowing he had got it right. The second repetition (4) makes the habit stronger, or gives the student a second chance if he did not perform well the first time.

SUBSTITUTION DRILL

Tape:	*Johnny's in England. France.*	(1)
Student:	Johnny's in France.	(2)
Tape:	Johnny's in France.	(3)
Student:	Johnny's in France.	(4)

Tape:	Spain.	(1)
Student:	Johnny's in Spain.	(2)
Tape:	Johnny's in Spain.	(3)
Student:	Johnny's in Spain.	(4) etc.

In this case the first 'Johnny's in England' on tape is the *model* or *pattern*. The subsequent *France* is the *cue* or *prompt* or *stimulus* and other phases of response, reinforcement and second response are the same as in the repetition drill. This then is a type of pattern drilling.

Drilling in the classroom (as opposed to the language laboratory) normally follows a three-phase scheme. The final response by the student is omitted. Also the teacher rewards the correct response by showing his approval in some way, rather than simply saying the correct pattern for the student to compare it with his own.

Points for discussion

Look back at fragments A – C in the first section of this chapter. Mark the places where drilling occurs. Identify the cues, responses and reinforcement.

What methods of *cueing* were used in fragment C?

Can you think of other ways the teacher might provide positive reinforcement (reward) apart from saying 'Good!'? What methods do you use mostly with your classes?

What do you do when a student fails to produce the correct response? Discuss the various possibilities here and what effect these might have on the student. What is the effect of simply saying 'No' or 'That's not right'?

Introducing variety into the drill

There is an old joke amongst teachers of EFL which goes like this:

'*Dictionary definition:* Drill – a device for boring.'

One of the most frequent objections made to drilling is that the students find them boring. So the more variety that can be introduced, the better.

One simple way of making pattern drilling more varied is to use different kinds of cue while practising the same pattern.

Practical exercise

Imagine that the following short text appears in your textbook. You have presented the new structural items, the past tense forms, *went, saw, took, ate, drank* and *bought*:

> Jack and Lulu went to France last year. They saw the Eiffel Tower and Jack took some photographs. They ate snails and they drank champagne. Lulu bought a new hat.

The students have read the text, know all the new lexical items and understand the situation in the text. You now want to do some simple pattern drilling on the statement form of the past tense. E.g. you might do this:

> *Teacher:*   Champagne
> *Students:*   They drank champagne.

Can you suggest different ways of cueing the patterns? (Avoid asking questions to do this, because the natural way of answering a question such as *What did they drink?* would be *Champagne.* And anyway the students have probably not yet met the question form.)

The following blackboard lay-out might give you some ideas:

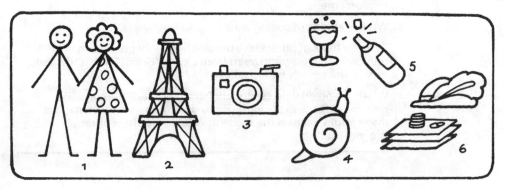

Check your results. Did you identify the following types of cue?

1   Word cue
2   Visual cue *(pointing)*
3   Number cue
4   Mime cue

Now practise doing this drill exercise with other teachers acting as students. Try to vary the cue the whole time. For fun, get somebody to time you and see how many responses you can cue in a minute.

Activity

Make up a text of about the same length containing examples of the *he/she* form of the simple present tense.

Using the other teachers as students, conduct a pattern drill, introducing as much variety into your cueing as possible. Begin the activity with some choral and individual repetition work.

Another way of introducing variety into drilling is to use different types of drill. Here are some examples of different drills. Examine them and discuss the answers to the questions.

DRILL 1

Teacher: They drank champagne – beer
Students: They drank beer.
Teacher: coffee
Students: They drank coffee.
Teacher: tea
Students: They drank tea.

DRILL 2

Teacher: The film was awful yesterday.
The weather
Students: The weather was awful yesterday.
Teacher: bad
Students: The weather was bad yesterday.
Teacher: last week
Students: The weather was bad last week.
Teacher: The children
Students: The children was bad last week.

Questions

1 Is drill 1 any improvement on repetition?

2 How else could the teacher have cued the responses?

3 What is the difference between drill 1 and drill 2?

4 In drill 2, why did the students make the mistake in their last response?

5 The teacher's last prompt 'children' really turns it into a different kind of drill. Construct another substitution drill in order to give your students practice in when to use not only 'was' but also 'were'.
Only change the first part of the sentence. Call this *drill 3*.

6 At what stage of the lesson would you use this drill?

7 Is it a learning or a checking device?

DRILL 4

Teacher: Are there any bananas?
Students: No, there aren't many.
Teacher: Is there any milk?
Students: No, there isn't much.
Teacher: Are there any sandwiches?
Students: No, there aren't many.

Teacher:	Is there any wine?
Students:	No, there isn't much.

Questions

1 Why is the teacher making the students do this drill?

2 How is doing it as an oral drill different from doing it as a written exercise?
Could this drill be used for written practice?

3 Is it possible for a student to understand the distinction between 'much' and 'many' and still make mistakes when doing this drill?

4 Can you think of a situation where a student was able to do this drill without making mistakes and yet had not understood the distinction between 'much' for uncountables and 'many' for countables?

5 Is it necessary for the teacher to ask the question prompt?
How could the teacher get the student to ask the question?

DRILL 5

Teacher:	He read 'The Times'.
Students:	What did he read?
Teacher:	He said 'Good morning'.
Students:	What did he say?
Teacher:	He saw 'Romeo and Juliet'.
Students:	What did he see?

Practical exercise

1 Continue this drill with three other examples of your own.

2 Can you think of a way in which this drill could be contextualized or made more realistic i.e. think of occasions when we might ask and answer questions like these.

3 Construct another drill to practise the present perfect verb form e.g. 'I have done', where the students have to perform some sort of transformation from one verb form to another.
Try to make the language as realistic as possible.

DRILL 6

Teacher:	It may rain. He'll stay at home.
Students:	If it rains, he'll stay at home.
Teacher:	It may be sunny. We'll go to the beach.
Students:	If it's sunny, we'll go to the beach.
Teacher:	It may snow. They'll go skiing.
Students:	If it snows, they'll go skiing.

Exercise

Give two examples of other structures which could be practised using this technique of combining two sentences or clauses.

DRILL 7

Teacher: They go to the cinema.
Students: They go to the cinema.
Teacher: on Sundays
Students: They go to the cinema on Sundays.
Teacher: always
Students: They always go to the cinema on Sundays.
Teacher: nearly
Students: They nearly always go to the cinema on Sundays.

Practical exercise

1 What is this drill being used to practise?

2 Construct a similar drill (not necessarily practising the same thing). Start with:
The man crossed the road.

Reading assignment

Read *Introduction to English Language Teaching* by John Haycraft, pages 36-39.

Activities

1 Comparisons of drills – match each drill with the name you think describes it best. The reading assignment may help you, although the drills given here are not all exactly the same as the ones given in Haycraft.

Drill 1	Expansion drill
Drill 2 (apart from the last prompt)	Mini-dialogue drill
Drill 3	Question drill
Drill 4	Clause combination drill
Drill 5	Progressive substitution drill
Drill 6	Simple substitution drill
Drill 7	Variable substitution drill

If you do not agree with the labels given to the drills here, try to think up your own which describe them better.

2 Would you necessarily use each type of drill at the same stage of your lesson i.e. would you use some of these drills later because they are more 'difficult'? Number the drills in order of difficulty on

the table below. If you consider any of the drills to be of equal difficulty, give them the same number.

3 Are there any of these drills which you would never use at all?
  Put a × by these.

4 Are there any drills you consider particularly useful?
  Put a √ by these.

	Question 1 Name	Question 2 Difficulty	Question 3 Useless	Question 4 Useful
Drill 1				
Drill 2				
Drill 3				
Drill 4				
Drill 5				
Drill 6				
Drill 7				

Revision section

By this stage, you should be able to:

1 give your students controlled practice in saying correct sentence patterns;
2 be able to do this in a variety of ways, by using a number of different oral drills;
3 have a command of a reasonable range of techniques to give variety in cueing these drills.

Now read the following passage and answer the questions which follow:

Controlled drills
It is by no means certain precisely what part controlled drills should play in the language learning process and indeed whether they should be used at all. The extent to which the teacher uses drills in the classroom is largely a matter of personal choice, but no

discussion of drills is complete without a look at the basic assumptions involved here.

Perhaps the main argument in favour of using this kind of pattern practice drill is that it helps the student to acquire fluency in the language by training him to produce language patterns automatically and without conscious effort. It trains him to speak without pausing to select the right grammatical combinations.

If the drills are well constructed, they will consist of fragments of realistic conversation. Consequently, the students will be getting practice in using language which can later be transferred to a situation where real communication needs to take place. For example, consider this 'realistic' drill to practise reflexives:

Cue: Peter's just fallen down the stairs.
Response: Oh dear! Has he hurt himself?

Even quite mechanical drills, requiring little conscious effort on the part of the student, can be made to resemble genuine conversational exchanges by the addition of expressions like *actually, you know, Oh dear!, Really?* and so on.

With large classes, drills are of particular use in that they maximize student participation. A one-word cue, or indeed a non-spoken cue on the part of the teacher can elicit a complete utterance from the students and an enormous number of such utterances can be produced within the space of two minutes. With judicious mixing of choral and individual drilling, each learner can have the chance to respond productively about five times a minute in classes of twenty students or fewer. Furthermore, if use is made of a language laboratory (to which such drills are ideally suited) the number of responses will be even greater and there is the added advantage that each learner can work through the drills at his own pace.

Assuming that one of the aims of pattern practice drills is to help the students gain control over grammatical structure, there can be no doubt that drilling is a much more interesting way of doing this than working laboriously through written exercises, which, in any case, are of dubious value for helping students actually speak the language. Drilling, on the other hand, can be positively beneficial in helping a student to develop his oral ability, especially if the teacher insists on correctness of pronunciation, as well as correctness of structure. Again if the drill is presented on tape and only a short time is given to reply, the student has to have the correct stress and rhythm, to respond in the time provided.

It is generally believed that when learning a language, a student will remember a grammatical rule far better if he has had a chance to work it out for himself, rather than having it supplied for him by the teacher. As the student works through a well thought-out drill, it is maintained, he will recognize the regularity underlying the changes he is being asked to make and will be able to formulate a grammatical rule for himself, thus obviating the need for the teacher to supply one for him.

One drawback of this approach however is that the drill itself must be extremely well structured, allowing for no possibility of misinterpretation. If the drill is badly structured, it is quite possible that the student may make the wrong generalization and draw the wrong conclusion, which would defeat the object of the exercise altogether.

Another point for consideration is that the language in the drills should be as close as possible to real language. Unfortunately, in many textbooks this is not the case: the cue and the utterance are all too often artificial. It is difficult to see how utterances, thus learnt, could ever be used in a real-life situation.

Perhaps the most frequently voiced criticism of pattern practice drills is that they are mechanical and can be performed by the student without understanding what is said. Even if understood initially, it is possible that, after frequent repetition, the pattern has become virtually meaningless, especially when the student's attention is being directed towards other goals, such as word pronunciation or intonation.

Again, if the structural pattern of a drill does not vary, the structure itself may fade into the background and not be learnt at all.

A complaint often voiced by students is that they find drills boring, especially if the drills are practised for hours on end in the language laboratory. Even in class, when drilled beyond the stage when the student can cope with the structure, tedium results and students develop a distaste for this type of learning. As motivation is a prime factor in language learning, the teacher cannot afford to allow this to develop. It is, in fact, all too easy for the teacher to stop drilling either too early or too late. Too little drilling, through fear that the students have become bored, may not be enough to ensure that the students have learnt the structure.

Too much intensive drilling, on the other hand, can develop in the students an inflexibility which prevents them from producing the practised pattern in situations which do not correspond perfectly to the verbal exchanges contained in the drill. Students often seem able to master a structure while drilling, but are then incapable of transferring it to other contexts.

The conclusion then, must be that pattern drilling is pointless unless the student is aware of the relevance of what he is practising to situations outside the classroom. Ultimately, the only proof that pattern practice has been successful lies in seeing the student apply his skill or knowledge creatively in totally new circumstances.

Written assignment

1 From the text you have just read, list the arguments in favour of and against using drills in the classroom. Do this in note form.

2 The writer says that drills should help a student acquire fluency in the language. Explain in your own words how drills can help a student to do this.

3 The writer says that drills should be made to resemble realistic conversational exchanges. Give an example of a 'realistic' drill to practise the change from affirmative to interrogative form of the simple present tense.
  e.g. Mary likes chocolate.
        Mary doesn't like chocolate.

4 What is meant by the phrase 'maximize student participation'?

5 What do you understand by the term *mechanical drill?*

Meaningful and realistic drilling

Points for discussion

In the previous section, the terms *meaningful* and *realistic* were introduced as applied to drills.
Before proceeding further with this section, check by discussing with other teachers that you agree on the meaning of these terms.

So far nearly all the drills we have looked at have been mechanical, although in some cases attempts have been made to make them more meaningful by contextualizing them; or more realistic by trying to make them resemble real language. In this section we shall be looking at more meaningful types of drill. David Wilkins in *Classroom techniques* (in *Ideas and guidance for teachers working with adults*, BBC Publications, 1976) has defined a meaningful drill as one where 'the student has to understand part or all of the sentence in order to be able to respond'. However it is still possible for a drill to be meaningful and yet highly artificial, i.e. the students understand the meaning of what they are saying and, indeed, must be able to do so in order to do the drill, and yet one could not conceive of a situation where the cue and response would actually ever be used together in real life.

One of our aims therefore should be to make drills not only meaningful, but also realistic.

Here are some more drills. How well do you think they succeed in being both meaningful and realistic? Can you foresee any practical problems with their use in the classroom?

DRILL 1
(Tape-recording of sound of running water)
Response: He must be in the bathroom.

(Sound of plates being washed up).
Response: He must be in the kitchen.

DRILL 2
Picture of house with windows cut out. Yellow strip of paper inserted through the windows.

Responses
He must be in the kitchen.
He must be in the hall,
etc.

DRILL 3
Cue: I've been working hard all day.
Response: You must be tired.

DRILL 4
Cue: Beer
Response: They drank beer.
Cue: Spaghetti
Response: They ate spaghetti.
Cue: Film
Response: They saw a film.

DRILL 5
Cue: Paul's 28.
Response: He'll be 29 next year.
Cue: Mary's 35.
Response: She'll be 36 next year.

DRILL 6
Cue: My cat's just died.
Response: Oh dear, I'm sorry to hear that.

Cue: I broke my favourite vase yesterday.
Response: Oh dear, I'm sorry to hear that.

DRILL 7
Cue: I failed one of my exams.
Response: Oh dear, I'm sorry to hear that.
Cue: But I still managed to get a place at university.
Response: Congratulations!
Cue: It wasn't really the university I wanted to go to.
Response: Oh dear, I'm sorry to hear that.

DRILL 8

Cues: Response: What did he eat?

Cue: Response: What did he drink?

Questions for discussion

1 What is the method of cueing drill 1?
   What other structures could be drilled using this sort of cue?

2 Which two drills use pictures cues? Why is one more realistic?
   Construct one other drill containing a picture cue which is both
   meaningful and realistic.

3 What is the cue being used in drill 5? Can you think of any other
   language items which could be drilled using this technique?

4 Fill in the following table and discuss your results:

	Type of cue	Meaningful (Marks out of 10)	Realistic (Marks out of 10)
Drill 1			
Drill 2			
Drill 3			
Drill 4			
Drill 5			
Drill 6			
Drill 7			
Drill 8			

Discussion and practical work

Try to get hold of one or more of the following books.

> *Access to English,* Book 1 *(Starting Out),* Coles and Lord, O.U.P.
> *Active Context English,* Book 1, Brinton *et al.,* Macmillan
> *Cue for a Drill,* Harkess and Eastwood, O.U.P.
> *English in Situations,* R. O'Neill, O.U.P.
> *Incentive English,* Book 1, Fowler *et al.,* Nelson
> *Lado English Series,* Book 1, R. Lado, Regents
> *Signpost,* Book 1, Austen *et al.,* Nelson

If you cannot get hold of any of these, choose any beginner's textbook containing drill exercises.

Now look at the following:

1 *How are the drills arranged in the book?* Are they based on a text, picture or any other form of situation? Are there examples of correct patterns? Are there words arranged in boxes or tables? What other form of help is there for the student?

2 *How meaningful and realistic are they?*

3 *How would you use these in the classroom?* Exactly as they appear in the book? Adapted? With some preparation beforehand?

4 Choose one drill which you like and try it out on other teachers or on your class.

Written assignment

Suggest two different kinds of drill which you would use to teach the structure contained in:

> I've been waiting for ages.

From *R.S.A. Certificate for Overseas Teachers of English* June 1980

Techniques, methods and approaches

So far in this chapter we have considered two aspects of TEFL: the initial phases of *presentation* and *controlled practice*. We have also introduced a variety of techniques for presenting and practising structural items.

It is worthwhile discussing briefly the difference between three words which are often used when talking about TEFL: *techniques, methods* and *approaches*.

When we use the word *approach* we mean that an idea or theory is being applied: that whatever the teacher does, certain theoretical principles are always borne in mind. When we talk about a *technique*, we mean a procedure used in the classroom. Finally, a *method* is a set of procedures or a collection of techniques used in a systematic way which it is hoped will result in efficient learning.

A *technique* then is the narrowest term, meaning one single procedure. A *method* will consist of a number of techniques, probably arranged in a specific order. The word *approach* is much more general and has the implication that whatever method or techniques the teacher uses, he does not feel bound by these, but only by the theory in which he believes. If he can find new and better methods or techniques which will fit in with his approach, then he will adopt these.

We therefore have a hierarchical system:

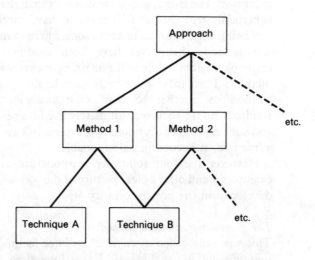

It follows from this that different approaches may share the same techniques and even the same methods; and different methods may share the same techniques.

We have already introduced the scheme of behaviourist learning theory. In this case it makes sense to talk about 'the behaviourist approach', but 'the audio-lingual method' (page 18). We can also talk about different drilling 'techniques'.

A final word of warning. *Approach* is used formally in the sense we have described. The behaviourist approach has been introduced; later we will introduce the mentalist approach and the communicative approach. However, *approach* is often used *informally* to mean something closer to *method*. We might say, for example, that a teacher should 'vary his approach when teaching different types of class'. This does not mean that the teacher should change his theoretical beliefs for each type of class!

Some techniques have developed independently, but many of the important ones have arisen from particular methods. In the next section we shall examine a number of methods which have all contributed to the range of techniques currently used in TEFL.

Methods of language teaching

In this section we will take a brief look at four methods of language teaching which have been used at various times in this century. Although we shall present these in a sequence which corresponds roughly to their historical development, it should not be assumed that each method in turn was totally abandoned in favour of its successor. The situation is more complex than that. To begin with, it is certainly true that all four methods have survived intact and are still being used by some teachers somewhere in the world. Moreover the methods themselves have been modified by teachers and textbook writers, while still remaining recognizably the same basic method. Then there have been considerable borrowings from one method by another so that some amalgamated versions have resulted. As we shall see, ultimately the idea of adopting a method and sticking to it or abandoning it is unsatisfactory. The very idea of a 'method' is becoming unfashionable.

However the four following methods are archetypes – classic examples – and offer a clear picture of the way language teaching has developed in the present century.

The grammar-translation method

This was only called a 'method' by later methodologists who were pointing out its weaknesses. For a long time, it was uncritically assumed that this was the only way languages should be taught.

The method consisted of giving the students grammatical rules and *paradigms*. Paradigms are lists of forms arranged according to a grammatical pattern.

For example:

Simple present indicative active tense of the verb 'to go'

	Singular	Plural
1st Person	I go	We go
2nd Person	You go	You go
3rd Person	He She goes It	They go

or

Personal pronoun system

Number	Singular					Plural		
Person	1st	2nd	3rd M	F	N	1st	2nd	3rd M F N
Nominative	I	you	he	she	it	we	you	they
Accusative	me	you	him	her	it	us	you	them
Genitive	mine	yours	his	hers	its	ours	yours	theirs
Dative	me	you	him	her	it	us	you	them

Students were also given lists of vocabulary (lexical items) together with their translation equivalents in the mother tongue (L_1).

And they were given grammatical rules such as the rule for the usage of *some* and *any* (see fragment A), together with any exceptions to these rules.

First the students had to memorize all these 'facts' about the language and they were often tested on their knowledge by being asked to recite the paradigms or give the translation of words. Or they were asked to 'parse' words. E.g: *He goes* is the third person singular of the simple present indicative active tense of the verb 'to go'.

Next the students were made to put their knowledge to use by translating sentences or texts from mother tongue (L_1) to foreign language (L_2) or vice-versa.

In retrospect, there were many serious disadvantages to the grammar-translation method. Here are some obvious ones:

1 The grammatical analysis was very neat and satisfactory for the grammarians who had devised it, but it often made facts about the language very confusing to the students. (Look at the analysis of personal pronouns on the previous page.)
2 The method put a tremendous strain on students' memories.
3 Word-to-word translations were often unsatisfactory.
4 The students had to learn a lot of grammatical terms (*noun, tense, indicative* etc.). In fact, they had to learn a new language for talking about language!

Activity

Make a list of additional serious disadvantages to the grammar–translation method. If you have ever studied a language by this method, describe the difficulties you experienced. What were the *results* of teaching by this method?

The direct method (Sometimes called the oral method or the natural method)

It has often been pointed out that the direct method was developed as a reaction to the grammar-translation method. This is true, but in fact people have been learning languages by this method at least as early as Roman times, when young men were provided with Greek tutors to teach them Greek, the cultural language of Europe in those days and an essential part of one's education.

The simple idea behind the direct method was that we learn languages by hearing them spoken and engaging in conversation: reading and writing can be developed later.

Practitioners of this method immersed their students in a flow of examples of the spoken language, while actively demonstrating the meaning of what they were saying, if possible suiting their actions to the words. At the same time they would encourage the students to speak (*cue* them), often by asking questions.

Reading assignment

A good description of this technique can be found in *The Techniques of Language Teaching* by F.L. Billows, (pages 1 – 5, Sections 1 – 3). Read this passage and then discuss the questions which follow.

1 'He makes a good many mistakes at first, but the nearest grown-up patiently repeats the correct form and does what is expected.' (page 1). From your own experience, would you say that this is in fact always true?

2 The main principle of the direct method was to immerse students in the target language. As you can see from Billows' examples, the aim seems to have been to give the students a rich sample of the forms of the structural or lexical items being taught, to envelop them in a continuous stream of the language. Some questions are appropriate here:
(a) How natural is the teacher's use of language? (Remember this method is sometimes called the 'natural' method.)
(b) What percentage of time do you think would be occupied by the teacher's voice during oral work?
(c) Do you think this type of lesson would be easy to teach?

The audio-lingual method

We have already mentioned this method in connection with drills (page 18). It could be said that this method consists entirely of drilling in one form or another.

Audio-lingual means 'listening-speaking'. The method consists of presenting an oral model to the student, on tape or in the teacher's voice, and carrying out a series of pattern drills based on the model. We have already seen (pages 18ff) examples of language laboratory four-phase drills produced by audio-lingual course designers. The classroom version would be similar but three-phase.

The following principles were applied:

1 Students should first *listen*; then *speak*, then *read;* and finally *write* the language. (In extreme forms of this method, students had to listen for many hours before they were allowed to speak!)

2 The 'grammar' should be presented in the form of model patterns or dialogues. Drilling consisted of forming new utterances on the basis of the original pattern. This was called 'analogous pattern drilling'. That is, the students formed the new utterances by *analogy*.

3 Drilling should follow the stimulus – response – reinforcement scheme. Students should always be rewarded when they responded correctly, by seeing that they had got the answer right.

4 Students should proceed by very easy steps, starting with simple repetition and going on to simple drills, then more complex drills and so on. Ideally the possibility of a student making an error should be avoided altogether, because positive reinforcement (reward) was considered more effective than negative reinforcement (punishment). This principle was called *error prevention*.

5 By repeating the stages of stimulus – response – reinforcement, students would develop correct language habits. Once a habit had been formed, a student could produce examples of the pattern effortlessly and without thinking about how to do so. The student was then regarded as being *fluent* in that pattern.

Activities

1 Look through *Introducing variety into the drill* again. Find a drill which seems to correspond well to the audio-lingual method as represented by the five principles mentioned above. What problems might you expect if your classes consisted almost entirely of this kind of activity?

2 What similarities does the audio-lingual method share with the direct method?

3 Do you agree with the principle (1 above) that practice in the language classroom should follow the sequence: listening, speaking, reading, writing? When introducing a new word or structure, do you ever write it up on the blackboard before getting your students to repeat it? If not, how long do you wait before writing it up? Explain the reasons for your own procedure.

Reading assignment

Read *Teaching Foreign Language Skills* by Wilga Rivers, Chapter 2. Pages 32-36 deal with the background to the audio-lingual method and may be skimmed quickly. Look carefully at the last two sections (*Evaluation of the Audio-Lingual Method* and *Areas of Controversy*) and discuss these ideas with other teachers.

Critics of the audio-lingual method would focus mainly on the fact that much of the method consists of *mechanical drilling* (see page 27). Practice activities tend to be repetitive and boring. More serious is the danger that students might produce analogous patterns without realizing what they are saying. The next method, in reaction, places its emphasis on establishing meaning.

The structural-situational method

This method is widely used at the time of writing and a very large number of textbooks are based on it. But it also has important links with the audio-lingual method, especially as far as the way the language to be taught is organized (the 'structural' ingredient). New language is presented in the form of model patterns or dialogues. Much use, too, is made of repetition and analogous pattern drilling.

However, great care is always taken to present and practise language *within a situation*. Billows explains the word 'situation' in the passage you are about to read. The purpose of the situational ingredient is to ensure a meaningful context for language practice. (Another word for this is 'contextualization'.) In other words it aims to avoid meaningless and mechanical practice.

Reading assignment

Read *The Techniques of Language Teaching* pages 6-12.

1 Do you agree with Billows when he says (page 12) 'All new language material must be made familiar in the inner sphere before it is brought to bear on action or situation in the second or third spheres'? Can you think of structural or lexical items which might be difficult to present within the inner sphere?

2 Describe the stages you would follow to do a situational presentation of the structure contained in the sentence: *Mr Smart wanted Mary to type the letters.*

Now read *Selected Articles on the Teaching of English as a Foreign Language* by L.A. Hill, pages 84-89.

Notes:

1 'The old idea of teaching languages' (page 84) can be identified as the grammar-translation method.

2 *Vocabulary selection* and *The structural approach* are really more to do with design of textbooks and syllabuses than *methods* of teaching. However their inclusion in this article helps to put the development of methods into historical perspective.

3 *The drill method* may be identified as the audio-lingual method, although Hill's description of it is brief and not very flattering.

4 The *situational approach* combined with the *structural approach* may be regarded as the *structural-situational method*.

An eclectic approach

Read this passage and answer the questions which follow.

Probably most teachers of EFL nowadays, if asked what method they use, would reply that their approach is 'eclectic'. By this, they mean that they do not follow any single method, but rather that they use a selection of techniques. Such an approach to TEFL has many advantages. For one thing, it is much more flexible and can easily be adapted to suit a wide variety of teaching situations. Perhaps its biggest advantage is that a teacher who approaches TEFL eclectically is less likely to become fixed in one single method and more likely to keep an eye open for new techniques and approaches.

Although much research has been conducted on the effectiveness of different methods of teaching foreign languages, it is really very difficult to demonstrate scientifically what is or is not a 'good' method. The truth is that a lot seems to depend on factors such as the personal qualities of the teacher and his ability to get on well with his students, which are difficult things to measure.

Because we have lacked solid scientific evidence, the teaching of foreign languages in general has been for a long time the victim of fashion. D.A. Wilkins writes (in *Linguistics in language teaching*, page 208):

'Viewed historically, language teaching has always been subject to change, but the process of change has not resulted from the steady accumulation of knowledge about the most effective ways of teaching languages: it has been more the product of changing fashion.' In other words, though teachers have tended to leap from one method to another as each new fashion turns up, they do not seem to have become any wiser.

If then we decide to stop looking for the one definitive and perfect method, and concentrate instead on acquiring skills and techniques, what should be our criterion for selecting these? Which should we adopt and which reject?

The answer must be simply: adopt those which are successful. If it works, use it.

There is, of course, still the problem of knowing what we mean by 'success'. Every language teacher should begin by considering what the aims of his pupils are, both in the short and the long run, and judge success by whether these are achieved. The question of objectives will crop up again and again in this book; and it is one which should never be far from our minds, whatever aspect of TEFL we are considering.

We began this section by favouring an eclectic approach to TEFL and encouraging pursuit of successful techniques rather than methods.

A word of warning is appropriate at this stage. 'Eclectic' is a convenient term, but it is also vague. If we condemn blind chasing after methods, we should also condemn the blind adoption of techniques. It may turn out that an eclectic approach to TEFL is nothing more than a bundle of techniques which a certain teacher has encountered by chance and adopted quite arbitrarily. It is important, therefore, that teachers should be aware of some of the theoretical principles which lie behind the major trends in foreign language teaching. Without this background knowledge, teachers will be merely practitioners of a technology which has been passed on second-hand. Teachers owe it to their profession to go deeper into their subject than this. Ultimately, they are the ones who know most about the practice of TEFL, and they are the ones who should contribute to progress in the field by developing a critical attitude to all approaches that appear on the horizon and deciding whether they are valid or not. The opinion of the teacher is invaluable, but only if it is *informed* opinion.

Questions

1 What is meant by an 'eclectic approach' to TEFL?

2 Why is it difficult to test the effectiveness of TEFL methods?

3 The writer ends paragraph 3 with the words: '... they (teachers) do not seem to have become any wiser.' In your own words, explain what he means by this.

4 Explain what is meant by the word 'criterion' in paragraph 4.

5 What is the 'warning' given in the last paragraph?

6 What do you understand by the phrase 'informed opinion' in the last sentence?

Revision

The following terms have been introduced in this chapter. Try to explain them in your own words. If you have difficulty, refer back to the pages where they first appear.

Presentation (page 9)

Structural, lexical and
    phonological items (page 10)

Structural grading (page 11)

Situational presentation (page 12)

Individual repetition (page 15)

Habit formation (page 16)

Reinforcement (page 16)

Four-phase drill (page 18)

Pattern or model (page 19)

Cue (page 19)

Visual cue (page 20)

Mime cue (page 20)

Mechanical drill (page 25)

Realistic drill (page 25)

Meaningful drill (page 27)

Paradigm (page 32)

Error prevention (page 35)

Eclectic approach (page 37)

Bibliography

A look at some common techniques
A university grammar of English, R. Quirk & S. Greenbaum (Longman)

Situational presentation of a structure
Introduction to English language teaching, John Haycraft (Longman)

Repetition
Teaching oral English, Donn Byrne (Longman)

Introducing variety into the drill
Introduction to English language teaching, John Haycraft (Longman)

Meaningful and realistic drilling
Ideas and guidance for teachers working with adults, Julian Dakin (BBC Publications)
Access to English, Book 1, M. Coles & B. Lord (O.U.P.)
Active context English, Book 1, E. Brinton *et al.* (Macmillan)
Cue for a drill, S. Harkess & J. Eastwood (O.U.P.)
English in situations, R. O'Neill (O.U.P.)
Incentive English, Book 1, W.S. Fowler *et al.* (Nelson)
Lado English Series, Book 1, R. Lado (Regents)
Signpost, Book 1, E. Austen *et al.* (Nelson)

Methods of language teaching
The techniques of language teaching, F.L. Billows (Longman)
Teaching foreign language skills, Wilga Rivers (University of Chicago Press)
Selected articles on the teaching of English as a foreign language, L.A. Hill (O.U.P.)

An eclectic approach
Linguistics in language teaching, D.A. Wilkins (Edward Arnold)

2 Useful classroom techniques

Reading

After finishing this section, you should be able to:

(a) check your students' comprehension of a text by asking them suitably graded questions;

(b) introduce a text using any one of a number of different ways;

(c) have command of a reasonable range of techniques for exploiting the text.

Points for discussion

Answer the following questions and discuss your answers with the rest of the group.

1 Choose the textbook you use most frequently.
Is a reading passage included in every chapter?

2 What is the purpose of the reading passage?
e.g. to improve your students' reading skill
to reinforce structure
etc.

3 On average how many new words are included in the passage?
How do you deal with these?

4 When introducing the text in class, who reads?
(a) you
(b) the students aloud
(c) the students quietly

5 Can you think of any arguments in favour of letting your students read aloud?

6 Can you think of any arguments against letting them read aloud?

7 In textbooks you use do questions follow the reading passage?
If so, do these questions check your students' comprehension of the text?

8 Are the questions in any sort of order?
e.g. from easy to answer to difficult to answer
Do the parts of the text which provide the answers to the questions follow the same order as the questions themselves?

A Reading comprehension

1 Choosing and grading questions

Read the following text.

TEXT 1

Gregory is about forty-five and his hair is starting to go grey. Everybody knows Gregory because he reads the news on television. He has done this for ten years and enjoys it very much. He likes it when people stop him in the street or when they point at him and whisper to their friends.

Yesterday his boss suggested Gregory changed his job. Gregory knows his boss wants a younger man to take his place and doesn't care what happens to Gregory. The new job could never be as good as his old one. He has no-one to discuss the problem with at home and this makes it worse.

Activities

Do the exercises which follow drawing on your own practical teaching experience or read Donn Byrne *Teaching oral English* pages 45-48.

1 Grade the following questions in the order you might put them to your students, going from easy to answer to difficult to answer.
   (a) What is Gregory's job?
   (b) Does he enjoy his job?
   (c) Does Gregory read the news on television or on the radio?
   (d) What did Gregory's boss suggest yesterday?
   (e) What sort of company does Gregory work for?
   (f) Why do people point at Gregory?
   (g) What colour is his hair starting to go?
   (h) Has Gregory had the same job for a long time?
   (i) What is going to happen to Gregory?

2 Which of the above questions do not really check comprehension i.e. which questions could the students answer correctly without having really understood the text?
   Is there any point in asking questions like this?

3 Consider the following questions.
   Would they be suitable for checking comprehension? Why/Why not?
   (a) Does Gregory have anyone to confide in at home?
   (b) In Gregory's opinion, will his new job be an improvement on his present one?
   (c) Is Gregory's superior concerned about Gregory?

4 Now consider the following questions.
   (a) What is Gregory's problem?
   (b) How old is Gregory?
   Which of these two questions do you find easier to answer and why?

Which of these two questions better checks the students' overall understanding of the passage?
Make up one more global question like question (a) and one more specific question like question (b).

Global questions such as (a) check whether your students have understood an idea which is central to the whole text. Usually students have to read most of a text to be able to answer a global question.

Specific questions focus on some point of detail. This need not be an irrelevant detail, as often it is necessary to understand some small point in order to grasp what follows later on in a passage. Students can usually find the answer to specific questions from just one sentence.

Global questions can be put before the text as pre-questions. If the question is set before students read the text, this ensures that as they are reading, their attention is focused firmly on the text and they are reading for a purpose.

Questions

Occasionally more specific questions are asked as pre-questions.
Do you think this is of any value?
What skill do such questions help to develop in the students when set as pre-questions?
How is this type of reading different from the type of reading your students would be doing if you set them a time limit to read a text and asked them a global question?

2 Varying your question technique

Read through the following answer to an exam question and complete the title of the question.

Reading comprehension questions do not always ...

Questions that follow the reading of a passage are usually intended to check whether the class as a whole has understood the passage or not. In practice, what invariably happens is that the same brighter students answer all the time, while the others stay quiet. In many cases, it is impossible for the teacher to tell if these others have really understood nothing or whether they are just too lazy to put up their hands.

One way of ensuring that all the class does participate is to make the students answer the questions in writing. The questions should, of course, be carefully graded, going from very easy to more and more difficult to answer. The activity will finish when the first student has answered all the questions. In this way, each student can work at his own speed and within his own limitations. The weaker students will have answered only the earlier, easier questions while the brighter students may have answered them all.

Asking comprehension questions may even be disguised as a game by writing each question on a piece of card and distributing these cards among the students. When a student has finished answering the question on his piece of card, he then asks the teacher for a different question or exchanges his card with another student. The first person to have answered all the questions is the winner.

A more thorough way of checking comprehension is to use *true or false* statements. The teacher gives the class a statement such as: Gregory isn't a newsreader. The class then has to say whether the statement is true or false. It is easy to involve the entire class by asking them to put up their right hands for true and their left hands for false. In this way the teacher is able to check comprehension at a glance. It is also easy to imagine this activity as a game. The class is divided into two teams and each team chooses a representative. At the front of the class are two chairs – a true chair and a false chair. The two students stand midway between the two chairs. The teacher or one of the other students from the class makes a true/false statement and the students at the front have to go to the appropriate chair and sit on it. The first student to sit on the appropriate chair wins a point for his team.

So, with very little effort on the part of the teacher, checking comprehension of a reading text need be neither boring nor limited to only a few students, but can be an interesting activity which all the class can take part in.

Questions

The exercise you have just done – supplying a title to a text – could be used with your students. What exactly would you ask them to do?

What specific reading skill would they be practising?

3   Types of comprehension question

Exercise

Consider the following questions:

1 Is Gregory's hair black?

2 Why do people point at Gregory?

3 Gregory is young (*true or false*).

4 Tick the right answer:
  Gregory (a) has just lost his job.
        (b) has been replaced by a younger man.
        (c) is going to be replaced by a younger man.

5 Gregory enjoys his job because ...

Look at the questions above and decide, from the list below, what kinds of question they are:

  Multiple choice question
  True or false statement
  Open-ended question
  Open-ended statement
  Polar question

Which of the above types of question do you think is most difficult to construct?
Do any of these questions test purely the reading skill?
What other skills do the other questions test?

Activity

Take a reading text from a textbook that you use. Look at the questions which follow the text and consider the following points:

  Are the questions global or specific?
  What kinds of question are they?
  What is the proportion of polar questions (which students need to answer only with yes or no)?
  Do the questions go from easy to difficult?
  Could the students answer any of the questions without having understood the text?
  Are the questions natural?

Write a short report of your findings and compare them with teachers who have examined other books.

B Handling a text

1 Dealing with long texts

Texts in textbooks are frequently very long and can be very tiresome to work through from beginning to end if you just go ploughing through the text. Often the first thing to be done with a text is to split it up into shorter, more manageable parts.

Consider the following text and decide how you are going to break it up.

TEXT 2

It was an extremely hot summer's day and the four tourists were on the beach, enjoying the sun. Mary was sitting, looking at the mountains and it was her idea to go for a walk. So they put on their shorts, sandals and tee-shirts and set off up the hill, buying a map at a shop on the way.

They had been climbing for about an hour and were becoming thirsty. 'We should have taken some water with us,' said John. Mary looked at the map. 'Never mind, there's a spring not far away. Let's make for that.' And off they went.

The path leading up to the spring was not as good as the path they had been on before, but after about forty-five minutes they reached the spring. It was rather disappointing. Only a trickle of water was coming out of it, as it was the middle of summer, but at least they managed to have a drink.

'We'd better go back now,' said Mary. 'It'll be dark in an hour or two.' They were all getting cold, as well. They wished they'd taken more clothes. But worse was to come. On the way down the rough path, Jane slipped and twisted her ankle. What should they do now?

2 Planning a lesson involving a text

Choose a text from your textbook that you are going to be teaching shortly. If it's too long, split it into manageable sections. Decide how you are going to introduce each section. Choose from the suggestions below.

Methods of introducing a text
Fill in the ways we have already dealt with.

1 ....
2 ....
3 Students read aloud after the teacher.
4 The text or part of the text is written on the blackboard. In this way the students see a different script and their attention is focused on the teacher and not on their books.
5 The text is built up orally with the help of the pictures.

e.g.

Teacher:	Was this story in summer or winter?
Students:	Summer.
Teacher:	What sort of day was it?
Students:	Hot.
Teacher:	Very hot?
Students:	Yes.
Teacher:	That's right. It was an extremely hot summer's day.

(Students repeat)

The picture is added to.

Teacher:	Where are these people?
Students:	On the beach.
Teacher:	How many of them are there? etc.

6 An alternative to the above is for the students to ask the questions with the help of picture or word cues.

7 Jumbled sentences on card, stuck on the blackboard.

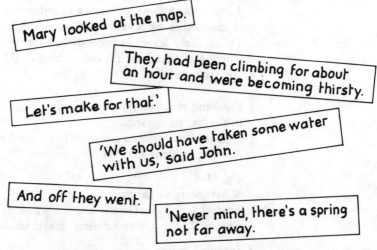

(a) Students read and put the sentences in the right order
or
(b) Students read the text in their books, and then put the sentences in the right order.

8 The text can be represented as a gap-filling exercise (just remove every seventh word or so).

Again the students can either read the text and fill in the missing words, or they can read and fill in the missing words without having previously seen the completed text.

In the latter case, a simpler exercise, where only the easy words are deleted, can be used.

e.g. The path leading up ...... the spring was not ...... good as the path they ...... been on before, but after about forty-five ......, they reached ...... spring.

9 Paired story completion.
Students A and B are given copies of the story in which different information has been left out. The two copies are so prepared that students A and B can fill in their spaces and thus complete their texts by asking their partners questions. e.g.

Student A	Student B
They had been ...... for about an hour and were becoming .... 'We should have taken some ...... with us,' said John. ...... looked at the map.	They had been climbing for ...... and were becoming thirsty. 'We should have taken some water with us,' said .... Mary looked at the map.

If you are to have a balanced lesson, as well as one which will be interesting, it is as well to include a variety of activities. These need not be confined to reading activities, but can also include the other skills.

Look at the following practice activities which can be done on a text and decide what skills they are practising.

Do all these activities necessarily have to be controlled by the teacher? Put a cross by the ones which could be done in pairs or small groups.

1 Find and point to a word beginning with 'a' and ending with 'e' in the last paragraph.
2 One student makes a question from word prompts.
Another student answers the question.

e.g.
What/tourists/wearing?
Student 1: What were the tourists wearing?
Student 2: They were wearing shorts, sandals and tee-shirts.

3 Jumbled letters
What is this word 'rekltic'? Write it down.
4 Finish this sentence:
Teacher: They had been climbing ...
Students: They had been climbing for about an hour.

5 Find this word | rough | and point to it.

6 *Teacher:* Find 'rough' and point to it.
7 Jumbled words

e.g. Jane ankle the her path down On slipped the and rough way twisted.

Students arrange the words in the right order, either without having the text in front of them or, depending on the ability of the class, they can read the text and put the words in the right order.

8 Jumbled sentences

9 Jumbled paragraphs

10 Find all the four-letter words in paragraph 2 and write them down.

11 Students retell the story orally using picture or word prompts.

12 Students write a dialogue based on the text.

e.g. Write a short dialogue of what the four friends said when they saw the spring.

13 *Teacher:* Is this word in the text? `tickle`

Teacher: What about this word? `trickle`

14 Structure practice based on the text.

e.g. They didn't take any water.
They should have taken some water.

They didn't tell anybody where they were going.
They should have told somebody.
etc.

15 Revelations
Teacher has a word written on a piece of card e.g. 'spring' and reveals the word to the students letter by letter.

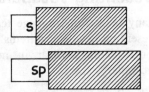

At each stage the students try to guess what the word is.
Once the word has been guessed, students tell the teacher what the next letter is going to be, thus checking spelling.

16 Parallel story
Students use the original text as a base and substitute various points of information to produce a completely different story.

e.g.It was an extremely hot summer's day and the four tourists were on the beach, enjoying the sun.

Prompts for substitution
winter   explorers   mountain hut   hot coffee

Activity

Now go back to the text you chose at the beginning of section 2. You will have already decided how you are going to introduce it. From the above activities choose and prepare the ones you are going to use.

Teaching vocabulary

Points for discussion

Look back to Question 3 in the *Points for discussion* on page 41.

1 What do you think is the optimum number of words which can be taught in any one lesson?

2 Are the sort of students you are teaching going to affect this number in any way i.e. can some students learn more words than others?

3 Does this number depend in any way on the words which are being taught i.e. are some words easier to learn than others?

4 We have mentioned teaching new words when doing a reading text. Do you think it is desirable to present new words at the same time as presenting a new structure?

5 Do you think it is a good idea to give your students a list of words to learn for homework and to test them on this the next day?

A Presenting vocabulary items

Many books on language teaching mention the different ways of presenting new lexical items.

Some points to bear in mind, however you present the new vocabulary, are:

1 Teach and practise the words in spoken form first, otherwise your students will try to pronounce the words as they are written.

2 Unless you only want the students to have a passive knowledge of the lexical items, you must put them into context and get the students to practise them.

3 As with teaching anything else, revision is essential, otherwise the new words you have taught will be forgotten.

4 Always check your students have understood the new words, no matter how they have been presented.

5 Students will remember new vocabulary better if it is presented in a memorable way to start with.

Activity

List ways in which you yourself have presented vocabulary items to your students. For ideas, read Haycraft: *Introduction to English language teaching.*

1 drawing pictures on the blackboard

2 ....

3 ....

4 ....

5 ....

6 ....

7 ....

8 ....

9 ....

10 ....

Are any of these ways of presentation 'better' in that you have found they help students remember the words more effectively?

How do you check that students have understood the word you are teaching?

Which of the above ways would you use to present the following words: elephant, honesty, to dance, a matchbox, a box of matches, broad (adj) an only child, accident.

Exercises for discussion

1 What is the opposite of short ......
                            thin ......
                            old ......

2 Look at the following and translate into your own language:

   the head of a table
   the man's head
   the head of a match
   the head of a school
   the head of a bed

3 What is a synonym for broad?
   Do both broad and the word you have chosen fit into the following sentences?

   The two cars crashed because the road wasn't ...... enough.
   He's got very ...... shoulders.
   She is very ...... minded.

4 Consider the following exercise.

   Will you help me make the dinner. Can you
   (a) shell
   (b) peel
   (c) crack
   (d) skin
   the peas?

   Why are the other words wrong?

In English which of the following can we peel, which can we shell, which can we skin? Tick √ the boxes.

	shell	peel	skin
potatoes			
oranges			
eggs			
shrimps			
nuts			
tomatoes			
grapes			
fish			

How does this compare with your own language?

5 (a) What is this?   and this?

If you were teaching the word, how would you draw it for your students?
(b) Can you think of any other common objects which look different in your own country and Britain?

6 (a) If you explained to your students that a letter-box is a box in which we post letters, do you think they would be able to find one when they went to Britain?
(b) Is there any way of getting these cultural differences over to your students?
(c) Is it necessary to get them over?

7 Students learn words more easily if they are grouped together in a memorable way. Which of the methods of presentation you listed is particularly suitable for teaching a related set of words (lexical set)?

B Consolidation and checking

In the previous section you discussed the pitfalls of presenting new lexis in certain ways and probably came to the conclusion that all methods of presenting new lexical items are open to ambiguities. The teacher must, therefore, ensure that all new lexis has been properly understood by using a different method of checking from the one that has been used to present the new lexical item.

Even so, the fact that the students understand the lexical item is no guarantee that they are going to be able to use it. Understanding or passive recognition of the new words may be all that we are aiming for in which case nothing further needs to be done. However, more frequently, we wish our students to be able both to understand and produce the new lexis, in which case we must provide our students with adequate practice in using the new words.

Some ways of doing this are listed below. See if you can add to them.

1 *Word games or puzzles*

(a) Each student chooses a letter of the alphabet and fills in the following text with words beginning with that letter.

> I know a *(adjective)* man whose name is *(man's name)*. He lives in *(country)*. He is a *(job)*. He likes *(verb)*ing. He eats *(food)* and he drinks *(drink)*. He has a *(animal)*.

Here is a completed example with the letter 'B'.

> I know a *bad* man whose name is *Brian*. He lives in *Britain*. He is a *butcher*. He likes *bowling*. He eats *beef* and he drinks *beer*. He has a *bear*.

Now each choose a different letter and do the same.
Make a list of the letters which are more difficult.

(b) Another word game which is very useful for revising or checking vocabulary is Word Bingo. One way of playing it is for each student to have a card with six or more words on it, that the teacher wants to practise. The teacher reads out definitions of the words and if the student has the word on his card, he covers it up. The first student to have covered up all his words is the winner.

(c) Odd one out.
Students have to pick out the word which doesn't fit.
e.g. table chair desk horse bed

List all the other word games you can think of and explain to each other how they are played.

For more about other types of games see page 95.

Look back to section A *Exercise for discussion* 4. Construct an exercise similar to this which your own students can do. Think of two verbs which they confuse e.g. look, watch; get off, get out of, and provide them with a list of nouns to be matched with the verbs.

---

2 Picture compositions are a useful way of activating known vocabulary. If you draw the pictures, you can control the vocabulary which is being practised quite effectively.

3 Another way of activating your students' vocabulary and helping them to organize words they know into 'sets' is to give them a word e.g. *tree* and then give them one minute to write down all the words they can think of which are connected with this. Any unusual word associations need to be explained by the students. The students can then write a text including all the words they have listed.

4 One of the most difficult areas to check comprehension of, and to give students practice in, is the use of words which are similar in meaning. For example, a house, a flat and a bungalow can all be described as places in which people live, but it is difficult to check whether our students have grasped the distinction.

The following is one way of doing this:

(a)List all the places you can think of in which people live.

(b)Fill in the following table:

Places in which people live	No. of floors	No. of rooms	Big/ small	Town/ country	Old/ new
1 palace	more than one	20+	big	either	either
2 hut	one	one	small	country	usually old
3					old
4					
5					
6					
7					

Based on an idea in *Self-help lexis* by G. Broughton, *IATEFL Newsletter No 70 page 21.*

Make a list of any other ways you can think of, of checking and consolidating vocabulary. Other more formal ways of checking vocabulary can be found in the section on testing.

C On whether to pre-teach vocabulary when doing a reading test

---

Activity

Look at the title above. Now consider which of the following words you might expect to find in this section.
  graded questions
  extensive reading

intensive reading
substitution drill
antonym
infer the meaning of a word
lexical item

Some people state very prescriptively that all new vocabulary should be pre-taught when handling a reading text. There are arguments both for and against this.

By pre-teaching the vocabulary, the teacher makes sure the students have no problems with the new words which crop up in the text and he is thus able to concentrate on whatever his main aim in doing the text may be. The students' attention will not be distracted, as it would otherwise have been, by difficult vocabulary. Also, as there will be a short time lapse between the presentation of the vocabulary and the reading of it in a text, when the student comes across it for the second time during reading, this will provide further consolidation of the lexical item.

However, pre-teaching vocabulary can be very 'bitty'. If you have six words you want your students to learn for active use, it doesn't make for a smooth lesson to present the word, practise it, check its meaning has been understood etc. and then to repeat this process for another five totally unconnected words. Furthermore, we may be depriving our students of the opportunity of acquiring the useful skill of inferring the meaning of words from the context. Even with younger children it may not be necessary to pre-teach the vocabulary, although extra help can be given to aid comprehension as in the following example where the words *hair, jacket, tie* and *dress* are new lexical items for the students. The students will get a great deal of satisfaction from working out the meaning for themselves, and in the example which follows comprehension is checked at the same time.

This is Mr Smith. He's Suzy and Dave's father. He's a tall man, and his hair is black. His tie is red and his jacket is grey.

This is his wife, Mrs Smith. She's a thin woman with glasses. Her hair is brown and her dress is blue.

With more advanced classes, it is often quite difficult to predict exactly which words are going to be new to the class and also different words may be unknown to different students. In cases like this, it is easy to waste ten minutes at the beginning of a lesson, pre-teaching lexical items already known to some students. A way of overcoming this problem is to use an exercise similar to the one you did on pages 54-5. This checked whether you knew the meaning of all the words on the list, as well as acting as a sort of pre-reading task which tuned you in to the sort of thing you were going to read.

A slightly different exercise which fulfils the same function is to be found preceding the section on *Extensive reading*, on page 58.

Yet another variation which helps activate known vocabulary and gets the students to teach each other new words is the following. The students are told they are going to read a text about e.g. hospitals and are then asked in groups of three to make a list of ten words they think they are going to find in the text.

In conclusion, each individual teacher will have to decide for himself whether to pre-teach vocabulary or not, and his decision will depend on many factors, such as the difficulty of the text, whether he wants the students to acquire the words for active or passive use and, most important, it will depend on the students themselves.

D Teaching in word groups

Activities

1 We have already mentioned that students remember words more easily if words belonging to one area or lexical set are taught together. We frequently teach groups of words like this together without consciously being aware of it, when teaching a structure, as some lexical sets fit in conveniently with certain structures. e.g. There is/there are + furniture.

   What lexical sets could you teach in conjunction with
   (a) some/any
   (b) I've got
   (c) possessives
   (d) much/many

2 In a beginners' course you may decide to teach 'family relationships'. List five other lexical sets you might include.

3 We can easily help our students to increase the vocabulary they already know by making them aware of simple facts about word formation in English. Our students should be taught to recognize prefixes and suffixes as well as the part of speech indicated by the suffix.

(a) Think of three words to which prefixes can be added.
What do prefixes often do?
(b) Think of three words to which suffixes can be added.
What do suffixes often do?

4 What are the opposites of the following words:
    polite
    legible
    convenient
    regular

Think of other words, beginning with the same letters, which form their opposites by using prefixes.
Is there any regularity underlying their formation?
Is it worth teaching your students these rules or are there too many exceptions?

5 What part of speech is indicated by the suffix -ness?
What about -ful? Is it worth pointing this sort of thing out to your students?

6 Think of five compound words (e.g. newspaperman) in English. Think of an exercise which will help your students learn these.

E Micro-teaching assignment

Choose one of the lexical sets you listed in *Section D*, question 2 to teach to a class. Decide how you are going to present the new lexis and devise some practice activities for your students.

Written assignment

1 Two teachers were heard discussing their work:

Teacher A: 'I always translate new vocabulary for my pupils. They understand the words very quickly then.'
Teacher B: 'I never translate anything for my pupils. I always use objects or pictures and I explain everything in English.'

Comment on these two teachers' opinions and state what principles you follow in the presentation of new vocabulary. (Say which age-group or level you are referring to in your answer.)
(30 minute question from the R.S.A. Certificate for Overseas Teachers of English June 1980.)

2 The following vocabulary items are similar in meaning. Explain briefly the techniques you would employ in the classroom, in a more advanced class, to make the pupils aware of the difference and to use them correctly.

destroy, smash, break, ruin

3 The following is part of a story which you are presenting to an intermediate class. Pick out the *vocabulary* which you think you would need to present to them and describe how you would do so.

The child lay on the rough straw mattress tossing feverishly. The old woman took one look at his flushed face and heavy eyes and realized that he was seriously ill. That morning the doctor had come out from the village. He had diagnosed a slight chill and recommended rest and a light diet. It was clearly more serious than that.

(Specimen question paper R.S.A. Certificate for Overseas Teachers of English.)

Extensive reading

So far, we have dealt only with intensive reading, which consisted of our students' working through a relatively short passage under the teacher's supervision, and examining it in detail. In this section we shall be looking at extensive reading. Here the student is reading in quantity, without bothering to check every unknown word or structure. Our main purpose in helping our classes with extensive reading should be to train the students to read fluently in English for their own enjoyment and without the aid of a teacher.

You are going to read an exam question answered by a teacher trainee. The title of the question is:

'Students are given guidance for intensive reading, but not for extensive reading. How would you help students to read extensively in English?

Why do you think extensive reading should play an important part in the foreign language learning process?'

Exercise

The following words and phrases are to be found in the essay. How do you think they might be used?

keep in contact with
reinforcement
on his own
pleasure
feedback
infer the meaning of
dictionary
subscribe to

Now read the essay and answer the questions which follow.

Extensive reading should play an important part in the foreign language learning process for several reasons. Firstly, it is an activity that can be carried out by the student on his own, outside the classroom. Furthermore, it may be the only way a student can keep in contact with English after he has completed his course.

Extensive reading also provides valuable reinforcement of language and structures already presented in the classroom, as well as giving students useful practice in inferring meaning from the context when structures and vocabulary are unfamiliar.

As extensive reading is, or should be, reading for pleasure on topics that interest the student, it increases his motivation and gives him a more positive attitude towards the target language. It may also be the only opportunity the student has to increase his reading speed, as this is a skill rarely taught in the ordinary English lesson. As the student is reading for pleasure, he will be eager to see what happens next and will therefore try to read more rapidly. The more a student reads extensively, the faster he learns to read.

Undoubtedly, the main way in which the teacher can help the student to read extensively is by directing the student's attention towards reading material that he is going to find interesting. If there is a British Council library in the students' town, they can be shown how it works and encouraged to join. Another way of providing students with extensive reading material is for the teacher to have a set of class library books which the students can borrow. Some students, once provided with the reading material, will then read quite happily with no further encouragement from the teacher; others, however, will require further incentive. One way of giving them such an incentive is for the students to be given some sort of task to do after reading a book. At the same time, this will give the teacher some sort of feedback as to who is reading the most books and which books are the most popular. Older students can be asked to fill in a book report form, furnishing details of the plot, the main characters etc., as well as a personal opinion of the book, while with younger students a card such as the one below could be used.

```
Author .............................................
Title .................................................
I started this book on ....................................
I finished it on .............................................
It was about ...................................................
   .................................................................
   .................................................................
It was very good/OK/not very good.
```

Better still, a chart with a list of all the books available down one side and the names of the students in the class along the top, and including some sort of grading system to show which books were enjoyed most, works extremely well to motivate students, especially children.

With older students, a class magazine library often proves very popular and the teacher can encourage the students to subscribe to magazines themselves.

Although it is true that the students will not read unless they are interested, the teacher can help the students to acquire the specific skills they are going to need for extensive reading. One such skill is the ability to infer the meaning of unknown words and structures. Students can be taught certain techniques for inferring meaning; for instance, they should consider whether the unknown word is a noun or a verb by its position in the sentence; whether (if it is a noun) it is singular or plural, countable or uncountable; whether it is similar to any known words; whether it may be a derivative of a known word. Students should also be made familiar with suffixes and prefixes and their significance, and whenever they learn a new word, they should be made aware of its derivatives.

Even with this help it is going to be impossible for the students to understand every single word in a reader and it is important that the students should be willing to tolerate less than one hundred percent comprehension. The teacher can show the students how it is possible to understand the storyline of a book, even when there are quite a lot of unknown words. If students are given reading practice using passages a little more difficult than their level, which contain a few unfamiliar words and structures, they are made aware that they *can* understand the general meaning of the text, without complete comprehension of vocabulary and structures.

Sometimes, despite all the training he has had, a student may find it impossible to guess the meaning of a vital word in the text. In this case, he should be able to look it up in the dictionary. A useful skill the teacher can help students to acquire is the ability to use a dictionary quickly and efficiently. A lot of helpful ideas for exercises of this nature can be found in the workbooks which accompany many EFL learner's dictionaries.

Students are not going to read for pleasure if they read so slowly that they have no chance to get interested in the content of what they are reading. We have already mentioned that students should not be slowed down by words and structures they don't know, but it is also helpful to give the students practice in reading quickly. One exercise the teacher can do is to give the students a time limit to read a text and ask them to provide a title for it, thus making them aware that they can understand the gist of something even when they read very quickly.

Above all, extensive reading should be reading for pleasure and not a chore. It is therefore not usually a good idea to set deadlines by telling students they should have read so many pages of a book by a certain time. If the teacher makes the students read, it will tend to reduce the enjoyment and satisfaction they would have got out of doing something for themselves. In conclusion, it must be remembered that forcing students to read defeats the object of the exercise and it is the duty of the teacher to introduce the reading programme in such a way that the students are interested in spite of themselves.

Questions

1 List briefly the reasons why, in the writer's opinion, extensive reading is important.

2 What are the sources of extensive reading mentioned in the essay? Can you think of any others?

3 Design a book report form to be used by more advanced classes.

4 Fill in the following table:

Skills needed for extensive reading	How teacher can help develop these skills

5 The writer mentions that the students need to be taught to 'use dictionaries quickly and efficiently'.
Think of one exercise which might help them to do this.

Writing

By the end of this section you should be able to:

1 Make your controlled and copying activities as interesting and as varied as possible.

2 Compose your own substitution tables and make their use in class more interesting to your students.

3 Produce a reasonable range of guided writing materials.

4 Understand the necessity for adequate preparatory activities before plunging students into free writing.

Of the four skills, writing is the skill most frequently neglected. A lot of modern ELT 'methods' under the influence of the audio-lingual method stress the importance of speech, with writing coming a very poor second. It is no wonder that, frequently, writing is taught very sketchily, if at all. All too often, when written work is set, it is assumed that if students can say something, they should be able to write it. Thus, little preparation is done for written work in class and assignments which are far too difficult are set. Some teachers seem to think that at elementary level, an example of an easy writing task is 'Write a short paragraph about what you did at the weekend.' If this sort of free writing exercise is set too early on, students will find it difficult to keep within the limits of their English and will inevitably translate from their own language.

It is therefore essential to work gradually up to the stage where your students can express themselves freely.

A Handwriting

This section will be of most interest to teachers whose students do not know the Roman script. If your students are unfamiliar with the Roman script, your first stage will obviously be to give them practice in forming the letters. You may wish to do shape recognition exercises and will do a great deal of straightforward copying of letters. Some useful books are:

J.A. Bright & R. Piggot, *Handwriting* Teacher's Book and
    Workbook, (C.U.P.)
Neil Butterfield, *Crescent English Course* Handwriting Books
    (ELTA/OUP)
For children, the *Oxford Junior Workbooks* are useful.

Points for discussion

1 Would you make sure your students could read quite well before you taught them any writing?
Would you introduce some writing, of letter shapes for example, at the same time as your students were learning to read?

2 Students must obviously be able to recognize letters before they write them. List three exercises which would help your students to recognize letters.

3 Which letters do your students frequently confuse?
Is it a good idea to teach these letters together?

4 You are probably not going to teach all the alphabet at once. How would you split it up for teaching purposes?

5 Would you teach capital and small letters at the same time? If not, which would you teach first?

6 Do you think the script on page 65 is a good script to teach your students?

Do you necessarily need to begin with unjoined script?
What possible advantages might there be to beginning with
cursive (joined) script?
What difficulties do you anticipate in teaching joined script as a
first script?

7 If a 'print' type script is taught, does a joined script *need* to be
taught later on?

Pupils who are unfamiliar with the Roman script will obviously have
to begin by copying. However, copying an unfamiliar script is not as
easy as it may seem, even to those of us who have had to learn the
script ourselves.

What for example if the pupils' own script goes from right to left,
or top to bottom? Those pupils will have to accustom themselves to a
totally new concept of moving their pen hand from left to right
across the paper. A perfectly valid beginners' exercise is to get them
to draw horizontal lines across the page in the right direction. If this
is then varied by getting them to draw rhythmic patterns corresponding to movements in Roman script, they will become gradually
familiarized to what is expected of their pen hands. Here are some
examples:

The *Oxford Junior Workbook I* contains many more examples of this
type of activity.

Note that pupils should be made aware of the proportion of parts
of the letters by following guidelines. To begin with, four lines
should be used. Later, the two middle lines; and still later, the base
line only is used.

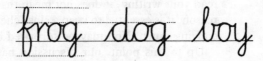

At this stage, a decision must be made as to whether pupils should be
expected to begin writing cursive script from the start. This may
seem desirable and may work if they have plenty of study hours

available. But the main difficulty this approach causes is that, when imitating models, young pupils have a serious problem identifying the separate letters. For this reason, many teachers and education ministries have preferred to start with a simplified form of printing, which is designed to lead easily into cursive writing at a later stage. This consists of fairly simple curves and straight lines:

abcdefghijklmn

However, it is not enough to get students to copy these letter shapes: they must also acquire the habit of making the pen movements in the right directions at the same time. If this is done, they will readily learn to write cursively later on; if not, they will probably develop an idiosyncratic, slow, awkward method of semi-joined printing, which they will use for the rest of their lives.

To take an example:

        can easily become:

However:

        will cause endless problems.

When starting with young beginners, another important point is the size of the letters you ask them to read and copy. Very young children still have difficulty coordinating their hand movements and this degree of control varies from child to child. Large letters are easier to manage to begin with. A reasonable size to begin with is that of the examples above.

It goes without saying that those teaching beginners of any age who are unfamiliar with the Roman script will have to pay particular attention to their own handwriting, especially when writing models on the blackboard. Many experienced teachers faced with this situation for the first time have found it necessary to teach themselves to write a special blackboard script. Just because you can read your writing, it does not mean that your students can. For this reason, it is essential to keep a close check on what your students are copying down. You may be surprised by what you see!

Up to this point, our discussion has assumed that copying is a purely mechanical activity. However, this need not be so, as we will attempt to show in the following pages.

B From copying towards guided writing

Example 1

tea	glass	cat
bike	girl	daughter
dog	coffee	boy
white	three	blue
mother	frog	water
cup	car	plane
man	red	train
two	sister	four

1.	tea	coffee	water
2.	_____	_____	_____
3.	_____	_____	_____
4.	_____	_____	_____
5.	_____	_____	_____
6.	_____	_____	_____
7.	_____	_____	_____
8.	_____	_____	_____

Question

Can you think of any other ways in which the copying of single words can be disguised as a game or can be made more interesting or meaningful? For ideas, read Donn Byrne *Teaching writing skills* pages 38-39.

Example 2
Copying only the correct sentence

Students are given a picture with three sentences underneath. They have to choose which sentence describes the picture correctly and copy it.

Activity

Make up a worksheet of similar length to Example I to illustrate this activity.

Does this type of 'copying the right sentence only' exercise
necessarily have to be done in conjunction with pictures?
How else could it be done? Give an example.

Example 3
Look at the following example:

What are their names?

1 _____ 2 _____ 3 _____

Mr Smith is wearing a white shirt. His hat is black
and his tie is white. He's carrying a black umbrella
in his right hand. His shoes are black.

Mr Jones is wearing a white shirt. He's wearing
glasses. His tie is black and he's carrying a bag.
He isn't carrying an umbrella. His shoes are black.

Now write about Mr Thomas:

_____

Question
Would you say that this was still a copying exercise?
Does this sort of exercise necessarily have to be done with pictures?

Example 4
Correct the wrong sentences.

Students have to rewrite sentences carrying false information, in
conjunction with pictures where necessary.

Example 5
Look at the following example:

Can you play the guitar, Mary?

Yes, I can.

1. Now ask your friends and write their answers.

Name:				
play the guitar				
speak French				
sail a boat				
ride a bike				
ride a horse				
swim				
make coffee				
make a cake				
draw very well				
play tennis				
play chess				

2. Now write some sentences about your friends in your exercise book.

Activity

Make up a similar but shorter questionnaire, which will enable your students to write a connected paragraph and at the same time give them practice in the present simple tense.

C Substitution tables

Substitution tables are a traditional type of 'copying' exercise used in the classroom often when a piece of language is being presented for the first time. They allow for the formation of large numbers of correct sentences.

Consider the following types of substitution table:

Type 1

| He
She
Mary | goes to | school
work
the cinema
the theatre | on | Mondays.
Tuesdays.
Wednesdays.
Thursdays. |

Type 2

| If | he
she | had some | money
flour
matches | he
she | would | light a cigarette.
buy a car.
make a cake. |

Type 3

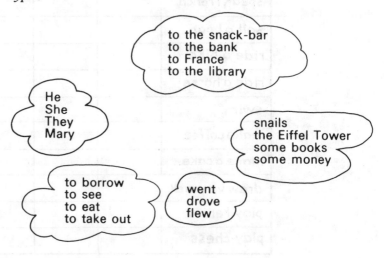

Questions

1 What is the difference between a Type 1 and a Type 2 substitution table?

2 What is the difference between a Type 2 and a Type 3 substitution table?

3 At what stage of learning would you use the different substitution tables?

4 With what level classes e.g. beginners, elementary etc., would you use the different types of substitution tables?

5 List some structures which are particularly suitable for use with a Type 3 balloon substitution table.

6 Many textbooks now include substitution tables. Would you allow students to work directly from the substitution tables in their books or do you think anything is to be gained from transferring the substitution table to the blackboard?

If substitution tables are over-used, the novelty will soon wear off, so it is as well to vary the way we use them in class. The following are just a few of the ways in which we can make substitution tables more challenging for our students.

1 One 'column' of the substitution table that is particularly easy can be missed out.
2 Certain words can be missed out.
3 Picture prompts can replace some of the words.
4 Writing from substitution tables can be turned into a game by giving students a certain time limit and seeing who can make the most sentences.
5 Interest can be increased by increasing student participation i.e. involving the students more. The whole class can help the teacher make up the substitution table.
6 The teacher can rub out sections of the table and get the students to make different but correct replacements.
7 The teacher can get the students to read the substitution table and then he can gradually erase parts of it. The teacher can erase only a small part of the table, half or nearly all of it, depending on the ability of the students.

Activities

1 Make up a Type 2 substitution table to give your students practice in the first conditional.

   e.g. If it rains, I'll stay at home.

   Suggest a way you can make this activity more challenging for your students.

2 Make up a Type 3 substitution table to practise adverbs of frequency.
   i.e. sometimes, often, always etc.

3 How would you encourage students to copy in whole word sequences rather than copying word by word?

4 Is it necessary to include a substitution table in most 'presentation of structure' lessons you do?
   What other controlled writing activities could you do instead?

5 A Type 2 substitution table could be extended into a homework worksheet giving your students writing practice e.g.

	zoo.		film.
Yesterday John went to the	beach.	He saw a	tiger.
	cinema.		shark.

   (a) Complete this example so that students can write a complete story.
   (b) Write a set of instructions explaining to students what they are expected to do.
   (c) How could this exercise be made a little more free?

D From guided writing towards free production

It is obviously not possible to go straight from modified copying activities to writing free compositions. There must be certain bridging activities.

Exercise

Some of the following activities are still highly controlled, others come quite near to free writing. Number them in the order in which you might use them in the classroom going from the most controlled to the freest.

1 Open-ended dialogue
   e.g.

A: Hello Jane. Well, this is a surprise.

B: ....

A: Yes, it must be three years. What are you doing with yourself these days?

B: ....

A: Oh, so you don't work at the bank any more, then.
   etc.

2 Give your students a text and ask them to write a dialogue. Newspapers are often a good source of texts which lend themselves to this. e.g.

Passenger with pole reaches breaking point

A CANADIAN who arrived at Heathrow with a 20-foot-long brown paper parcel over his shoulder explained that it was a fine and valuable example of delicate craftsmanship covered in carvings and insisted it must travel with him to Toronto in the jumbo jet, to avoid damage.

When airline staff said the pole could not be accommodated in the passenger section, he demanded his money back and said he would travel by sea. Then he whirled round, clearing a 20-foot space and stormed out of the exit.

But as his parcel swung round, it hit the door, snapped in half, and fell to the ground. After a few seconds of silent thought, he picked up the two halves and returned to the check-in desk, which allowed him to take the items on the aircraft as hand baggage.

3 Give students the beginning and end of a paragraph. They have to write the middle.

4 Give students a set of guided and sequenced questions which when answered will form a well set-out description. e.g.

Answer the following questions in full sentences.
Q: What did you do for your holidays last year?
A: Last year, I ...
Q: Who did you go with?
   etc.

5 Give students pictures to describe, possibly supplying relevant vocabulary. The teacher's handbook to Donn Byrne's *Wall pictures for language practice* contains ideas for composition work using the wall-charts.

6 Picture composition. Students describe a whole sequence of pictures, telling the story.

7 Give students prompts from which they can write essays. These can be detailed word prompts:
Mary/never/be/England/before.
or

8 They can merely be ideas for how the essay should develop. e.g. Man wakes up in middle of night/thinks he hears noise downstairs etc.

9 Students are given a short paragraph where link words, such as *therefore*, *whereas*, *however* etc. are missing. They have to supply the missing words.

10 Students are given a longer paragraph where sentences which provide a bridge between ideas and arguments are missing.

Activities

1 Construct an exercise like no. 9 for your students. It might be a good idea to write the missing link words at the top.

2 Prepare a set of guided and sequenced questions which when answered will enable students to write a description of their house. You may need to supply the first word or two of their answers in some cases.

E Using tables and diagrams

1 A diagram or a table is similar to a text as its purpose is to provide information. There are however obvious differences. What do you think is the most important difference between (a) and (b)?

(a)   Letters

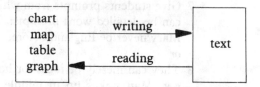

	1st class	2nd class
up to 60 grms	15½p	12½p

(b) Postage rates depend on whether you wish to send your letter first class or second class. The cost of sending a letter first class is 15½p and 12½p for second class, providing it weighs no more than 60 grms.

The information contained in (a) and (b) is effectively the same but conveyed by different means. Writing in the classroom can be done meaningfully in the *transfer* of information from a table (or diagram, or graph or map). Reading comprehension can be encouraged by the transfer of information from a text to a table, diagram, chart, map etc. The following diagram summarizes this:

```
┌──────────┐                    ┌──────────┐
│  chart   │      writing       │          │
│  map     │  ───────────────►  │   text   │
│  table   │  ◄───────────────  │          │
│  graph   │      reading       │          │
└──────────┘                    └──────────┘
```

2 At the early stages students will probably need practice in actually getting information from tables etc. just the same as they would from a text. How would you go about giving them this sort of practice?

3 When and to which type of class would you teach the following?

Look at the graph below and then read the text.

(a) *German Export of Pens to Britain*

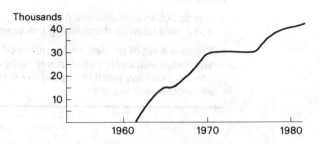

Germany started to export pens to Britain in 1962. By 1970, the number of items exported yearly had risen to 30,000, but for the next five years this figure did not increase. In 1975, however, demand began to rise once more and the present figure stands at over 40,000 per annum.

Now write a paragraph about the export of televisions from the US to France, using graph (b). Use text (a) as a model.

(b) *US Export of Televisions to France*

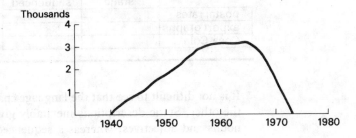

4 An alternative to the parallel text above is a fill-in text based on information from a diagram, in this case, a flow diagram which shows the steps in a production process.

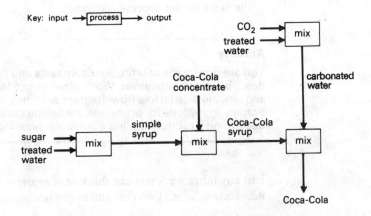

The production of Coca-Cola ..... with the process of syrup making. Measured quantities of sugar and ..... are mixed to form what is called '.....' ..... concentrate is ..... poured into this basic syrup and is ..... with it. Meanwhile, carbon dioxide ..... with treated water to make ..... Next, this is mixed with the ..... to produce the finished drink. Finally, it is bottled and is then ready for consumption.

(based on R.V. White *Functional English 2* page 48)

5 As yet we have not looked at the *kind* of language used in this type of writing. The three examples we have looked at have been either of the 'static' type or the 'sequenced' description type – but which is which?

Activity

Fill in the following table:

	static	sequenced
postal rates		
export graphs		
Coca-Cola		

It is not difficult to see that the language changes from one type to the other. Static descriptions inevitably give greater emphasis to nouns and adjectives, whereas a sequenced description attaches more importance to verbs and expressions of time. Notice, for example, the use of the passive (it is mixed) and of time expressions (begins with, then, finally) in the Coca-Cola passage.

Read the final version of the passage again and pick out the 'sequencing' words (those words which tell you the order in which the steps in the process occurred).

Activity

You are now ready to write your own texts and flow charts to describe simple processes. Work either from a text (using the sequencing words) to a flow diagram or from a diagram to a text. Some suggestions for processes are baking bread, making glass, decorating a room, mending a puncture, planting seeds.

List any other ways you can think of of representing information in a non-textual form. Two that you might not immediately think of are:

(a) *Pie-chart*
    e.g. The distribution of new cars sold in Britain

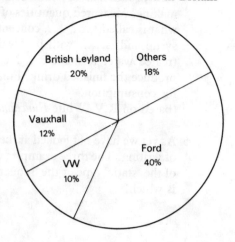

(b) *Histograms*
e.g. The population of Wivenhoe

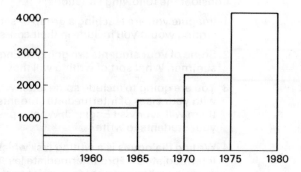

Planning
The planning part of composition work is one of the most ...

As a first step, the student may analyse a passage, and in note form, make a list of .... These may then be reordered into .... This technique is essential for writing precis or summaries. Next, the student may practise writing notes on his own thoughts before .... Finally, a student should find suitable ways of beginning and .... and suitable illustrative and supportive material to include in it.

Helping with the linguistic content
Here the teacher will provide help with both vocabulary and .... All the vocabulary that the students will need should not have to be formally taught, but instead will .... As far as language other than vocabulary goes, obviously different language is going to be needed for .... e.g. describing processes will require a lot of passives and sequencers, writing instructions will .... and argumentative essays may require the use of linking and contrasting devices. Once the teacher has analysed the title of the composition and decided .... , he can then give the students practice in ....

F Matching our writing tasks to suit the needs of our students

The sort of free writing we will want our students to do will depend very much on their aims. A group of students studying for a formal examination will obviously want training in writing the types of composition mentioned in the previous section, but in view of the difficulty of the task, is it realistic to expect other groups of students to do the same?

Activities

Consider the following situations:

1 Imagine you are teaching a group of secretaries. What types of writing would you include in their course?

2 Some of your students are going to England for a short time this summer. What sort of writing will they need to do?

3 You are going to include some letter writing as part of your course with your class of intermediate students. It is unlikely that any of them will ever visit England. What types of letters would you train your students to write?

4 Writing dialogues is a writing task which is frequently set at intermediate and pre-intermediate level. Can you think of any occasion when your students might actually need to write a dialogue? Of what value is this type of exercise?

5 You have been asked to say which of the following types of writing should be included as part of the language component in a one-year course for trainee teachers of English. Tick only those types you think are directly relevant to teachers.
1 Writing a curriculum vitae.
2 Writing a letter (a) of application
                  (b) asking for information
                  (c) giving information
                  (d) ordering something e.g. books
                  (e) of apology
                  (f) of complaint
3 Writing essays.
4 Writing summaries.
5 Writing a reference for students.
6 Writing a notice.
7 Writing instructions.
8 Filling in forms.

6 Think of the sort of information-seeking letter a teacher might actually have to write. Compose an essay title for this type of letter. Write a model letter to compare with the version written by the students on the course.

Dictation

Points for discussion

1 How frequently do you give your students dictation?

2 Do you use dictation
(a) as a test?
(b) as a practice activity?

3 What do you think dictation practises most?
(a) listening
(b) writing
(c) memory

4 Do you think dictation *can* be given as a test for anything?

5 Do you think it is possible for a student to do a dictation successfully without understanding the general context of what is being dictated?

6 At which stage of teaching a structure can dictation be used effectively?

7 Is it a good idea for dictations to contain unfamiliar material (words and structures)?

8 (a) Will your students ever have to write down anything as it is being said i.e. will they ever have to take down a dictation in real life?
(b) If so, what sort of material might possibly be dictated?

9 (a) What do you do about the mistakes your students make in dictation?
(b) Is it a good idea to make them write out their mistakes three times?

A   Problems which may arise when giving dictation

1 At elementary level, there may still be problems of script.
2 Students may react against dictation if they look upon it as a test.
3 Students may just be completely unable to make any sense at all of a passage. This can be for a variety of reasons e.g. a student may be unable to pick out individual words from the stream of sounds etc. It is often very difficult for the teacher to tell exactly why the student has not understood.
4 Some students become flustered when asked to remember exactly what they have heard.
5 Often passages from books which the teacher gives for dictation are designed for other purposes, such as to be read aloud. In passages like this, there may be pronunciation traps to catch out the students. These passages are therefore not suitable for dictation.

B   A suggested approach to using dictation

1 Don't use texts from your textbook for dictation, as it will then just be a memory test. It is better to write your own passage for dictation. Decide which things you want to reinforce or test and compose a passage round things previously done. There are also

commercially published books of dictation passages, such as *Sounds and spellings* by L.A. Hill, which link spelling to pronunciation and help with both.

2 Don't try to trip the students up. Progress from dictating simple words to simple messages, then gradually increase the length of the students' scripts.

Remember that as dictation is quite a difficult activity, your students' concentration span will be quite short, so do not make your dictations too long.

3 As dictation is largely a listening exercise, read the passage at normal speed, (reading slowly and carefully can be just as bad as reading too fast) and dictate the passage in short but meaningful segments.

4 Think of what might possibly be dictated in real life (see *Discussion point* 8b on page 77) e.g. messages, telegrams, instructions etc. and dictate this.

5 If you're not using dictation as a testing device, try to make it as friendly as possible. Remember that in real life the recipient of anything being dictated has the opportunity to request that something is repeated, so why not in the classroom? There is no reason to restrict yourself to reading the dictation only twice. It is often useful to allow students to ask questions and diagnose their own problems.

6 Have the corrected version masked on the overhead projector or blackboard or on an easel-type blackboard facing away from the class. You could also get a bright student to write the correct version on the board. In this way, if the dictation is marked by the students straight away, they will get immediate feedback.

7 Instead of the teacher reading the text again once the students have written it, get one of the students to read it back.

8 Give your students a text with gaps which the students fill in after listening. The gaps can either be structural or vocabulary based, depending on what the teacher wishes to practise.

9 Dictate things which may be of use to your students e.g. if your students keep a vocabulary list, dictate sentences which will help them with new lexis.

Questions

1 The writer says that it is just as bad to read slowly and carefully as it is to read too fast.
   Why do you think he says this? Do you agree?

2 How does allowing your students to ask questions make dictation a 'friendly activity' as the writer states?
   Why could this be thought of as an advantage?

3 What are the advantages of having the pupils mark their dictations straight away? Can you think of any disadvantages of doing this?

4 Look at 4 above and think of any other things that might be dictated in real life.

5 In 9 above the writer suggests dictating things which may be of use to the students. Think of one other thing it might be useful to dictate other than the example mentioned.

6 Make up a dictation with gaps as mentioned in 8 for your class of intermediate students who have difficulty with prepositions. Write your own completed version of the piece, indicating where you are going to pause, then write the version you are going to give your students, from which the prepositions and any other words you may choose are missing.

Listening

At the end of this section, you should

1 have an understanding of the role listening should play in your teaching;
2 have an understanding of the place of authentic materials in listening comprehension;
3 be able to construct a wide range of exercises designed to test the listening skill and the listening skill only;
4 be able to analyse the listening comprehension passages to be found in course materials and see how they can be exploited.

Points for discussion

1 Why do you think students frequently find it more difficult to listen to a taped dialogue than to read the same dialogue in a book?

2 In the early stages, if students are finding listening to the spoken language very difficult, would it be a good idea for them to follow what they are listening to on a tape-script?

3 In the early stages is it better to listen to a listening comprehension text sentence by sentence and then put it together, or should you let students listen to the whole thing and then deal with individual sentences if necessary?

4 Some writers distinguish two types of listening exercises – intensive and extensive listening. On the basis of the work you have done on reading, what do you think is the difference?

5 Does listening actually need to be taught? If students are taught to speak doesn't it automatically follow that they will learn how to listen?

A   The importance of listening

Without actually having been taught to listen, a student may be able to express himself orally, but he will never be able to communicate with speakers of English if he is unable to understand what is said to him.

Often students arriving in England find the listening skill the most difficult, yet in a lot of cases it isn't actually taught – because it is a passive skill, many teachers seem to assume that it's quite easy. However, as listening is the most varied medium, over which the student has no control, it would seem logical that it should be actually taught along with speaking, and the learner should be exposed, quite early on, to as many different types of listening as possible.

B   The first level of listening

1   Sound recognition

Obviously a student will be unable to make any sense at all of what he hears if he cannot recognize the distinctive sounds.

Look at Chapter 7, pages 211-2 and 230ff and list the different ways you can help your students to discriminate between sounds.

2   Recognizing and identifying the different intonation patterns

Activity

Look at Chapter 7, pages 218-226 and list some ways in which you can make your students aware of the meaning of different intonation patterns.

Our aim in doing listening comprehension activities is to make our students aware of what is being said to them.

Do you think they are more likely to misunderstand if they have a poor appreciation of sounds or of intonation, i.e. is it more important for a student to be able to discriminate between sounds or to be able to recognize basic stress and intonation patterns?

Think of an example of a situation where a misunderstanding may occur through a student's inability to discriminate between two sounds e.g. /æ/ and /ʌ/ as in cap and cup.

Think of an example where a misunderstanding may occur through
a student misinterpreting an intonation pattern.

The problems of discrimination of sounds, intonation and stress
patterns are however only a few of the elements involved in
understanding the spoken language.

C Some background to listening

1 The information content of words

It is important to remember that students can only absorb a certain
amount of information at any given time.

Wilga Rivers gives the following examples of the information
content of words:

1 'This is a book', said while someone is holding a book, will have a
   very low information content.
2 'He is reading' will have a high information content if the person
   reading is not visible to the listener.

In other words, in example 1, context gives us a lot of clues as to the
meaning of the word, whereas in example 2, context does not help us
at all.

In view of the above, how might you help students at the beginner's
level gain confidence in their listening?

Now read Wilga Rivers *Teaching foreign language skills* pages
136-140.

---

2 Redundancy

Every language uses several grammatical devices simultaneously to
express the same meaning. For example in 'I went there yesterday',
past time is marked both in the verb 'went' and in the adverbial
expression 'yesterday'. Furthermore, in natural speech, the same
information is often repeated more than once. Consider the
following extract from an interview with a social worker. It is taken
from *Viewpoints* by Robert O'Neill and Roger Scott (Longman) and
is an example of a 'spontaneous, unscripted conversation.'

The social worker is talking about how people react when they
know they are going to die.

Interviewer: I notice that old people sometimes say, 'Well, I won't be around
much longer.'
Social Worker: Yes.

Interviewer:	They don't seem particularly disturbed by the thought, somehow, I mean they don't seem...
Social Worker:	It could be that they've come to terms with it.
Interviewer:	Um?
Social Worker:	You can come to terms with it.
Interviewer:	You can see people who come to terms, who've come to terms with death?
Social Worker:	Yes, you... you can come to terms with these things.

It is useful to remember that some classroom dialogues unwittingly omit redundancy and may therefore be all the more difficult to understand.

Now read David Wilkins *Second language learning and teaching* pages 14-16.

D Types of listening comprehension

1 Intensive listening

Two possible types of intensive listening exercises can be distinguished.

1 Exercises which focus on detailed comprehension of meaning. This can be done through:
(a) Comprehension questions. As with reading comprehension questions, these can be:
(i)   factual (where the answer is clearly stated somewhere in the passage);
(ii) inferential (where the student has to make some sort of connection for himself. This can be a connection between two parts of the passage or between something in the passage and the student's knowledge of the outside world);
(iii) personal (where the question is related to the student's own experience or opinion).
(b) Summary questions, where the student listens to a passage and then has to summarize what he has heard. One possibility is that the student takes notes as he listens. The summary could be written up in the form of a letter or a newspaper report.
(c) Logical problems, e.g. 'All Frenchmen speak French, but not everybody that speaks French is a Frenchman.'
Questions based on sentences such as the above should encourage very careful intensive listening.
2 Intensive listening for language. Teachers often do more detailed work on language once the students can understand what they are listening to. It is usually more effective if the linguistic exercises

are somehow related to each other and to the passage and are not just unconnected bits and pieces.

It is useful to remember that questions for both language and comprehension work need not necessarily be asked at the end of the passage, but can be asked in the middle, as this will lighten the memory load.

2 Extensive listening

With extensive listening, the student is not reinforcing a structure or practising a grammar point which is linked to the rest of the course work. Extensive listening exercises are those where a student is primarily concerned with following a story, or finding something out from the passage he is listening to.

As students can sometimes be overawed by the prospect of doing extensive listening, the teacher can prepare the students for listening to a passage by telling them something about the topic of the listening text or by giving them key words.

3 Summary

To a large extent, however, the division between intensive and extensive listening is somewhat artificial. Listening does not lend itself neatly to this type of categorization in the way that reading does. It is perfectly easy to use the same listening passage for both extensive listening and more detailed work.

Read through the passage below and answer the questions which follow:

> Listening to a language involves participation – not in the classroom sense of answering questions, but in the 'real world' sense of dealing with the message received. Spoken language is not understood in isolation. The listener is actively involved in
> 5 the communication process and understanding is, therefore, not a purely receptive process.
>
> The listener is engaged in anticipating what the speaker is going to say and constantly checks and readjusts his predictions as the speaker provides him with further clues. If a flow
> 10 of speech were cut off in the middle of a sentence, the listener could make a reasonable guess about the remainder of the utterance. It follows then, that in the classroom, pupils should be encouraged to develop their sense of anticipation in order to prepare for using the language in the real world. This can be
> 15 done by stopping a tape/reading in mid-flow and asking the students to guess what is coming next.
>
> In the real world, people usually have a purpose in listening to something, for example, they may switch on the radio to listen to the weather report because they want to go out

20 somewhere, or they may want to check the time. If we are
listening to the news and we want to know about the condition
of the roads, we will first listen, then identify and then reject
those items we are not interested in. Similarly, students can be
given tasks which involve selecting and rejecting information.

25 It is particularly important, however, to make sure that we
always give students a reason for listening. This could be done
by setting a pre-question. Assessing the attitude of a speaker
might be made an alternative goal of the listening, as might the
relationship between speakers.

30 Although it should be made clear to students that you do not
expect them to understand every word, it is useful if they can
understand or recognize certain signal devices. Signal devices
are built into the spoken (and written) language and they alert
the listener to a change in the content. They may indicate the

35 end of a long continuous flow of speech (a lecture)

e.g. In conclusion...
I'd like to finish by...

or review the points made and draw a speech to an end

e.g. By way of summary...
40   To sum up...

They may indicate a continuation of the same opinion, or a
supporting fact

e.g. moreover, furthermore, also, another point is

The attitude of the speaker can often be inferred through the
45 use of modal verbs

e.g. it would seem that...
it could be that...

or through more overt phrases such as

e.g. in my opinion...
50   I think/believe that...

Although the devices mentioned here may be peculiar to
certain types of listening text, they form a framework for the
information to hang on to. Whenever there is a switch of focus,
an introduction of new ideas, the listener is made aware by

55 such devices that what follows will be similar, different,
related, unrelated etc. to what has gone before.

Questions

1 How, according to the writer, is listening in the real world different
from listening in the classroom?

2 What are two ways in which a teacher can *teach* (as opposed to
test) listening comprehension?

3 Can you anticipate how people are going to finish their sentences in your own language? If this is a skill people have in their first languages anyway, is it something which needs to be taught? Do you find it more difficult to predict the end of a sentence in English than in your own language?

4 Think of some signalling devices which would indicate that an opposite opinion would follow.
e.g. We do not wish to handcuff the teacher to his materials ... we wish him to feel free to adapt them to the special needs of the class.

5 The writer mentions that the signal 'devices mentioned here may be peculiar to certain types of listening text.' What type of listening material would you expect to find them in?

6 To what word or words in the passage does each of the following refer:
his (line 8)
him (line 9)
this (line 14)
this (line 26)
they (line 31)
they (line 33)

E Isolating the listening skill

Exercises designed to practise listening nearly always involve the other skills as well, e.g. students listen and respond in writing; the teacher asks questions and students respond orally etc. This is perhaps as it should be. We have seen from other sections that it is not always easy or desirable to separate one skill from another. However, in some cases, it is difficult to see whether or not students have understood a listening passage without isolating the listening factor. For example, some students may have understood, but get stuck over formulating a correct answer; others understood but can't remember; a few students may be just too lazy or apathetic to put their hands up to answer. In many cases, students' level of understanding is ahead of their writing or oral ability. One way of practising *only* listening is by asking students to respond to what they hear in non-linguistic ways.

An example at elementary level might be:

Example 1

Students listen to teacher reading or on tape.

Jane isn't as tall as Mary.
Put a circle around Jane.

More interesting would be a connected text where students have to identify more than one person.

Activities

Make up a listening text to go with this diagram. The students must be able to write in the names and ages of all the members of the family.

You may, of course, have to explain the symbols (=etc.) to your students first.

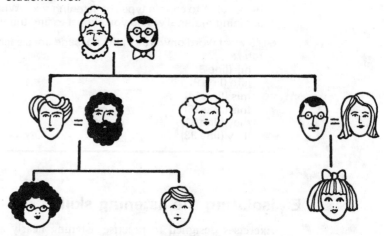

At what level could you use this particular listening exercise?

Example 2

A similar task likewise relying on visuals is 'identify and number'. The students have a series of pictures, e.g.:

Students hear on tape or the teacher reads:

Number 1   It's got four legs. It's quite big. You can ride it.

Number 2   It's got four legs. It's small. It likes cheese.
etc.

Activities

Construct a similar exercise, but instead of animals use different
sorts of clothes.
e.g.

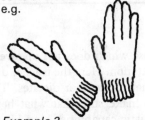

They are made of wool.
There are usually two of them.
We wear them on our hands.

Example 3

How could any wall-chart, flashcard or magazine picture be used for
listening comprehension? Use the following picture and make up
ten sentences to help test listening.

Example 4

Students have a map. They have to listen and identify the buildings.

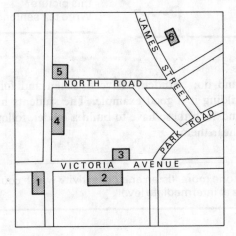

Write the text to
accompany
this map.

Now read J.B. Heaton *Writing English language tests* pages 57-82, where you will find lots of similar ideas for listening comprehension exercises.

Exercise 5
Another useful exercise which does not involve reading, writing or speaking is picture dictation. Here the teacher dictates a passage and the students draw what the teacher dictates. The teacher must, of course, be careful to make sure that what he is dictating is well within eveybody's artistic capabilities, and he should make it clear that it doesn't matter how badly people draw. Follow-up work can be done which also involves speaking practice, by asking students to 'read back their dictations' by describing the pictures they have drawn, or alternatively the teacher can ask the students questions about their pictures.

Make up a text for picture dictation connected with colours for an elementary class.

Example 6
Another related activity is to give students a partially completed picture to which they have to add details as they hear a description, e.g. students are provided with pictures of an empty street and they hear details of what is happening in the street, which they must then draw in.

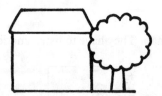

What could you dictate to go with this picture?
Write ten sentences.

Example 7
Listen and do: Students have to listen and follow instructions. *Lego* building is a good example. The students have a set of *Lego* bricks and with these have to build a model, following instructions as they hear them.

Think of one more 'listen and do' activity which could be used with students at intermediate level.

Example 8
Grid listening: Students here have a table which they have to fill in, as they listen to the text. In this case, a little bit of reading is usually involved. This is a frequently used technique in ESP (English for special purposes, where students will be working with scientific and technical materials) but can equally well be used at elementary level. e.g.:

	cat	dog	age
John	✗	✗	13
Mary	✓	✓	12

Text
Mary, who is twelve, loves animals and has a cat and a dog. Her friend John is a year older than her, but he has no pets.

Although grid listening may involve just (✓) or (✗), it could also involve some writing.

F Authentic listening material

By the time students are at an intermediate level it is likely that they will be moving towards using ungraded and unscripted listening material.

Authentic listening materials at the early stages

Generally speaking, listening material can be selected which does include structures and vocabulary beyond the ability level of students, providing the task the students have to perform after the listening is within their capabilities. In other words, the activity and not the material is graded. However, it does not follow that *any* kind of authentic material will be successful with a class of 11-year-olds because of the choice of *topic*. It is much easier to pay attention to an interesting text than one on an irrelevant topic.

So long as the topic of the text is chosen with care, authentic material can be used even at the beginner stages. The activity must, however, be graded. For example, the teacher can play extracts from different types of radio programmes to the students, who have to identify what type of programme (news, sports commentary etc.) they are listening to. Listening to the news, students can be asked to identify the main news items. If real conversations are used, they can try to identify where the conversations took place and what is happening, or they can try to gauge the attitudes of the speakers – are they angry, friendly, happy, sad etc.

Authentic materials are also important as a motivating device. Students get real satisfaction from having made some sense out of real-life language at the early stages. If teachers can show students how easy it is to understand *something* from authentic material rather than how difficult it is to understand *everything*, then students are more likely to want to understand more.

Points for discussion

Do you agree with the following? Give reasons.

1 Authentic material is easier to understand than specially scripted texts as there is little redundancy in the latter.

2 If our aim in doing listening comprehension is to train students to understand normal spoken English, it would seem more sensible to use authentic material rather than trying to write our own 'normal sounding' dialogues which are never quite the same as natural speech.

3 In using authentic material, we plunge students into the type of language they will be hearing outside the classroom. Given time they will learn to understand what they are hearing.

4 Authentic material is often too fast for the students to understand very much.

5 Authentic material often contains too many strange accents and ungrammatical language.

6 Using ungraded authentic material is not a very economical way of teaching students listening comprehension.

7 Even at elementary level, it is possible to use authentic material with our students. One very useful activity is to ask students to listen to a piece of authentic language e.g. a radio or television advertisement, and pick out two or three words.

G Using listening comprehension dialogues in class

As we have already seen, many listening comprehension passages, especially the longer ones to be found in published course material, are suitable for other types of work, too, e.g. structure practice. In cases like this, many of the techniques for presentation and practice we talked about in the section on reading comprehension can be adapted to listening, so if a text is too long, it can be divided up and global pre-questions can be set, followed by more specific post-questions. Likewise, many of the practice activities we mentioned can equally be used with a listening passage.

As well as presenting the dialogue on tape, shorter dialogues can be presented orally by the teacher. This need not involve the teacher leaping from one end of the classroom to the other in an attempt to play the part of two characters. Use can be made of glove puppets or the teacher can simply point to the characters on the blackboard.

Presenting the dialogue on tape, however, has obvious advantages. The teacher has a constant and unvarying model and can focus attention not only on structural and lexical points which need clarifying but also on points of phonology, including drawing attention to things like irony and sarcasm conveyed by tone of voice. Having the dialogue on tape has the further advantage that the teacher can stop the tape where necessary, e.g. if he wants to check comprehension of small details. The tape can also be stopped to ask the students to use contextual clues to predict what is going to come. e.g. 'Well, I don't think it's going to rain, I think ...'

Reading, writing and speaking work can also arise naturally out of listening comprehension dialogues.

Practical exercise

Take a dialogue, for example, from your textbook, and write a lesson plan, saying how you would exploit your dialogue in class.
Pay attention to the following:

(a) Decide how you are going to present the dialogue and whether you are going to need to split it up.

(b) Write out any pre-questions you are going to ask.

(c) Decide how many times you are going to play the tape and if you are going to get the students to repeat any parts of it.

(d) Decide if you are going to stop the tape at any point during the second or third playing to ask questions.

(e) Make sure that your students have understood what the tape is all about.

(f) Don't forget about follow-up activities. Try to include a little reading, writing and speaking work.

Written assignment

1 What place should authentic materials play in listening comprehension?

2 List as many sources of authentic listening material as you can and say how and at what level they could be used.

3 'Children learn listening skills through the give and take of discussions and through actively participating in a variety of experiences.' (Chenfeld)
What activities have you found most successful in training your pupils in the various listening skills? (Say which age group or level you are referring to in your answer.)

From *R.S.A. Certificate for Overseas Teachers of English,* July 1981.

Songs

In this section we shall be looking at:

A How to justify the use of songs in the classroom.
B How to choose and evaluate them.
C Some ways of using them in the classroom.

A How to justify the use of songs

Some teachers are very wary of using songs because they feel self-conscious about their own singing ability and think the students will likewise feel self-conscious. Others are unable to see any usefulness or relevance in teaching songs, except possibly to very young children. In fact, there are many arguments in favour of using songs in language teaching for all age groups. Songs can increase motivation to learn the language as students, especially weaker ones, feel a real sense of achievement when they have been able to learn a song. As well as being a break from the usual routine, songs, like structure drills, give students intensive practice in selected patterns, but without boredom. They also have the added advantage of being memorable – it is much less likely that your students will forget the song, and therefore the language practised in it, whereas language practised in even a well constructed drill is usually very quickly forgotten. If songs are carefully chosen, they will also give the students pronunciation practice – in stress and rhythm as well as in individual sounds. Furthermore songs can provide students with an insight into English culture. Finally singing songs is a group activity, an act of cooperation, which helps to bring the group together and breaks down the barriers of reserve which can sometimes prevent students learning a language effectively.

B How to choose and evaluate songs

Activity

We can here distinguish between different types of songs. Look at the following table and give at least one example of each type of song.

Type	Description	Example
1 Special occasion songs	Songs which are sung in England only on certain occasions or at certain times of the year. Teaching this sort of song to students may give them an insight into English culture.	
2 Songs and games	Songs, usually children's songs, which are sung to accompany certain games.	
3 Action songs	Songs which require actions or some sort of mime to be performed while singing them. Ordinary songs can be made more meaningful by devising a series of actions to accompany them.	
4 Songs where one structure or a lot of lexis is repeated over and over again.	Specially written songs for teaching can be included here.	
5 Songs which tell a story.		

Considerations in choosing songs

Activities

1 Each take a different song from the examples you have listed and write down all the essential vocabulary and structures that your students will need to know.

Your first consideration therefore is structure and lexis and whether they are known, or indeed of any use to your students.

2 Decide what language level (elementary, intermediate or advanced), the songs you have listed are suitable for.

So your second consideration is ...

3 Are any of the songs only suitable for one particular age level?

Consideration 3 is ...

4 Many songs are unsuitable for language teaching because they have unnatural stress patterns or sometimes words are pronounced wrongly to fit in with the tune. You should therefore

bear in mind that the songs you choose for teaching should have words which fit the tune naturally. Each take one song on the list and check that this is the case. You can do this by singing the song to yourself and seeing if the words fit in with the beat of the song.

5 Would any of the songs be more appealing to your students? Why is this?

So your final consideration should be ...

C How to teach with songs

As we have mentioned, there are different types of songs and the way we teach and the practice activities we do are going to depend to a large extent on the sort of song we have chosen. However, although we may wish to use a few songs for listening purposes only, the majority of songs we will probably use for student participation.

There are many ways we can go about teaching the actual song. The following is one suggested procedure that can be followed:

1 Pre-teach words and idioms.
2 Play the whole song to the students.
3 Repeat the words chorally, tapping on the desk to establish the rhythm (verse by verse if the song is quite long).
4 Put the words to the tune (verse by verse if necessary).

Activities: exploiting other possibilities

Listen and respond
With most songs, we will probably want to do some question and answer work to check comprehension. Which type of song, in particular, lends itself to asking comprehension questions and retelling the story?

Listen and write
(a) Choose one song that is easy enough for students to write down the words of as they listen to it.
(b) Choose one song that could be used for a 'Listen and fill in the blanks' activity. Write out the text of the song you would give your students. The blanks should not be too difficult or long.

Listen and do
Take any song and work out a series of actions or mime for your students to do as they sing it. 'My Bonnie lies over the ocean' is a good one.

Listen and point
Consider the following song:

I like coffee
I like tea
I like Harry
And he likes me.

How could you have a 'listen and point' activity for this song?
What pictures would you need to draw on the blackboard?

Exercise for written work
At what stage of a lesson do you use songs and why?

Games

Games are often wrongly regarded as an end-of-term activity or something to fill in the last five minutes of a lesson. In fact they can be used at all stages of practice from controlled to free.

Look back to the section on songs. Which of the reasons for using songs in the classroom also apply to games?
What other reasons can you think of that justify the use of games?

A Games to practise structures

1 Memory games

1 Kim's game is an extremely versatile game which can be used for teaching several structures. The basic principle is that the teacher displays a wall-chart or some realia, etc., which the students have to study carefully for a minute or two. What was displayed is then hidden from view and the students then have to remember what they have seen.
e.g. For teaching *there was/there were*.
The teacher displays ten or so objects on his desk for one or two minutes and then hides them with a cloth – the students have to remember what there was on the desk.

Think of three other structures or areas of language that Kim's game could be used to practise.

2 In the early stages of practice, after presenting a structure, the teacher often tries to get the students to produce sentences containing the structure by asking questions. This can be a fairly meaningless activity, especially if the structure has been presented through visuals and all the pupils can clearly see the answers to the questions being asked. Even an exchange such as:

Where's the red pen?
It's on the book.

can be made more meaningful by asking students to sit on their desks facing away from the board or the surface on which the visuals are being displayed and asking them to answer questions from memory.

3 A wall-chart showing as many people as possible is displayed. Students are allowed one minute to study it before the teacher masks one of the people in it. The students then have to describe this person. To add realism, they can be told that this person is a notorious criminal and they are being asked to give the police his description.

What structure apart from the past continuous could be practised here?

---

2 Guessing games

Guessing games are even more versatile than memory games. The following is just one example using magazine pictures to practise 'has he got':

The teacher covers over the picture of the plate and students then have to guess what Napoleon has got in his hand by asking questions such as:
Has he got a gun?
Has he got a book? etc.

Activity

Either from your own experience or with reference to one of the books on language teaching games such as:

W.R. Lee *Language teaching games and contests* (2nd Ed.)
A. Wright, D. Betteridge, M. Buckby   *Games for language learning*

find or think of a guessing game to practise:

1 prepositions
2 present simple
3 some/any
4 second conditional

One drawback with guessing games is that although all the students may be interested in the activity, only one student is able to speak at a time, and some of the shyer students may not participate at all.

Question

Can you think of a way of playing this sort of guessing game and making sure that all the students take part?

3   Other games to practise structures

1 *Adverb game*
Student A leaves the room while the rest of the class think of an adverb e.g. *slowly*. Student A is then called back and asks the other students to do certain things in the manner of the agreed adverb.

e.g. Marios, open the door.

Marios has to open the door in the manner of the adverb chosen, in this case, slowly. Student A has to guess the adverb which has been thought of.

2 Look at the following Bingo game:

Example of student's card   *Example of teacher's cards*

went	walked
saw	hit
met	gave
got	drew

What structure is this Bingo game practising?

Activities

Write a set of instructions for other teachers, explaining how this game can be made and how it should be played.

Can you think of a way in which a Bingo game can be used to practise prepositions? In this case, the students' cards will probably have pictures and not words on them. Draw one example of a student's card and an example of the sort of card or other material the teacher will need.

As well as being able to use games at different stages of the lesson, we can also use games to practise all the different skills, although inevitably a game practising one skill will probably overlap with another skill or structure.

B Reading games

1 Flashcard game

The teacher needs pieces of card with various commands written on them e.g.

One student then stands behind the teacher. The teacher holds up the flashcard to show the rest of the class, who then have to obey the command written on the flashcard. The student standing behind the teacher has to guess the exact words written on the card. This is especially good for practising personal and possessive pronouns. e.g. if *Point to me* is written on the card, the student must say this and not *Point to you*.

2 An elementary reading/listening game to be played in pairs

Students are arranged in pairs facing each other. Each student has one card. On the card is a list of words, some of which have an x next to them. This means the student must read out the word. His partner decides whether the word he has on his card is the same or different.

A		B	
x	1. dog		1. boy
	2. school	x	2. school
x	3. blackboard		3. blackboard
	4. mouth	x	4. house
x	5. car		5. car
	6. cat	x	6. hat
x	7. glass		7. glass
	8. cup	x	8. cap

The words on the cards are those words which the students confuse. Teachers should keep a close check on the students' pronunciation of the words, otherwise the game reinforces errors.

3 Describe and arrange

This is a game made from magazine pictures. The student has a board and a set of pictures.

Write a set of instructions for your *students* so that they will be able to play this game.

4 Matching game

The idea here is for students to make up completed recipes by matching the right title and ingredients to the right instructions. Cut up three or four recipes into the three sections, and paste them on cards. What other things apart from recipes could your students match? Remember they do not need to match words to words, but you could also have a game which required matching words to pictures.

5 Jigsaw picture/text game

This can be made quite simply. You need a piece of strong card but one which can be easily cut up into jigsaw shapes. Stick a picture from a poster or calendar on one side of the card and a text on the other. Finally it can be cut into jigsaw shapes. If the text and picture are connected and are on a subject of interest to the students, then it can be a highly motivating game for low-ability students.

6 Translation game

For this you will need two texts, one which is the translation of the other. The English version is cut up into paragraphs or individual sentences and stuck onto card. The L_1 text is kept whole and used as a model to reconstitute the English version. A source of texts of this type is tourist information.

C Listening and writing games

Activity
Make a similar short list of games to practise writing and one list of games to practise listening.

D Pronunciation games

Exercise
Explain how you think the following games would work:

1 Phonetic snap
2 Phonetic bingo

3 Give your students a list of words which they have to sort out into sounds e.g. if you have been practising /ɪ/ and /i:/ give your students a shopping list to be divided into two lists, one containing items which have the sound /ɪ/, one items with the sound /i:/.

Make a list of ten words which you could include on the shopping list you give to your students.

4 This is a more complicated extension of the same game.

This is Jim.
Jim only likes things containing the sound /ɪ/.

This is Eve.
Eve only likes things containing the sound /i:/.

	Write down the following:	
where they live	India	Greece
favourite colour		

job		
favourite food		
favourite drink		
favourite animal		

5 Look at the section on teaching vocabulary, *Section B*, exercise 1 on page 53. How can the game mentioned be adapted for use as a pronunciation game?

E Ways of disguising an ordinary activity as a game

1 *Making sentences practising recently learnt structures*
The class is divided into two teams O and X.

1 much	2 There is	3 any
4 Are there	5 a lot	6 many
7 How many	8 some	9 How much

Now write a set of instructions to accompany the above game to be included in a teacher's manual.
What stage of practice could a game like this be used for?

2 *Answering the teacher's questions*
One way of introducing a game-like quality into this is simply to divide the class into two teams and give them points for answering the teacher's questions correctly. With children, further interest can be aroused by using the 'football game'. The following is drawn on the blackboard and a ball made of card is stuck in the middle.

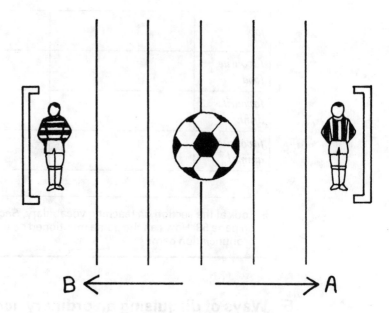

If Team A answer a question correctly, they move one step nearer towards scoring a goal. If they answer incorrectly the ball goes one step nearer to their own goal. Do not have too many steps between goal and centre line, otherwise the game becomes a bore.

Written assignment

1 Give one example of a guessing game. What language structures are being practised?

2 Give two examples of different sorts of games to practise the past continuous.

Revision

How would you define the following? Try to use your own words.

1 Open-ended question
2 Graded readers
3 Lexical item
4 Authentic material
5 Guided writing
6 Substitution table
7 Extensive reading.

Bibliography

Reading
Teaching oral English, Donn Byrne (Longman)

Teaching Vocabulary
Introduction to English language teaching, John Haycraft (Longman)
Self-help lexis, G. Broughton in IATEFL Newsletter No.70, p21

Writing
Handwriting, J.A. Bright & R. Piggot (C.U.P.)
Crescent English Course Handwriting Books, N. Butterfield (ELTA/ OUP)
Oxford Junior Workbooks, C. Carver (O.U.P.)
Teaching writing skills, Donn Byrne (Longman)
Wall pictures for language practice, Teacher's handbook, Donn Byrne (Longman)
Functional English 2, R.V. White (Nelson)

Dictation
Sounds and spellings, L.A. Hill (O.U.P.)

Listening
Teaching foreign language skills, Wilga Rivers (Univ. of Chicago Press)
Viewpoints, R. O'Neill & R. Scott (Longman)
Second language learning and teaching, D.A. Wilkins (Edward Arnold)
Writing English language tests, J.B. Heaton (Longman)

Games
Language teaching games and contests (2nd Ed.), W.R. Lee (O.U.P.)
Games for language learning, A. Wright *et al.* (C.U.P.)

3   Teaching aids

Blackboard

The blackboard is perhaps the most useful of visual aids and the majority of teachers would feel hampered in a classroom which did not have one.

Activity

Think of all the things you have used the blackboard for in the last week. Pool all your ideas and make a comprehensive list of uses of the blackboard.

A   Considerations when using

Unfortunately many teachers do not make full use of the blackboard or they use it badly by neglecting to take the following points into consideration.

Questions

1 What effect might it have on the students if the blackboard has not been cleaned at the start of the lesson and is still full of things written by the previous teacher in the last lesson?

2 Do you think it's a good idea to rub out things on the blackboard as soon as you've finished with them or as soon as they've been copied?
Or do students benefit by seeing the things you're trying to teach them exposed throughout the lesson?

3 What are the disadvantages of writing in capital letters? Consider the following.

HE SAID, "NO, I WENT THERE ON THURSDAY".

4 What is wrong with this example?

I didn't know

5 Is it a good idea to write in cursive script? e.g.:

When using the blackboard, go round and check that all the students can see and if they can't, move them.

6 Try out different coloured chalks on the blackboard and see which one shows up the best. Is it, in fact, white?

7 Some colours can't be seen very clearly at all. What colours are these?

8 Are the colours which are difficult to see any use for anything? When is it useful to have different coloured chalks?

9 When doing a dictation, it might be a good idea to write the dictation on the blackboard before the lesson and mask it with a piece of cloth or card, only revealing it when necessary.

In what other circumstances might masking be useful?

B Increasing student participation

If you are laboriously copying something long onto the blackboard, it is very easy to turn round and find your students' attention wandering. This can happen especially if you are engrossed in copying a blackboard drawing in small detail.

The answer is to try to involve the students as much as possible. The following are just a few ways of doing this:

1 Talk to the students as you are writing and turn round frequently to face them.
2 Ask the students what to write as often as possible and get examples from them.
3 Ask them what they think this word or picture is going to be.
4 Get them to read things as you write them.
5 Ask them to spell the difficult words for you.
6 When writing try standing on the right of the board as the students see it. This has the advantage of forcing you to write in straight lines; you are facing the class, and what you write is revealed to the class as it goes up.

C Planning your blackboard work

Much of the chaotic and untidy work on blackboards can be avoided if the work is planned in advance and included as part of the lesson plan. Ideally the blackboard can be sectioned off into areas. There are various ways of dividing it up, but it is as well to keep one section free for things that crop up in your lesson, that you had not foreseen. One way of dividing up the blackboard is the H model which effectively divides the blackboard into four.

Thus part of the board can be kept for pictures, part for writing tables and for lists, or part can be kept for planned work and part for impromptu work. Also, although you will rub most things off the board when they have been copied and are no longer needed, you could have one permanent section for vocabulary items, which probably benefit from being exposed on the blackboard as long as possible. The permanent part of the blackboard also serves at the end of the lesson to refresh the students' memory of the different activities that have been done and the language which arose out of them.

Don't forget that you are not limited to the blackboard itself. The areas on either side can be used equally well for display purposes.

D Blackboard drawing

Many teachers are reluctant to try their hand at blackboard drawing, saying that they *can't* draw, often without ever having tried. However, simple stick figures are not beyond even the most hopeless artists and, with a little practice, every teacher can learn enough to draw simple pictures for drills or picture compositions.

The following section contains only a few examples of blackboard drawing; there are many books on the market which are useful for copying practice or as reference before a lesson. Some of these books are:

A. Wright *Visual materials for the language teacher*, pages 117-127 (Longman)
Johnson *et al. Stick figure drawing for language teachers* (Ginn)
J.S. Crichton *Blackboard drawing* (Nelson)
The teacher's books accompanying *Contact English*, published by Heinemann, also contain a lot of good ideas.

Exercises

1 *Jobs*
Using basic stick figures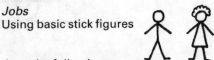

draw the following:
doctor, nurse, policeman, pilot, schoolgirl, secretary, farmer housewife, cook, mechanic.

You may sometimes need to draw objects as well to make things absolutely clear e.g. with the mechanic, you could draw a spanner.

2 *Transport*
(a) Draw a plane, a train, a bus and a lorry.
(b) Below are the first few steps in drawing a bicycle. Add details to make your drawing complete.

(c) Look at the way in which we can show in which direction these people are looking.

Draw a car and show in which direction it is travelling.
(d) What are these two men doing?

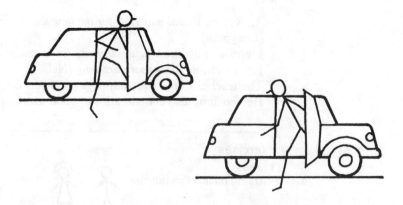

Now draw the same two actions, but use a bus not a car.

3 *Facial expresssions*
Match the adjectives with the faces below. There are more
adjectives than faces. Four adjectives are not supposed to
describe any of the faces.

sinister	embarrassed	surprised	drunk
worried	interested	shocked	crying
cunning	frightened	smiling	neutral
angry	annoyed	cold	excited
laughing	tired	hungry	dizzy
sad			

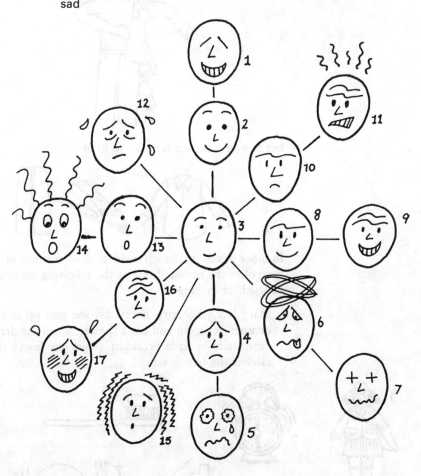

(a) How are these expressions achieved? Which features are
important?
(b) Experiment with each combination of different features. What
expression results?
(c) Try to draw some of the expressions *not* identified in the above
list.
(d) Do you think it matters if it is not immediately clear to your
students what all these expressions mean?

4 *Speeding up your blackboard drawing*

The obvious way of speeding up our blackboard drawings is to practise until we can do them very fast, but there is one other way of speeding up drawing. Imagine you were asked to draw 'he got dressed'. We could draw:

but it would be much easier to draw:

In other words it is much easier to draw pictures of objects which symbolize the action. Look at the following sequence which can be used for drilling.

Mary is a schoolgirl. Every day she gets up at 6 o'clock. She brushes her teeth and has a shower. Then she dresses and goes downstairs to have breakfast. Then she leaves the house and catches the bus to school.

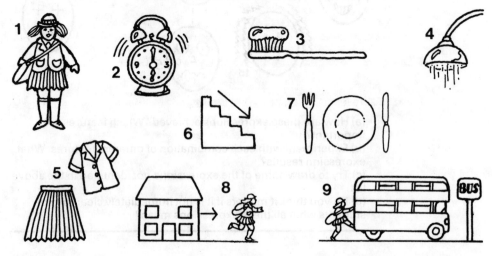

Activities

Now in pairs draw the pictures for the following story:

Mr Johnson is a businessman. Last October he went to Paris. The weather was bad. It rained a lot. He stayed at the Hilton. He had three important meetings. He ate snails and drank champagne. He went to cabaret shows in the evenings. His wife didn't go with him.

Micro-teaching assignment

1 Write a similar short story practising one main structure.

2 Work out the blackboard drawings you are going to do.

3 Plan a 20-25 minute lesson based on your drawings:
   (a) First present the story through the pictures.
   (b) Then drill the language items in the pictures.
   Here are some types of drill you could use.

Drill	Cue
Simple statement e.g. He ate snails.	Picture Word Mime
Question and answer e.g. Where did he stay? He stayed at the Hilton.	Point Question word Mime
Negatives He didn't drink tea	Wrong word Wrong statement

(c) Include some practice activities to exploit the pictures further. Here are a few ideas:

Retelling the story
Writing the story (after exposure to written form)
Game e.g. Noughts and Crosses, 'Football' game
(see section on games in *Standard Techniques*)
Changing to 1st or 2nd person
Writing a dialogue
Parallel story.

E Picture compositions on the blackboard

Picture composition can be made a lot more interesting by drawing the pictures on the blackboard rather than having them on specially prepared flashcards. More suspense can be created among students if the pictures go up on the blackboard as they are watching.

Practical exercise

Look at the following lesson notes. Refer back to page 106 Section C and make a plan for your blackboard for each stage of the lesson. Include any blackboard drawings you will have to draw. Decide which things are going to stay on the board for the whole lesson and at which stage you are going to rub the other things off.

Time: 1 hour   *No. of pupils in class:* 16

Aids: blackboard, flashcards

Aim: First presentation and practice of the infinitive of purpose. Students will practise saying sentences such as:
He went to the bank to take out some money.

(In the following lesson notes, new lexical items are italicized.)

Stage one
(a) Blackboard picture of John (very well off man)
      T: Questions – Is he rich? etc.
(b) Blackboard picture of John's car (very big and expensive)
(c) Blackboard picture of Fred (very poor)
      T: Questions – Is Fred rich?
                           Has he got a car?
                           Does he want a car?

Stage two
T sets situation.
Fred was very *jealous* of John, so one night he went to John's house and he took a bottle. (Blackboard picture)
He took a bottle to break the window. (Blackboard picture)
He broke the window to get into John's house. (Blackboard picture)
He got into the house to *steal* some money. (Blackboard picture)
He stole the money to buy a car like John's.

Stage three
Composing sentences from substitution table on the blackboard.

Stage four
Cardboard cut-out of John without his clothes on.
T: Question – Is money the only thing Fred took?

Cardboard cut-out of row of shops and John's head on a stick.

John's head first appears through the window of the bank.

He went to the bank to get some money. Cardboard cut-out of money put into John's hand.

John's head now moves to other windows in the line and the procedure is repeated. (New lexical item – *jacket*)

Stage five
Balloon substitution table with four different balloons written on blackboard.

Homework   Writing Activity.

F Other sorts of boards

Read *Visual materials for the language teacher* – A. Wright (Longman) and make a list of other sorts of boards you could have in your classroom. Say how they differ from the blackboard in the way they can be used.

Other visual aids

The blackboard is probably the most useful visual aid available to us, but our lessons can be enlivened enormously if we have other aids at our disposal.

Activities

1 In two minutes make a list of as many aids as you can think of.

2 Pool all your ideas. Make two lists on the blackboard, one for visual aids, one for aural.

3 Look carefully at the list of visual aids.
Circle those aids which are also mechanical.
Underline all the aids which you yourself have used.
Tick all the aids you can make yourself.

A   Realia

Questions

Which of the following definitions best describes realia?
Realia are:
(a) real objects
(b) examples of the world outside brought into the classroom
(c) things made out of natural materials
(d) everyday objects that most of us recognize

Uses

(a) For presenting vocabulary.

(b) For presenting new structures.

(c) To help students get into character when acting out a dialogue or doing role-play e.g. if someone is acting the part of a policeman, he can be given a policeman's helmet etc.

(d) As props for dialogues or role-play, so if a scene is taking place in a shop, a lot of realism can be added if real money or real objects are used.

(e) Aids for various games e.g. Kim's game (see page 95).

Activities

(a) Give some examples of vocabulary items that can be easily and quickly presented by using realia and which would take far longer if they were presented in any other way.
(b) What objects would you bring into a classroom for a first lesson on prepositions of place?

B   Flashcards

1   Picture flashcards

Picture flashcards have the advantage that the teacher can prepare them at his leisure at home. In this way, they can be made more attractive and colourful and can include details impossible to include in a hastily drawn blackboard picture. Although they will probably be used in much the same sort of way and for much the same sort of purpose as blackboard drawings, they have the advantage of cutting down greatly on time as well as providing variety. One can also make double-sided flashcards to use when drilling certain contrasting language items. e.g.

Side One She usually drinks tea

Side Two but now she's drinking champagne.

Activity

Look at the following example:

John's rich now, but he used to be poor.

Think of five more similar sentences containing the same structure and make six double-sided flashcards that you can use with the whole class.
Remember when making double-sided flashcards, the second side should be the opposite way up to the first, so they can easily be flipped over.

Think of one other language item you could practise using double-sided flashcards.

Question for discussion

What sort of things would you have to take into consideration when making your own flashcards for use with the whole class?

---

2 Word flashcards

We are not necessarily confined to having pictures on our flashcards. Writing on flashcards can also be used to great effect.

Activity

If necessary, go back to the section on Reading (pages 50ff) and find one reading and one writing activity that can be done with flashcards.

Word flashcard game for groups
Word flashcards can also be used for structure practice. The teacher thinks of a sentence containing the structure. The same number of students as there are words in the sentence come to the front of the class. Each student takes one word card, and they must form themselves into a line, so that the sentence reads correctly. With several groups this can be a highly competitive game.

Making your own word flashcards
One problem with word flashcards is that very often you find that you use word or sentence flashcards once and don't use them again. Many teachers are put off doing jumbled sentence or jumbled word activities because they think it is a waste of card. This difficulty can be overcome by making reusable word and sentence flashcards. Simply cut the card to the required size and length. Then cover with transparent sticky covering of the type that is used to cover books. (*Transpaseal* is one make.) You will then be able to write on these cards with water-soluble felt tip pens and use them as often as you wish. Remember to use the water-soluble felt tip pens as you can rub out with a damp cloth anything you write on the plastic surface. The permanent felt tip pens are just ... permanent.

C Magazine pictures

Magazine pictures are one of the most useful visual aids available to teachers. Firstly they provide variety from other visual aids, e.g. blackboard drawings, and they are often much more imaginative than commercially produced wallcharts and flashcards. The students can be presented with completely unusual situations in magazine pictures, which at the same time are stimulating and colourful.

Magazine pictures are also easily accessible to everyone – they are cheap and easy to find. As well as in magazines, pictures found in calendars, greetings cards and free pamphlets and brochures can be used. They also have the advantage that they can be used for a variety of purposes. We have mentioned in other parts of this book, how they can be used to present new situations and vocabulary and how they can be used in games. They can also be used for types of drilling as well as pair-work activities.

Something which often deters teachers from using pictures is that they only think of the pictures they need an hour or two before the lesson, and it is often impossible to find all the pictures one needs or exactly the pictures one wants in so short a time.

Often when a teacher does find the magazine pictures he wants, they get used for one lesson, put away and then forgotten about. One way of overcoming this is to build up a magazine picture library – storing and filing magazine pictures, so that one has a ready-made collection from which to draw. An excellent book to which you will be referred in this section is *The magazine picture library* by Janet McAlpin, published by Heinemann in their *Practical language teaching* series. It will inspire you to build up your own magazine picture library if you have not already done so. This can be done either as a joint venture at your school or privately at home.

1 Criteria for selection and classification

Questions
Why would you reject the following picture as unsuitable for inclusion in your library?

So pictures must be:
 (a) ......
What other criteria would you use to select your magazine pictures?
 (b) ......
 (c) ......
Big pictures can be used for ......
Small pictures can be used for ......

Reading assignment
Now read Janet McAlpin pages 20-36 and answer the following questions.
How would you classify your magazine collection?
 (a) by syllabus
 (b) by subject matter.

If you would classify them by subject matter, do you agree with the way of classification she suggests?
Do you think all the different categories she suggests are necessary?
Make a list of the different headings you yourself would classify your magazine pictures under.

2   Visuals for talking about and visuals for talking with

Janet McAlpin refers to the distinction Pit Corder draws between visual aids for talking about and visual aids for talking with.

We have already talked about 'visuals for talking with' in the section on blackboard drawing, when we said it is quicker to draw an object to symbolize an action rather than drawing the action itself. So a 'talking about' use for the following drawing would be

 It's a white tie.
It's made of silk.

whereas a 'talking with' use would be 'He put on his tie' or 'He got dressed.'

Reading assignment

Read Janet McAlpin pages 41-46 about how magazine pictures can be used for 'talking with' and think of one 'talking about' and one 'talking with' use for the following pictures.

3   Using pictures in sets

You will rarely want to use only one magazine picture alone – you will probably want to use more than one and it is useful to think of your pictures in sets.

Imagine that you wanted to present the past simple tense using a story that you could later use for drilling, for example:

Last Friday, John got up very early. He had breakfast and left the house at 8 o'clock, etc.

It is very unlikely that you will be able to find pictures of the same person doing all these things but you will be able to find pictures which could represent these actions.

Activity

Continue the story and say what magazine pictures you would use.

Reading assignment

After reading Chapter 7 in Janet McAlpin, or from your own experience, answer the following questions.

Questions

1 *Presentation*
(a) How would you use magazine pictures if you were presenting a structure through a situation or a dialogue?
(b) How could magazine pictures be used before presenting a text?

(c) What sort of magazine pictures would you need to present 'should/shouldn't' e.g. He should go to bed earlier.
Think of the pictures you will need as well as the sentences you hope to elicit.
(d) What structure can the following pictures be used to present?

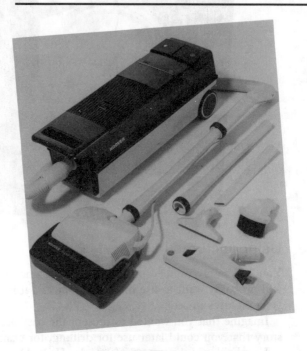

2 Pair-work

Once the class is familiar with a structure, you can get them drilling in pairs. You can either have a standard stimulus in which case only the response needs a magazine picture, for example:

Stimulus (Student 1):
What does Jane want for Christmas?

Response (Student 2):
I think she wants a ring.

or both the stimulus and response can be cued from two connected magazine pictures glued onto the same card, for example:

Student 1:
I bought Jane a ring for Christmas.

Student 2:
She didn't want a ring.
She wanted a handbag.

3 Reading and writing

Question

How could you use the following picture for reading and writing practice?

Room designed by Habitat (1981/82 Catalogue)

4 Games

Magazine pictures can obviously be used in many different ways for games, for example, in guessing games, for bingo games, for memory games, and generally as cues.

Practical exercise

1 Make a set of pair-work cards for a class of sixteen to practise the comparative. The practice should take the form of a two-line dialogue or two-phase drill.
Choose three or four magazine pictures you could use to practise the drill with the whole class first.
Write, in the form of detailed lesson notes, how you would make the transition from presenting the dialogue to the whole class, to the class working in pairs.

2 Find a set of pictures you could use to present an intermediate structure to your class.

3 Prepare one work card you could use for reading and/or writing practice with an elementary class.

4 Prepare a game for use with an intermediate class.

D Wall-charts

We have mentioned in other parts of this book how wall-charts can be used for listening comprehension, games and presenting structure. They can also be used for picture composition, and their usefulness is further increased if certain parts of them can be made to change or move e.g. things can be masked or certain objects can be added to the picture with Blu-Tack and moved around. This is especially good for practising prepositions. If you cut slots in the wall-chart you can even practise 'behind'. Things can also be stuck over other things, so a window can be broken, then mended etc. This would provide practice in the passive or causative *have*.

Take any wall-chart and make a series of cut-outs that you can stick over things in the wall-chart to practise the present perfect passive, e.g. It's been cleaned.

The tape-recorder

A Why use a tape-recorder at all?

The tape-recorder has come to be an invaluable aid to the language learner and teacher, and after the blackboard, is probably one of the most commonly used pieces of equipment in the classroom. However, as we have seen, many listening activities can be done in the classroom without it.

Activity

Look at the points below and decide whether a tape-recorder is essential to achieve the objectives mentioned, whether a tape-recorder is an improvement over the teacher, or whether the tape-recorder is not really necessary at all to achieve the objective in question.

1 To allow the students to listen to a variety of different accents and varieties of English.

2 To allow students to listen to conversations and dialogues involving more than two speakers.

3 To improve students' reading ability by allowing them to read along while listening to a text.

4 To do pronunciation work by imitating a model.

5 To introduce an element of variety and liven up drilling.

6 To allow students to listen to 'authentic' material (see page 89).

For more on the advantages of using a tape-recorder, see page 90.

B Uses of the tape-recorder

The tape-recorder can obviously be used for all the listening activities mentioned in the section on listening on pages 79ff. Here are a couple of other uses:

1 Sound effects

(a) These can be used as cues for drills as we saw on page 28.
(b) Sound stories.
These consist of a sequence of sounds which suggest something happening when taken together. Here is an example from a published source of sound stories.

(On tape)
Airport lounge – bustling noises – 'FAG announce the departure of flight FAG 61 to New York and Los Angeles. Passengers are requested to proceed to gate number 20 ...' – feet – more bustle – whine of jet engines – feet on tarmac, up stairs into plane – ffff of seats being sat on – 'Please fasten your seat-belts and do not smoke until we are airborne.' – crescendo of jet engines and take-off – spectral voice: 'Here is an important announcement: this is the first completely automatic flight. There are no aircrew aboard. There are no hostesses. There are no pilots...' – Excited gabble – 'Please do not be alarmed. Everything has been carefully tested. Nothing can possibly go wrong – go wrong – go wrong – go wrong – go wrong – ...'

(from *Sounds interesting* by Alan Maley & Alan Duff – Cambridge University Press)

The book by Maley & Duff contains ideas for exploiting sound stories, including written work, vocabulary building, etc.

2 Jigsaw listening

For this you will need more than one tape-recorder. Usually you will need three. The class is split up into three groups and each group listens to their tape and extracts relevant information. The groups then exchange the information they have found out.

The groups can be given different parts of the same story so they don't discover the whole story until they have exchanged information. Alternatively, they can be given a problem to solve – the best route for a prisoner to escape, for example. They are only able to solve the problem by pooling all their information.

Jigsaw listening can be an excellent way of integrating the skills. A published source of material is *Listening links* by M. Geddes and G. Sturtridge. (Heinemann)

C Other hints for using the tape-recorder

As we pointed out earlier, listening is a skill which requires a great deal of concentration, so it is a good idea to limit the time spent on continuous listening.

What is the maximum length of time you have found it possible to do continuous listening with students?

To lessen the memory load, you could stop the tape occasionally to ask students a question or to get them to repeat the last sentence they heard.

Will doing this break up the continuity of the tape and if it will, does it matter?

So far, all the activities we have mentioned have used the tape-recorder for playing back previously recorded material. Another frequently neglected use of the tape-recorder is for making recordings in the classroom, particularly of the students themselves. The teacher can record the students during a discussion etc., and can thus diagnose problem areas more easily.

Tape your students and decide which two consonant sounds and which two vowel sounds they need remedial practice in.

A very motivating activity for students is to let them write and record their own dialogues. You could also record students telling a story. Later on the story could be written in good English and the text could be used for reading practice.

D Practicalities

1 Criteria for choosing taped material

Points for discussion

Comment on the following statements:

1 Taped material chosen for use in class should be of interest to students, or else why should they bother to listen?

2 A disadvantage of taped material is that, unlike in real life, there is no non-aural context to aid comprehension.

3 Taped material chosen for classroom use should be as natural as possible. It should include redundancies, as well as the 'imperfect' speech of real life. Hesitations, false starts etc. must all be included.

4 With published material, very often, the tape adds nothing at all to the printed text, as in the case where passages are read aloud by a single voice.

5 It doesn't really matter if the quality of the tapes isn't that clear, since, in the real world, students will have to listen with a lot of distracting background noise.

2 Positioning the tape-recorder

Remember to check which is the best position to place your tape-recorder and also check that all your students can hear. Try to use a speaker which directs the sound at the students; after all, you're not teaching the ceiling. Extension loud speakers are cheap to obtain and can be fixed on a wall facing the students (while the teacher has the machine within reach to operate easily). Such speakers frequently improve the sound quality of small portable cassette-recorders.

3 Using the tape-recorder – some practical problems

The following exercise can be done by using either a cassette or tape-recorder. Do the exercise in pairs. Each pair will need access to a cassette or tape-recorder, preferably of the type you intend using in the classroom. Answer a question (a) and then (b) do what the question suggests.

---

1 (a) How does the machine get its power?

Mains plug ☐   Batteries ☐

(b) Now either plug it in or check the right number and type of batteries are in the machine.

2 (a) How do you know that the power is reaching the machine?

Lights ☐   Power meter ☐   Movement ☐

(b) Check power. If negative, check the following:

- plug switched on?
- wires connected, inserted properly?
- batteries weak, properly inserted?

3 (a) Where do you put the tape?
Does it go from right to left or from left to right?

(b) Place the tape on the machine.

4 (a) How do you start/stop/pause the machine?

(b) Practise using these buttons so that you can use them without looking. Do this by staring ahead of you and imagine you're playing the piano.

5 (a) How do you replay a short part of the tape? This you may wish to do for drilling or pronunciation practice.

(b) Practise repeating a line of dialogue on your tape so that you can do it without looking and without any distracting mechanical noises. You will find the numerical counter (if fitted) useful for determining how far to rewind.

6 (a) What do you need to make a voice recording?
Is a microphone necessary?

(b) Assemble your equipment and get it ready to record.

7 (a) What must you check before recording?

- recording level control ☐
- microphone switched on ☐
- tape at right place ☐
- counter to zero ☐
- microphone properly plugged in ☐

(b) Set your machine for record. Now do it.

8 (a) How do you make a recording from the radio, another tape-recorder or record-player? Do you need:
a wire with five or three pins on one end and five or three pins on the other;
a wire with a single pin at either end;
a mixture of the above.

(b) Connect your two machines, check recording level and record away.

4 Follow-up

In order to bring these simple techniques up to standard you will have to practise in your own time and very soon you will find everything becomes automatic.

Written assignment

Choose one of the instruction writing tasks below:

either
1 Write a series of instructions to show how to play a dialogue twice on the tape-recorder in your classroom. The instructions should be suitable for inclusion in a manual for teachers.

or
2 Write a paragraph to show how you make a voice recording on your classroom machine. Imagine you are writing it for someone who has never used a machine like yours before.

R.S.A. Certificate for Overseas Teachers of English

15 minute question
Suggest three different classroom activities in which a tape-recorder might be used. How would you use the tape-recorder to the best effect during each activity? (June 1981)
30 minute question
In what ways can a tape-recorder be used effectively with a large class? (June 1980)

The overhead projector

Overhead projectors project horizontally-placed transparencies onto a screen. They can be used both in daylight and artificial light. They are used with long rolls of acetate or special cellophane paper which can be written or drawn on during a lesson. Material can also be prepared beforehand on acetate squares, and a library of these can be built up for future use. It is possible to write with either water-based pens (which can be rubbed out) or spirit-based (which are permanent). It is also sometimes possible to photocopy directly onto acetate squares. The cost of OHP transparencies is quite reasonable.

The OHP is very useful with large classes as the teacher can face the class as he writes. The writing position is better than writing on a blackboard, as you are writing on a horizontal surface. An OHP is also less messy than chalk.

Masking is very easy with an OHP. The teacher simply needs to place a piece of paper over whatever he wants to obscure. Overlays can be used, where one transparency is placed over another, and so an increasingly complex picture can be built up. Cut-outs can be used and these can be made to move by being slid across the transparency.

List some advantages that the OHP has over the blackboard.

Look at the following details of materials for the OHP. They are based on an article in *MET* vol. 6 no. 3 by J.Y. Kerr. Here are the instructions for how to construct the faces. The man's name is Humphrey.

'Humphrey is easily constructed. First draw the outline of a man's head seen full-face on, on a piece of thin card, which should be big enough to cover the whole surface of the OHP plate. Then cut out the inside area of your drawing to produce a projection of a head in brilliant light against a black background... (Also cut out thought bubbles.) ...

Humphrey's nose is made by laying a toothpick in the centre of the outline face, and his eyes are little paper circles (taken from an office paper punch) laid on either side. His mouth is a small elastic band, which can be rearranged to express happiness, and his moustache made of broken pieces of toothpick or matchstick; V-shapes will show happiness or surprise. In this way, it is possible to change Humphrey's expression very rapidly and one might simply practise....'

(from *Silhouette images and the OHP* J.Y. Kerr - *MET* vol 6 no. 3)

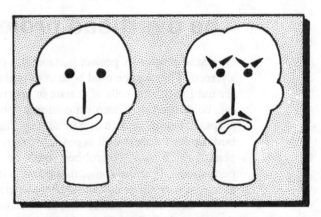

What do *you* think the silhouettes could be used to practise?

Criteria for judging the effectiveness of aids

Activity

Take any two of the aids we have talked about in this section and fill in the following table:

1 Cost.	
2 Does it need electricity?	
3 Is it suitable for use with large classes?	
4 Portability, convenience – e.g. some aids are difficult or impossible to carry round and take a lot of time to set up.	
5 Static v. changeable – e.g. once you have drawn a flashcard, unless you have made a moveable one, you can't change it.	
6 Laborious to prepare.	
7 Dramatic impact and interest (although most aids will lose this if over-used anyway).	
8 Sophistication – beware of over-sophisticated equipment unless you are proficient in using it. The simplest aids are often the best.	
9 What can it be used for? Is its use limited or is it versatile?	

Exercise

Now look back to the comprehensive list of aids you made towards the beginning of this chapter. Make a note of the aids which have not so far been dealt with.

Each find out as much as you can about one of the aids and prepare to talk about it for 10 minutes. While you are hearing about the other aids, fill in the table above.

Written assignment

1 You have been told you can have any two aids you wish in your classroom. Which would you choose and why?

2 How can magazine pictures be used at various stages of your lesson?

3 In what different ways can magazine pictures be useful in class?

4 Describe the use of wall-charts in class at the intermediate level.

5 What part can word flashcards play in E F L classes at the elementary level?

6 If you had to choose one set of picture flashcards as being the most useful and versatile, which would you choose and why?

Bibliography

Blackboard
Visual materials for the language teacher, A. Wright (Longman)
Stick-figure drawing for language teachers, Johnson *et. al.* (Ginn)
Blackboard drawing, J.S. Crichton (Nelson)
Contact English Teacher's Books, C. Granger & T. Hicks (Heinemann)

Other visual aids
The magazine picture library, Janet McAlpin (Heinemann)

The tape-recorder
Sounds interesting, A. Maley & A. Duff (C.U.P.)
Listening links, M. Geddes & G. Sturtridge (Heinemann)

The overhead projector
Silhouette images and the OHP, J.Y. Kerr in *Modern English Teacher*, Vol. 6, No. 3.

4 Errors and mistakes

Points for discussion

Mary knowed the answer.
He asked me where do I live.

These errors are commonly produced by students learning English. What has caused them? Presumably the students have never come across sentences like these (unless they heard them produced by other students).
Try to find a commonsense explanation for these errors. Can they be explained by L_1 *interference* (the students confusing their mother tongue with the foreign language and transferring items from L_1 to L_2)? Or is the process more complicated than this?

As practising teachers we know only too well that students make errors. Until recently, theorists and methodologists seemed chiefly concerned with who should accept responsibility, some regarding the student as mainly responsible, and others the teacher, depending on their standpoint. However, this sort of speculation seems to have missed the point. Naturally, teachers can be blamed for causing errors by sloppy or careless teaching or planning. On the other hand, if teachers blame the students (and we must accept the fact that they often do), their accusations are usually directed at lack of motivation, self-discipline or general intelligence. But however much truth there may be on either side, we must agree that even the most intelligent, conscientious and motivated students *do* make errors, even when learning under the best possible conditions. It is much more fruitful to analyse the cause of these errors and apply the knowledge we have gained from this analysis to the teaching process.

This chapter, then, is concerned with the following questions:

1 What causes our students to make errors?
2 What can we learn from examining errors in detail?
3 What attitude and policy should we adopt towards errors when they occur?

Learning strategies

Learning a foreign language is, of course, different from learning one's mother tongue. The learner is more mature, has already acquired a language and has probably developed strategies for learning in general. Present research on adults learning a second language as immigrants seems to indicate they employ a combination of instinctive language-learning capacity similar to that possessed by the child learning its mother tongue, and learning strategies more similar to those used for solving problems.

Human problem-solving ability seems to consist of the capacity to make theories or generalizations and then put these to the test. If the theory does not appear to work, we go back and start again.

To what extent can this cognitive process be applied to the learning of languages? Is this model of language learning superior to the behaviourist stimulus-response model?

There are no clear-cut answers to these questions. This will become clear if we examine three different areas of language: the three types of language items introduced on pages 10 ff.

Phonological items – the sounds of the language – may be best learned by a simple process of repetition and reinforcement. Certainly this is the attitude adopted by most teachers. It is, of course, possible that students develop their own personal strategies for remembering sounds or sound patterns, but it is unlikely that the teacher will suggest these for them.

Lexical items can be learnt by frequent repetition and exposure, but there is also a strong possibility that the students will adopt memorization strategies when learning these. Teachers can aid this process by teaching new vocabulary in relation to a particular topic. Students are more likely to remember seven lexical items which are all thematically related (e.g. items of furniture, adjectives for describing people's mood, etc.) rather than seven items which are not related in any way.

When learning *structural* items, there is much stronger evidence that students are adopting hypotheses, although this often appears to happen unconsciously: if you ask the student to explain the rule, he is often unable to do so. One simple hypothesis adopted at some stage may be that the structure is exactly parallel to that in the L_1. The result is L_1 'interference'. However, the student's hypotheses may not have any connection with L_1: they may be based on the student's experience of structures previously taught in the L_2.

Let us look at an example of this process.

Structure 1: *It's a car.*
Structure 2: *It's a blue car.*
Student's response to question: *What colour is it?*
        **It's a blue.*

The student's error here could be attributed entirely to his experience of the L$_2$ and have nothing to do with his L$_1$.

Exercises

1 Find examples of errors made by your students which are probably caused by L$_1$ – L$_2$ interference. One way to do this is to find errors which *cannot* be explained by L$_1$ – L$_2$ interference. Explain the probable cause of these errors.

2 Find examples of L$_1$ interference (also called negative transfer) which appear to cause errors in your classes, by comparing structures in your students' mother tongue with structures in English. List at least three types of structural error which this causes and explain why these occur.

Check to see if other teachers agree with the causes of these errors.

Competence and performance

It is worth remembering that the behaviourists regarded language learning as the acquisition of skills, comparable to the process of learning to do something practical, like driving a car. The complex skill was broken down into a series of *habits*, which were drilled until they became automatic and unthinking. The habits were taught in a series of small steps, so as to avoid errors. The mentalist would say that a speaker of a language *knows* his language; the behaviourist that he *is able to perform in it*. This distinction between *knowledge* and *performance* is a crucial one for teachers of foreign languages. Not only does it reflect the characteristic difference between the behaviourist and mentalist models of language learning, but also, even if we accept many of the mentalists' principles, we must still consider the role of performance alongside that of knowledge in the teaching process.

Noam Chomsky, the distinguished American linguist, pointed out that native speakers make many 'errors' when speaking (when performing), even though a native speaker has, by definition, a perfect command of his language – perfect knowledge of grammatical rules, lexis and the sound system. The native speaker's perfect knowledge Chomsky called *competence* and he therefore made a distinction between *competence* and *performance*. Competence is knowing what is grammatically correct; performance is what actually occurs in practice. Chomsky regarded performance as a faulty representation of competence, caused by psychological restrictions, such as memory lapses and limitations, distractions, changes of direction half-way through a sentence, hesitation and so on. To see this distinction in action, let us look at a transcript of an English speaker 'performing':

'At the end of the road there was a..... a sort of...... Well, you know those ga........ gate..... Like a customs barrier, really. Well, yes, more like a barrier. Kind of a long..... um... pole across the...... the road. And anyway, by..... by this time.... we were, well, really.... yes, really going quite..... Ooh, we must of been doing.... what? Forty-five? Fifty? Something like that. And there was no..... no way we were going to .... well, you know..... stop in time.'

If this transcript were given to the speaker afterwards and he were asked to 'correct' it, he would have no difficulty in doing so. It would come out something like this:

'At the end of the road there was a sort of gate, like a customs barrier - a long pole across the road. By this time, we were really going quite fast. We must have been doing forty-five or fifty. Something like that. And there was no way we were going to stop in time.'

The relevance of this for language teaching is considerable. So far all incorrect forms produced by the student we have called 'errors'. Now we will have to make a distinction between genuine *errors* caused by lack of knowledge about the target language (English) or by incorrect hypotheses about it; and unfortunate *mistakes* caused by temporary lapses of memory, confusion, slips of the tongue and so on. If we are uncertain whether one of our students has made an *error* or a *mistake*, the crucial test must be: can he correct himself when challenged? If he can, probably it is a mistake; if not, it is an error.

Points for discussion

1 During a student-student question-answer practice activity, one student comes out with:
   Did he went to the cinema?
   What should the teacher do at this stage to find out whether this is an error or a mistake? Describe exactly what you would do in these circumstances. Do other teachers use the same procedure? Would you do the same thing every time an error/mistake occurred?

2 Imagine a teacher who corrected every error immediately it occurred. What are the advantages of doing this?

3 Do students in your classes ever correct one another? Do you encourage them to do this? What are the possible advantages of this? Are there any disadvantages?

4 When a student makes an error/mistake, how can the teacher indicate to him (and the other students?) the *place* in the sentence where it occurred, without supplying the correct form?

5 Is it possible that students make *mistakes* in their written work? If so, how would this affect our policy of correcting written work?

Teachers will also have to allow errors to go uncorrected on many occasions – something which the behaviourist would not feel happy about. If students are faced with the difficult task of sorting out the complexities of English, they will not be able to concentrate or control their performance on *every* aspect at the same time. As far as correction is concerned, teachers will tend to focus on one aspect of performance at a time. For example, if a new structure is being practised, the teacher will probably ignore minor pronunciation errors/mistakes provided that the target pattern is produced. Later, when the student is producing the pattern consistently and well, he might raise the level of challenge by insisting on accurate pronunciation as well.

Discussion points

1 If errors are not to be regarded as signs of failure, how can we make this attitude clear to our students? How can we encourage them to feel they are making progress even while they are making errors?

2 Presumably teachers should aim at a balance between making tasks too easy and making them too difficult. How can we know whether we have judged this correctly? It is not just a question of counting the errors which occur.

3 Give other examples of ways in which the teacher might focus on one type of error/mistake at a time.

Analysing errors

It is now time to look in detail at examples of errors which students produce. Careful thought about the cause of our students' errors can help us sort out their problems. It may also make us decide to modify our teaching policy. Let's begin this section by examining a few common student errors.

1 John is ill since four days.
2 What you doing now?
3 There are too many beautiful flowers in your garden.
4 He suggested me some good books.
5 She told she was on holiday.
6 I have a knife to mend the pencil.

7 Just drop in at my residence on your way to Jane's place.
8 He changed his dress before going out.
9 She in my chair sitting.
10 To school should have gone Maria.
11 She bought many new furnitures.
12 Mary is knowing the answer.
13 I've lost my ruler; can I lend yours?
14 She sent to me a lot of letters and I too.

Activities

1 Correct the mistakes by rewriting each sentence. That is, attempt a 'plausible reconstruction' by writing down what you think the learner was trying to say.

2 Compare your reconstructions with those of another member of your group. Discuss differences. Have you corrected more than is necessary? Have you tried so hard to find to find an unusual context that you have found some of the examples acceptable as they stand?

3 Single out what you consider to be the least serious mistake and, also, the most serious. Discuss your choices with a partner.

4 Attempt an initial classification of the mistakes by putting them into two sets. You might have one set containing the sentences which appear to be somehow similar to example 9, and the other set containing those which appear to be related to example 13.

5 Suggest useful labels for the two sets. Which examples are difficult to place?

You will have realized that it is necessary to indulge in a certain amount of guessing when attempting a 'plausible reconstruction'. The amount of guessing varies, of course. When dealing with isolated sentences without a real context, and when unable to discuss them with the learner, you may be forced to guess quite a lot. Take example 8, for instance. The error might be the use of a masculine pronoun instead of a feminine. It might involve a misunderstanding of the use of the noun 'dress'. If 'dress' refers to ceremonial or formal clothes, then the error does not exist.

What you have been forced to do so far is unrealistic, of course. You have been given no clues. Fortunately, teachers are not often required to assess and correct language in a vacuum as it were; they know their pupils and their limitations, and they are dealing with language that has some context. Often, there are opportunities for teacher and learner to discuss errors and, through discussion, for the latter to put things right for himself.

A Grammatical and lexical errors

Look again at example 5 and your own correction of it. There are
two ways of dealing with the error:

(a) She told*them* she was on holiday.

(b) She *said* told she was on holiday.

The first correction is grammatical; it changes the pattern by
indicating that the verb 'tell' requires an appropriate noun or
pronoun (a grammatical object) after it. Our reconstruction suggests
that the pronoun 'them' would be appropriate here, but it is no
more than a guess when we have no information about who she was
talking to.

The second correction is lexical; it merely substitutes a synonym
that fits into the existing pattern.

Activities

1 Comment on the following correction of the same sentence:
   She told us that she was on holiday.

2 Give a reason for preferring either the grammatical or lexical
   correction of example 5.

3 Discuss the advantages and disadvantages of the following
   reconstructions of example 13:
   (a) I've lost my ruler; can you lend me yours?
   (b) I've lost my ruler; can I borrow yours?

Within the errors that we have classified as grammatical, there still
appear to be differences. Let's look again at examples 10 and 12 and
compare them. Example 10 obviously indicates that the learner has a
chronic problem with the order of words in an English sentence. Or
is it a problem with the order of *groups of words*? Example 12 seems
to have the correct order or sequence of parts, but the use of the
present continuous tense of 'know' shows an error in grammatical
choice. You will almost certainly agree that the latter is a far less
serious error than the former. We can say that example 10 illustrates
an error in the chain of language and example 12 an error in choice.

B Chain and choice

It is useful to think of language both in terms of a linear sequencing
of structures and in terms of choices or substitutions at various
points. You are already familiar with the traditional substitution
table which makes use of a key pattern or chain in order to allow the

learner to practise various choices within it. This is fine as far as choice is concerned but it does not help the learner who is having problems with the chain of language (or syntax). Such a learner might well profit from an activity that required him to put various choices into a correct chain – more or less, a substitution table in reverse. Here is an example:

in the park there yesterday well	played was playing should have played	tennis football games	he she Jack the boy

The point we are making is that the learner who displays the sort of syntactic confusion exemplified by sentence 10 needs to go back to basic sentence building; he needs a substitution table related more to chain than to choice.

The concept of choice is both grammatical and lexical. In example 12 we see an instance of incorrect grammatical choice, and in example 7 we see an instance of inappropriate lexical choice. 'Residence' is not an appropriate choice when in the company of 'drop in' and 'place' – it is far too formal. Thus, looking at language as chain and choice gives us a very useful framework for error analysis.

Activities

1 Go back to example 9 and comment on it in the light of what we have said about chain and choice.

2 Do the same for example 14.

3 One choice, of course, is the zero choice. When we produce a sentence such as 'Birds fly', we have chosen *not* to use an article – we have made a zero choice. What is the zero choice in example 9? What is it in example 2? Bearing in mind that very young children, with English as their mother tongue, are quite likely to say 'daddy coming now', to what extent can we generalize about such zero choices?

One of the most useful things that a dictionary does is to give synonyms for the word we look up. In other words, it offers a number of other choices which might be used in that particular place in the chain. The danger is, however, that the foreign language learner is liable to use the dictionary in a rather indiscriminate way; he either needs to translate from his first language or wants to avoid the over-repetitive use of a word he already knows reasonably well. The result may well be the inappropriate use of a word such as 'residence' in example 7.

Activities

1 Look up the word 'residence' in the everyday dictionary you normally use. Does it simply list synonyms such as 'abode', 'home' and 'dwelling' or does it give some indication of the contexts in which the word is likely to be found? Now look up the same word in the *Oxford Advanced Learner's Dictionary* and comment on differences.

2 Another dictionary has the following entry for the word 'thrice': 'Adv. Three times'. Comment on this information, and on the sentence, 'I played football thrice last week'. Comment on the additional information given in the *Oxford Advanced Learner's Dictionary*.

It is not always easy to decide whether a wrong choice is grammatical or lexical, as we discovered when we examined example 5. It is tempting to treat the form 'furnitures' in example 11 as a lexical error, but it is a form that reflects an important grammatical contrast in the language. Remember that choices within words, such as 'smile/smiled' or 'face/faces', are grammatical. The learner who produced the form 'furnitures', in example 11, needed help with the grammatical distinction between countable and uncountable nouns.

Activities

1 Comment on the following three reconstructions of example 11:

   (a) She bought much new furniture.
   (b) She bought many new pieces of furniture.
   (c) She bought a lot of new furniture.

2 Suggest two reconstructions for example 8, one lexical and the other grammatical. Which is the more likely? Suggest a reason for the less likely reconstruction.

3 Suggest a sentence containing 'his dress' used appropriately.

C Implausible reconstructions

Knowing what to correct and when to leave well alone is often a problem. Without knowing the level of the class and the teaching context within which pupils' responses are made, it is quite impossible to be dogmatic. More advanced pupils need to be aware of language style – just being correct is not enough. Less advanced, or less able, pupils should not be be disheartened by over-correction. 'Yes, but can't you think of a better word, a more descriptive word, than "nice"?' may well be a fair comment in the first situation, but not in the second. Over-correction may well occur during oral practice because the teacher has an ever-present opportunity to 'improve' pupils' responses.

In error-analysis over-correction leads to implausible reconstructions. Don't go searching for errors that don't exist; correct all grammatical errors and those lexical forms that are obviously wrong ('lend' for 'borrow' in example 13) or obviously inappropriate ('residence' in example 7). You will, of course, still have a few problems as, for instance, having to decide whether to accept 'mend' for 'sharpen' in example 6.

Activities

Comment on the following reconstructions and compare them with your own:

1 John is ill and has been for four days.
6 I have a screwdriver to mend that propelling pencil.
7 Just call at the residence on your way to Jane's abode.
9 She who is sitting on my chair ...
11 She bought many new chairs, tables, bookcases, cupboards, etc.
13 I've lost my ruler; can I lend yours to my partner?

Causes of error

Pit Corder claims that there are three major causes of error, which he labels 'transfer errors', 'analogical errors' and 'teaching-induced errors'. See J.P.B. Allen & S. Pit Corder (eds), *Techniques in applied linguistics*, Oxford University Press 1974. This extremely useful book is volume 3 of *The Edinburgh course in applied linguistics*. We shall use the same categories but give them different names.

A Mother-tongue interference

Although young children appear to be able to learn a foreign language quite easily and to reproduce new sounds very effectively, most older learners experience considerable difficulty. The sound system (phonology) and the grammar of the first language impose themselves on the new language and this leads to a 'foreign'pronunciation, faulty grammatical patterns and, occasionally, to the wrong choice of vocabulary.

Activities

1 Write down five examples of sentences produced by your students containing grammatical or lexical errors which you believe to be due to mother-tongue interference.

2 Comment on the errors in the light of your knowledge of the mother tongue. Use the minimum of grammatical terminology.

3 Discuss your examples and comments with other members of your group. You may find that what you have attributed to interference could be partly attributable to other causes that we shall go on to discuss.

Example 1 would be quite acceptable if translated into a number of other languages. And the child who produced example 9 was clearly translating from his own language. If we transposed its syntax into English we should have 'She + in my chair + sitting is'. Note that this does not account for the omission of the auxiliary form 'is' which has already been touched upon as a zero choice. We are not suggesting that all choices are deliberate. The auxiliary may well be omitted because the learner does not hear it clearly in the new language in its contracted form. E.g. 'I've finished' is heard as 'I finished'. Can you suggest a phonological reason for this? Consider also 'I'd better ....'

B Overgeneralization

The mentalist theory claims that errors are inevitable because they reflect various stages in the language development of the learner. It claims that the learner processes new language data in his mind and produces rules for its production, based on the evidence. Where the data are inadequate, or the evidence only partial, such rules may well produce the following patterns:

15 Where you went yesterday?
16 Where you did go yesterday?
17 She drinked all the lemonade.

Activities

1 Comment on the overgeneralization in examples 15, 16 and 17. Is there a progression from 15 to 16?
Can you suggest an even earlier question stage than 15?

2 Look again at example 12. If we accept it as an instance of overgeneralization, what is being generalized? Consider other verbs such as 'understand', 'hear', 'realize', 'perceive' and 'think'. Do they form a class, and is this relevant?

C Errors encouraged by teaching material or method

Having related mentalism to overgeneralization, we can relate behaviourism to those errors which appear to be induced by the teaching process itself. Those who support the behaviourist theory, at least in its more extreme form, would deny that errors have any positive contribution to make to the learning of any skill, such as language. To them, error is evidence of failure, of ineffective teaching or lack of control. If material is well chosen, graded and presented with meticulous care, there should never be any error. It is fairly easy to accept this in the early stages of language learning when controls are applied in the shape of substitution tables, conversion exercises of a mechanical nature and guided sentence patterns, but more difficult at later stages. However, it might be salutary for us to bear in mind the possibility of some of our students' errors being due to our own teaching. Unfortunately, these errors are much more difficult to classify, and Pit Corder (*op. cit.*) admits this:

'It is, however, not easy to identify such errors except in conjunction with a close study of the materials and teaching techniques to which the learner has been exposed. This is probably why so little is known about them.'

Let's look at a few examples of teacher-induced error.

18 I'm go to school every day.

If a structural syllabus has placed great emphasis on one tense, such as the present continuous, there is the danger that the learners will over-use it when moving on to new patterns. The prolonged drilling of the 'I'm ...ing' structure is quite likely to produce 'I'm go'.

19 I did go to cinema. (not intended as the emphatic past)

In a brave attempt to persuade a reluctant student to use the simple past tense, a teacher may over-stress the auxiliary verb in his repeated question and then find it echoed in the response. Thus, example 19 might be the result of the following prompt from the teacher:

' Now, listen to the question. What DID you do yesterday?'

By this time, even the article has been frightened off.

The teacher can also induce errors by indulging in some overgeneralization himself. It is tempting to say that the third person singular of the present tense always ends in 's' (especially having listened to numerous sentences of the type 'He play football.') and forget about sequences such as: 'he can', 'does he play' and 'he doesn't play'. These forms together may well outnumber the 'norm' that the teacher is attempting to deal with.

Activities

1 Discuss within your group the extent to which the third category (teacher-induced error) is valid. Could it be argued that it is no more than a sub-section within the 'overgeneralization' category?

2 Discuss the extent to which you think teachers should be accountable for their students' errors.

3 What possible pronunciation errors might be encouraged by the teacher's correction of the missing articles in the following sentences:
    20   I got good book from the library.
    21   Where is pencil I gave you?

4 Comment on the correction contained in the following short dialogue:
  Pupil: He said he'd come tomorrow.
  Teacher: In indirect speech, adverbs of time have to change. 'Tomorrow' changes to 'the next day'. Now, try again.

The distinction between errors and mistakes should by now be clear. Let us examine a number of student errors in the light of this distinction.

Activities

1 Outline how you would deal with the incorrect form 'furnitures' in example 11 assuming that it is (a) a competence error and (b) a performance mistake.

2 Decide whether you think the incorrect forms contained in the following sentences are errors or mistakes:

  (a) Baby broked it. (2-year-old English child)
  (b) He going to school now. (1st year EFL learner)
  (c) If I'll get through the exam, I'll be the happiest person alive.
  (d) He just take the money and off he went.
  (e) I'm looking at this picture and I'm seeing many children.
  (f) He asked him to go their with him. (In written work.)

3 Discuss with other members of your group the extent to which the clues (either given in brackets or linguistic clues) helped you to decide.

The teacher's attitude to error

The teacher's attitude to error is of crucial importance. Nothing will undermine a learner's confidence as much as a series of derogatory comments on his language performance. Insensitive correction during oral work can be particularly damaging because it encourages a withdrawal attitude in the learner; harsh written comments have an unpleasant permanence in exercise books and discourage revision. Nevertheless, the teacher must have a positive attitude to error and be prepared to do something about it. As with causes of error, there is a link here between attitude and underlying theory.

A   The behaviourist attitude

We have already made the point that behaviourists view error as a symptom of ineffective teaching or as evidence of failure. They also view it as being due very largely to mother-tongue interference – interference that the teacher (which here must include course designer) has failed to predict and allow for. When errors do occur, they are to be remedied by a bombardment of correct forms. This bombardment is achieved by the use of intensive drilling or over-teaching.

Activities

1 Prepare substitution-type drills to remedy the following errors:
   20 Does the bus goes from here?
   21 I put the blue big book on the table.
   22 Didn't nobody help you?

2 Prepare a simple five-sentence conversion exercise to change statements into questions. Use example 20 as your model.

B   The mentalist attitude

When dealing with errors arising from overgeneralization, we suggested that the learner processes the new data in his mind and comes up with a succession of rules that produce new patterns in the target language. The learner is constantly attempting to solve problems and make sense of the linguistic evidence around him. Consequently, error is inevitable; it is, in fact, an integral part of the learning process and developing competence. Students will produce errors because their hypotheses about the new language are wrong or incomplete. Errors are not, therefore, to be regarded as signs of failure, but as evidence that the student is working his way towards the correct rules. Nor are errors harmful to the learning process, as the behaviourists suggest. On the contrary, students learn by making errors and having them corrected.

This attitude to errors removes much of the over-anxiety caused by the behaviourist insistence on eliminating them from the classroom altogether. At the same time, it allows teachers to adjust the level of difficulty according to their students' progress, motivation and so on. An effortless class is going to cause boredom: a sense of challenge must be included, as in any teaching task, but if a task is made challenging, errors/mistakes will be made.

The language teacher must be concerned about what is going on in the learner's mind and must be prepared to discuss language problems. He must be prepared to help his students to sort things out for themselves, and should not be too hasty in rejecting a controlled amount of grammatical terminology and mother-tongue explanation. Grammatical explanation alone, however, is most unlikely to be effective; it is better used as a back-up device or extra strategy at the revision stage.

Activities

1 Indicate to what extent, if any, you would use grammatical terminology and/or mother-tongue explanation when dealing with the following errors:

20 Does the bus goes from here?
21 I put the blue big book on the table.
23 I've seen him yesterday.

2 Different languages have different grammatical systems. A learner may find the English pronoun system very difficult if, in his own language, possessive pronouns agree with the nouns they modify. Bearing this in mind, what grammatical and/or mother-tongue explanation would you give when attempting to remedy the following error:

24 He told her sister about it. (that is, his own sister)

C An eclectic approach

As with other aspects of TEFL methodology, an eclectic approach is the one most commonly used in remedial work. Structural drills can be useful in attempting to eradicate error, but remember that the learner is doing his best to sort things out for himself and requires intellectual, as well as mechanical help.

Activities

1 Outline how you would attempt to deal with the following errors using an eclectic approach.

3 There are too many beautiful flowers in your garden.
4 He suggested some good books.
25 The men all worked hardly in the hot sun.

2 Discuss the main disadvantages of relying entirely on a single non-eclectic approach.

D   Errors of omission

Whenever we use language we find ourselves having to make choices, lexical and grammatical choices. Do we choose 'encounter', 'meet' or, perhaps, 'bump into'? Do we begin our classroom warning with 'If you don't ...' or with 'Unless you'...? The choices that our students make in free practice can be very revealing because they indicate stages in language learning. The neglected choices are just as informative. Some student compositions are lacking in linguistic ambition; their authors are preoccupied with 'playing safe'. There may be considerably more merit in attempting a phrasal verb construction and getting it wrong than in relying on a well-worn but safe alternative. (Following more closely the mentalist approach, there is some value in allowing learners to experiment with language, to play with new words and manipulate new patterns. They may, on occasion, be given activities which the teacher knows to be just a little too demanding for them, in the belief that the thinking, discussing and problem-solving processes are also language-learning processes – even when the final answer is wrong.) Check for language choices (sometimes called 'language contrasts') which seem to be conspicuous by their absence.

Activities

1 In answer to the same comprehension question you get the following responses:
(a) He couldn't tolerate such bad behaviour.
(b) He couldn't put by with such bad behaviour.
Discuss with other members of your group how you would react to (b) assuming (i) the pupil could have used 'tolerate' but was experimenting , and (ii) he was not able to offer an alternative to his attempted phrasal verb.

2 How would you assess the following sentences both produced by students in the same intermediate-level class:
(a) She said to the teacher, 'We went out to play and it rained and we got wet.'
(b) She told the teacher we'd gone out to play and got wet when it rained.
Assume that the pronoun 'we' refers to the same group of people in both cases.

3 Comment on the sequence of tenses in (b) above. Compare 'She'd been to Athens and seen the Acropolis.'

4 List some of the choices that your students try to avoid in free practice. Check the extent to which there is group agreement.

5 Outline a strategy to encourage the use of one of these 'missing' choices.

Remedial strategies

In spite of this particular heading, there are no exclusive strategies for the correction of error that do not exist elsewhere. In other words, there is no separate methodology for getting things right. The avoidance of excessive error will inevitably be one of the chief aims in any lesson or teaching programme. There is nothing more certain to produce error than an exercise where students are required to write sentences with newly introduced words. However, what has already been discussed under *Useful classroom techniques* will go a long way towards minimizing the possibility of error, and will do so without depriving students of a sense of challenge. After all, we could devise a series of substitution tables that become progressively more complex but fail to give their users very much more than a mere promise of freedom. (We might finish with a rather rigid programmed-learning course.) Having admitted that a certain amount of error is as useful as it is inevitable, we must return to the problem of what teachers can do about those errors that persist and, in so doing, become an obstacle to learning.

A Errors of syntax

We have already used, and illustrated, the terms 'chain and choice' and introduced the technical term 'syntax' for the former. (See page 137.) If we look again at examples 2, 9 and 10, we can remind ourselves of the chronic nature of some errors of syntax, and consider ways of going right back to basic sentence construction for remedial purposes.

There are four basic structures in the English clause, or simple sentence, and they can be illustrated as follows:

	subject	*verb*	*object or complement*	*adverbial*
1	John	is	ill	since four days
11	She	bought	many new furnitures	
2	you	(are) doing	What	now?
9	She	(is) sitting		in my chair
10	Maria	should have gone		to school

If the four structures are colour-coded it is not necessary to use any grammatical terminology at all. Learners can manipulate coloured cards to practise getting the structures, or sentence parts, into the right sequence. Intermediate errors will not be recorded and the physical handling of the structures will be an additional advantage. Note that we are making use here of a very simplified model of systemic grammar. Should you be interested in this, you might refer to M. Berry, *Introduction to systemic linguistics* Vol 1, Batsford 1975. It contains a most useful section on 'chain and choice'.

Activities

1 Using the same grammatical framework, analyse examples 3, 4, 6 and 12. Bear in mind that it is possible to have more than one object and more than one verb.

2 If we include all conjunctions, or linking words, with adverbials, and give them the same colour coding, we can process more complex sentences. Now attempt an analysis of examples 5, 8 and 14.

3 If we use cards with detachable grammatical endings (or morphemes) a number of important grammatical operations can be exemplified. Consider the following cards and discuss ways in which they might be used:

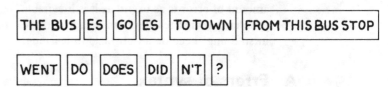

4 Suggest a colour coding for the cards and give them grammatical labels.
Note that a key to these activities is given at the end of this section (on page 151).

B Other errors in oral practice

When a learner makes an error in oral work he has an audience. Some members of that audience will not recognize it as an error, but others will and will show an interest in the teacher's reaction.

Activities

What would your reaction be in the following situations:

(a) You are talking informally to a group of students and one of them says:

26 'What you think about that film we saw?'

(b) You have prepared an oral activity for the class and, after adequate preparation, a student says:

27 'There was much trouble in the town.'

(c) You have asked a class of advanced students to prepare a class discussion or debate. Would you encourage, tolerate or discourage the use of the mother tongue at this preparatory stage? Give your reasons.

(d) Write a brief intervening dialogue, bringing in both teacher and second student.

> *Student 1*:   Does she plays the piano?
>   ....
>   ....
>   ....
> *Student 1*:   Does she play the piano?

(e) Discuss the role of the rest of the class in the correction of an individual student's error.

C Errors in written work

The student's usual audience here is just the teacher. Ideally, the teacher will check written work with the writer, but this gets increasingly difficult as the latter progresses beyond the elementary stage. It is very doubtful whether written corrections have much effect unless the writer is extremely well motivated. There is, of course, more than one way of indicating errors in written work.

Activities

1 Compare the following approaches to the correction of written work:

> A When his gard went for water,   guard
>   James managed escaping by   to escape
>   climbing on to his table and
>   squeezing through the bars, he   .He ...
>   was freedom at last.   free ...
>
> B When his gard went for water,   sp
>   James managed escaping by   gram
>   climbing on to his table and
>   squeezing through the bars, he   punct
>   was freedom at last.   vocab

(a) What are the advantages and disadvantages of the two approaches?

(b) In version B would it be more helpful for the teacher to indicate the position of the errors?

(c) How would you help a student apparently confused by the contrasting patterns: 'tried escaping' and 'managed to escape'?

2 Having corrected a piece of written work undertaken by the whole class, a teacher often feels it necessary to draw attention to, so-called, common errors. If, say, 20 percent of your students made the same type of error, how would you deal with it? What would you do with the 80 percent that got it right?

3 Discuss the extent to which we should give our students incorrect forms to be examined, discussed and corrected.

Reading assignment

Now read 'Correcting written English', article by Christopher Brumfit in *Problems and principles in English teaching* (pages 9-13), or in *Modern English Teacher*, volume 5, September 1977.

Extended activity

Handling a short text
Examine the following passage written by a student of below-average ability at an intermediate level of EFL:

> It was my sister's birthday Monday and all we wanted having a picnic. My mother she didn't know to where to go so my father he told that the weather was too warm so we should go for swimming. We did put all things in our car early and straght went to beachside.

Now, use the text for discussion and practice purposes within your group. Here are some guidelines:

1 *General impression* What is your first reaction to it? Does it communicate reasonably well? How serious are the errors? Is the syntax (sequence of structures) about right? Would you be likely to get this kind of writing from one of your students?

2 *Plausible reconstruction* Attempt a reconstruction and compare it with others. Compare, and comment on, the following alternative reconstructed fragments:

(a) ... and all we wanted was to have a picnic.
(b) ... and we all wanted to have a picnic.

Has your reconstruction caused you to modify your initial assessment in any way?

3 *Detailed examination* Comment on individual errors, either by relating them to grammatical categories such as subject, verb, object and adverbial and their structure, or dealing with them as they appear in the text. Whichever way you choose to deal with the errors, you might like to give some attention to the following issues:

(a) Is it obligatory to have a preposition in front of 'Monday' here? Is there a difference between informal speech and more formal writing?
(b) Are there other patterns which might encourage the structure 'wanted having'? e.g. 'start'?

(c) In what circumstances might we use a double subject? e.g. 'Mr Smith, he's a fine teacher.' Can we accept the double subjects in this text? (Your reconstruction will have answered this question, but elaborate on it a little.)

(d) To what extent is the use of 'too' for 'very' a common error in your situation? If it is a problem, outline a strategy for dealing with it.

(e) The preposition 'for' is often used to indicate intention. How would you deal with the confusion that might exist between the structures 'go for a swim' and 'go swimming'? Which is the more helpful reconstruction?

(f) Comment on the structure 'did put' in the light of the writer's handling of other past tense forms.

(g) The vocabulary of a modern language changes and develops. Are you prepared to accept the form 'beachside' (ignoring the lack of article for the moment) in this particular pattern?
Have you ever seen the word?
Would you accept it in the following pattern?

There were some lovely beachside restaurants.

4 *Assessment*
Give the short passage a score, a mark out of ten, and compare scores within your group.

(We are not, of course, suggesting that it is a good procedure to score small samples of work in this way; we are proposing it here simply as a convenient means of comparing assessment.)

Key to activities (page 148)

Activity	Example of error	Subject	Verb	Object or complement	Adverbial
1	3	There	are	too many beautiful flowers	in your garden.
	4	He	suggested	me some good books.	
	6	I	have to mend	a knife the pencil.	
	12	Mary	is knowing	the answer.	
2	5	She she	told was		on holiday.
	8	He	changed going	his dress	before out.
	14	She	sent	a lot of letters	to me and
		I			too.

3 Beginning with the sentence: *The bus goes to town from this bus stop*, the cards can illustrate necessary changes for *number, emphasis, negation, question, tense* and *rearrangement of structure*.

4 Any colour coding will do as long as it is consistent. Here is one example:

Yellow (Subject) `THE BUS` `ES`

Red (Verb) `WENT` `GO` `ES` `DO` `DOES` `DID` plus `N'T`

Blue (Adverbial) `TO TOWN` `FROM THIS BUS STOP`

NOTE If you choose to follow up our suggested further reading (Berry: *Introduction to systemic linguistics*), you will see that the terms *Predicator* and *Adjunct* are used in place of our *verb* and *adverbial*.

Written assignment

R.S.A. Certificate for Overseas Teachers of English examination questions:

1 Your students have done some written homework. You receive the piece which follows. How would you correct it as homework, and what steps would you take to remedy the errors?

> i am here since two months. i like not very much this place. i boring.

2 What procedures do you follow in correcting compositions? How do you deal with the situation where you find similar errors being committed by a number of pupils in the class?

3 'Pupils should be given plenty of opportunity to make mistakes.' (Brumfit).

'... everything that can be done to establish the correct forms, constructions, usages in the mental habits of the pupils must be done; because wrong forms are so difficult to eradicate ...' (Gurrey)

Comment on these two writers' opinions, and state what principles guide your own practice in this area.

4 Correct *all the errors* you can find in the following piece of writing. Underline the words or phrases you consider incorrect and write your corrected versions above them. If words need to be added insert them in the text where necessary. Where a word is not required underline it and cross it through.

You will receive *one mark* for correctly identifying an error. You will receive a *second mark* if your correction is acceptable.

> Last Sunday morning in about 10.30, I have been riding my bicycle along Western Avenue. I had been going in the direction of the park to playing football with some of my friends. I have a football under my left arm but I could still control my bicycle. I not usually ride one-handed, but there was not being much

traffic on the road and I am going very slowly. When I get near to the park I wanted to turn right into South Street where is the entrance to the park. As I was having the football under my left arm I could not giving a signal with the right hand to show that I going to turn, but I did slowed down. In fact almost I stopped and have been taking a quick look over my shoulder for seeing if nothing was coming. There was none car in sight in that moment. I started to move out towards centre of road and that was when I heard come a car up from behind. It sounded when it was moving pretty fastly but for that time I was in the centre of the road so, of course, I thought it had been passing by my left. However, just as I turned it has passed me by the right. The car has hit my front wheel and knocked me of my bicycle. It must had be going very fast because I have never started to turn right when I had seen or heard it coming.

Bibliography

The Oxford Advanced Learner's Dictionary of Current English, A.S. Hornby (O.U.P.)

Techniques in applied linguistics: Edinburgh course in applied linguistics vol 3, J.P.B. Allen & S. Pit Corder (Eds.) (O.U.P.)

Introduction to systemic linguistics, Vol.1, M. Berry (Batsford)

'*Correcting written English*' by C.J. Brumfit in *Problems and principles in English teaching*, C.Brumfit (Pergamon Press) (or in *Modern English Teacher*, Vol.5, Sept. '77.)

5 Planning and preparation

This chapter aims to help the teacher develop a more critical awareness of the language items that he has to teach. We hope to give guidelines that will enable teachers to judge the effectiveness of their textbooks, to exploit this material in a systematic way and to produce supplementary material in the form of exercises and drills. The chapter will be divided into five sections:

1 *The structural content*. Here we shall look at the factors involved in the learning of a new tense or structure; we shall examine carefully the various procedures that traditionally exist for the presentation and practice of the *form* of the new structure, its basic grammatical *meaning* and its *use*.

2 *The lexical content*. In Chapter 2 there is a section on *techniques* for teaching vocabulary. This section of Chapter 5 will deal more specifically with *selection* of vocabulary items for a given lesson, and above all with ways in which vocabulary work can be *integrated* into the main body of a structure lesson. We shall be suggesting 'links' between certain structures and certain lexical sets.

3 *Situational content*. Here we shall look at what we mean by a situation – the elements that go to make up a situation and how we select appropriate situations for different types of learner. We also suggest ways that situations can be handled in the classroom.

4 *Integrating material*. Here we look at examples in which there are strong, sometimes unbreakable, links between structure and vocabulary, between structures themselves, and how this can be exploited as a starting point for teaching a new structure or for creating *built-in revision*.

5 *Rounding off a lesson*. In this section we indicate certain ways in which the teacher can conclude his lesson by asking *key questions* to check whether the learners have in fact acquired the items that were being taught, or by providing a *summary* of the meaning and/or use of the items.

The structural content

Initial discussion points

1 The following conversation was overheard in an overseas secondary school teachers' room:

Teacher 1:   What did you do last lesson?
Teacher 2:   Well, I taught them the present continuous. I'll go on to the simple present next.

Which of the following statements do you think reflect Teacher 2's attitudes? Tick (√) the statements that you think Teacher 2 believes in.
(a) A tense of a verb is one teaching point only.
(b) The present continuous tense is a complex item that requires several lessons.
(c) Learners should be given the opportunity to use a tense in a variety of situations.
(d) Once presented the tense has been learned.
(e) There is only one use of the present continuous that needs to be taught at an elementary level.
Now put a cross (X) next to the statements that you believe in.

2 The following *paradigm* was written on the blackboard:

I am sitting
You are sitting
He/She/It is sitting
We are sitting
You are sitting
They are sitting

Read the following question and choose the best answer. Circle (a), (b), (c) or (d).

This *on its own* presents:
(a) The basic meaning of the tense.
(b) The grammatical form of the tense.
(c) The basic meaning and the grammatical form.
(d) A series of useful, meaningful sentences.

3 Look at the following language laboratory drill (which of course could also exist as a classroom drill) and then tick (√) the statement(s) underneath that you agree with.

Model: Tom is playing football.
Cue: John
Response: John is playing football.

Now you continue in the same way.

Cue: Peter
....
He
....
basketball
....

the piano

....

Mary

etc.

(a) This practises the form and meaning of the tense.
(b) This practises only the form of the tense.
(c) This helps the learners be able to use the tense.
(d) These are examples of real use of the language.
(e) These sentences are meaningless unless contextualized.

4 Look at the following list of sentences. These are most likely to be heard in one place. Where?

I'm opening the door.
She's drawing a house.
We are reading.
I'm sitting next to Peter.
What am I doing?
Are you standing?

Now tick(√) the statements below that you agree with.
The teacher is presenting:

(a) the form of the structure only;
(b) the form and the meaning of the structure;
(c) the form and one meaning of the structure;
(d) a series of commonly used sentences containing the present continuous tense.

5 Now look at the following question and answer exchanges. As you read them answer these questions:

Where does the exchange take place?

Who is talking? Who are A and B?

Write your answers in the table overleaf. The first one has been done as an example. Discuss your answers with your colleagues – you may be surprised at the range of answers.

(a) A: What are you doing?
    B: I'm making a bookcase.

(b) A: Where's John?
    B: He's playing football.

(c) A: What are you doing?
    B: I'm sitting.

(d) A: What's the boy in the red shirt doing?
    B: He's reading a book.

(e) A: Hi! Where are you going?
    B: To the park, are you coming?
    A: No, I'm going home.

(f) A: What's that man doing? There's nobody at home.
    B: It's the landlord. He's repainting the living room.

Example	Situation write *classroom* or *classroom + real world* or *real world only*	Speakers
(a)	Real world only	A: Son B: Father
(b)		A: B:
(c)		A: B:
(d)		A: B:
(e)		A: B:
(f)		A: B:

6 Read the following dialogue and underline all the examples of the present continuous tense.

A: Hello, Frank.
B: Hello, Jean. Where are you phoning from?
A: Torremolinos.
B: Torremolinos! What are you doing there?
A: I'm having a fortnight's holiday.
B: Well that's marvellous. How's it going?
A: Oh, fine. I'm really enjoying myself. The sun's shining all the time and I'm going quite brown. In fact I'm getting a very good tan.
B: Lucky you. It's raining here. I'm getting quite bored.
A: Why? Aren't you working?
B: Well, I'm spending more time in the pub than I am in the office. I'm feeling low, so I'm drinking a lot.
A: How typical! You're always drinking too much.
B: Oh, stop it. You're always complaining about that. Anyway, when are you coming home?
A: Oh, I'm flying back on Saturday. I'll phone you on Friday evening at about 10.
B: That's no good. I'm playing darts then. We're not finishing the match until 11.
A: OK, I'll be ringing at 11.30 then. Bye.

Now look at your underlined examples and match each of them with one of the grammatical categories of the present continuous tense listed below. Do this by writing the letter referring to the category next to the underlined example.

(a) an action happening now
(b) an action happening about this time but not necessarily at the moment of speaking
(c) a definite arrangement in the near future
(d) with a point in time to indicate an action which begins before this point and probably continues after it
(e) a frequently repeated action, often one which annoys the speaker or seems unreasonable to him
(Thomson and Martinet *A Practical English Grammar* O.U.P.)

A Form, meaning and use

Now read the following text and answer the questions below.

When preparing a lesson that will have as its main aim the first presentation of a new grammatical structure, the teacher first of all has to define his objectives clearly. What can help him do this? First of all he probably has a *syllabus*. In a lot of cases this will be nothing more than a list of items such as:

1 countable/uncountables
2 There is/are
3 present continuous tense
4 simple present tense
   etc.

The danger of putting such a document in the hands of an inexperienced teacher is that he may well think that the objective of the next lesson is nothing more than the next item on the list. This attitude results in conversations such as the example in *Initial discussion point* 1 on page 156.

However, 'teaching the present continuous' is something more complex. What this entails exactly may become clearer if we look at the problem from the point of view of the learner. What is it precisely that he has to learn?
There seem to be three main things that the learner has to acquire:

1 the *form* of the structure – the fact that it is **I am doing** but **he is doing** etc.,
2 the *meaning* of the structure – it is here that the teacher's first major difficulty arises. As there is not always direct correspondence between form and meaning, e.g. between tense and time, the teacher has to select one meaning from the many that may be listed in the grammar book (as in the example list at the end of *Discussion point* 6, on this page) and check that all his examples are consistent in meaning;

3 the *use* of the structure – this is an aspect that has traditionally been neglected. A typical grammar-translation method form of presentation separated form from meaning, using a paradigm similar to the one in *Discussion point* 2 on page 156 to present form, while the meaning was aided by some form of explanation e.g., 'The present continuous tense is used to describe an action happening at the moment of speaking.' Even when the grammar-translation method had been superseded, form often dominated and the type of mechanical drill (see *Discussion point* 3, page 156) that existed was intended to instil the habit of correct production of the form in the learner. This may or may not have been preceded in the classroom by a presentation of form and meaning simultaneously using such examples as those in *Discussion point* 4, page 157. In neither case was there any consideration of the use of the structure. But what do we mean by use?

Activity

Look at these following quotations from *Teaching language as communication* by Widdowson and then try to write a definition of what we mean by use:

1 '...when we acquire a language we do not only learn how to compose and comprehend correct sentences as isolated linguistic units of random occurrence; we also learn how to use sentences appropriately to achieve a communicative purpose.'(page 2)

2 'We are generally required to use our knowledge of the language system in order to achieve some kind of communicative purpose. That is to say we are generally called upon to produce instances of language use: we do not simply manifest the abstract system of the language; we at the same time realize it as meaningful communicative behaviour.'(page 3)

Now compare your definition with the one in the glossary.

The main aid to the acquisition by the learner of form, meaning and use is, of course, the textbook. Look at how different aspects of a structure can be presented in the textbook in the following examples.

Example 1
The sentences below are taken from a textbook unit that has as its main objective the initial presentation of the present continuous tense. They are accompanied by the appropriate illustrations.

He is riding a bicycle – He is riding a horse – He's eating an apple – He's sleeping in bed – She's combing her hair – She's telephoning a friend – She's reading a magazine.

Notice how the form of the structure is successfully presented by the following points:

(a) the transfer from *He is* to *He's*;
(b) the limiting to one form – the third person singular;
(c) an adequate number of examples to consolidate the presentation (seven). The meaning (an action happening at the moment of speaking) is, of course, made clear by the visuals. However, they are examples of what Widdowson calls 'correct English *usage*' (page 3). They are 'correct sentences as isolated linguistic units of random occurrence.' There is no indication of 'communicative purpose', no 'meaningful communicative behaviour'; in short they are not examples of *use*.

Example 2

Communication, of course, takes place in a particular situation, but the grouping of sentences according to a situation, although an improvement on the presentation of random sentences, does not in itself necessarily involve presentation of *use*. Look at the following sentences taken from another textbook, from the unit that is the initial presentation of the present continuous tense, and answer the questions below:

Penny is sitting near the window – Frank is opening the door – Carol is washing the plates – Mr Bell is reading the newspaper – Mrs Bell is watching television.

(a) What do you notice about the presentation of the form?
(b) What do you think the textbook contains in addition to these example sentences in order to present the meaning?
(c) If the textbook contains nothing more than these sentences (perhaps linked together in a short text) what would you, the teacher, have to do or add in order to present the meaning of the structure?
(d) What do these example sentences have in common?
(e) What do you think the 'situation' is?
(f) What is the 'communicative purpose' of these sentences?

Example 3

We hope that consideration of the above questions leads you to the conclusion that we are still in the realm of *usage* not *use* since, although the examples all describe what various members of a family are doing in the house, there is no reason why these sentences should be produced; there is no 'communicative purpose'.

In order to present a meaningful use of the structure the teacher needs not only to select a situation for presentation but to incorporate into his material a *function* of the structure, that is to say, the use of the structure for a particular communicative purpose. So we might modify the above material (*Example 2*), describing what members of the family are doing, in order to present one use of the present continuous tense, which we might define as 'Informing about a third person's whereabouts'. We might then have a piece of material for presentation that looks something like this:

Situation Mr Robinson is married and has four children. One evening he comes home from his office. Only his son John is in the living-room. Mr Robinson wants to know where the others are.

Mr Robinson:	Where's your mum?
John:	She's cleaning the car.
Mr Robinson:	Well, where's Philip?
John:	He's mending his bike.
Mr Robinson:	What about Ann?
John:	She's watering the flowers.
Mr Robinson:	And Paula?
John:	She's having a shower.

So the teacher could use the above material to present to the class the form and meaning of the present continuous tense and one of its uses.

Points for discussion

1 Now write out definitions of the following words and compare your definitions with those in the glossary:
form – meaning – usage – use

2 Taking into consideration the pedagogical adage that learners should be taught 'one thing at a time' do you feel that presentation of a new tense should be based on material that presents:
(a) form only
(b) form and meaning together
or
(c) form, meaning and use together?

3 Now look at the textbook you are using (or any textbook that you know if you are not teaching at this elementary level) and fill in the following form about the unit that presents the present continuous tense for the first time:

Form(s) of the tense introduced	
No. of examples of each form	
Meaning(s) of the tense introduced	
Total no. of examples of each meaning	
Uses of the tense introduced	
No. of examples of each use	

Now think of the implications of your answers for the exploitation of the textbook in the classroom.

B Language awareness

Activities

1 List A contains 18 examples of present continuous sentences, while list B gives 6 possible uses of the tense. Match the number of the sentence with the letter representing the category of use. (There are three examples of each.)

LIST A	LIST B
1 The bus is coming.	(a) Informing about a third person's whereabouts.
2 He's having a shower.	
3 It's getting dark.	(b) Pointing out something that is happening to a person who hasn't seen it.
4 The phone's ringing.	
5 I'm making a bookcase.	
6 I'm getting fat.	(c) Making comments about longer continuing actions.
7 She's cooking the lunch.	
8 It's raining.	(d) Explaining what you are doing when the listener is not clear.
9 I'm writing to my grandmother.	
10 His English is getting better.	
11 The taxi's waiting.	(e) Making a comment on something that is in the process of changing.
12 It's snowing.	
13 The baby's crying.	(f) Indirectly asking someone to do something that requires immediate attention.
14 He's watering the garden.	
15 The kettle's boiling.	
16 We're waiting for a friend.	
17 The plane's taking off.	
18 The sun's shining.	

2 Now add a further five examples of your own for each category (a)-(f).

3 Now take the two categories that you found easiest in exercise B and think of two situations for each. Write out five examples for each situation.

C Supplementary exercises on other structures

Activity

The future

Part 1 Match the sentence in list A with the sentence in list B that conveys the same idea.

LIST A
1 I'm seeing John today about the problem.
2 I'll see John today about the problem.
3 I'm going to see John today about the problem.

LIST B
(a) I promise to see John.
(b) I intend to see John.
(c) I've arranged to meet John.

Part 2 Match the sentence in list A with the function in list B.

LIST A
1 Mary's coming about five.
2 Mary'll come about five.
3 Mary's going to come about five.

LIST B
(a) an intention
(b) a fixed arrangement
(c) a prediction

Part 3 Look at the following exchanges, and paraphrase B's responses so that the full meaning is made clear.

1 A: The car needs a service.
   B: I know. I'm taking it to the garage this afternoon.

2 A: The car needs a service.
   B: I know. I'm going to take it to the garage this afternoon.

3 A: The car needs a service.
   B: OK. I'll take it to the garage this afternoon.

Part 4 From the above exercise it can be concluded that 'teaching the future' involves the teaching of more than the time reference. There is an additional meaning that is conveyed by the speaker's choice of future form.
Even when the same form is used the full meaning (grammatical meaning + function) may vary from sentence to sentence. Look at the following examples, taken from *A learner's grammar of English* by Norman Coe (Nelson).

1 My sister is going to buy a new car. (i.e. she has decided)
2 Our company is going to open a new office. (i.e. the decision has been made)
3 I can't go hiking because I'm going to wash some clothes on Saturday. (i.e. I have decided)
4 A: We need some salt.
   B: I know. I'm going to get some today. (i.e. I had decided before you spoke)
5 My wife's going to have a baby. (i.e. she is now pregnant)
6 The sun's going to come out. (i.e. the clouds are now moving away)

Now look at the following sentences. They are some of the answers to an exercise designed to practise the 'going to' future, taken from *A practical English grammar:Exercises 1:* Thomson and Martinet (O.U.P.). This exercise contains sentences with three different uses:

A expressing personal intentions;
B when the present situation contains the cause of something in the near future;
C to express a speaker's feeling of certainty.

Write the letter A,B or C against each sentence according to the use.

1 You're going to miss your train.
2 When's your husband going to cut the grass?
3 We're going to make the whisky bottle into a lamp.
4 What are you going to do with this room?
  I'm going to paint the walls in black and white stripes.
5 The umpire's going to blow his whistle.
6 You're going to eat all that?
7 That door's going to slam.
8 That bull's going to attack us.
9 It's going to rain. Look at those clouds.
10 The cat's going to have kittens.
11 He's going to grow a beard when he leaves school.
12 I'm going to stop here for a moment to get some petrol.
13 I'm going to have a bath.
14 There was very little blossom this Spring. Apples are going to be scarce.
15 These swans are going to eat all our sandwiches.

Part 5 Now take the following situations and uses of the structure and devise a series of model sentences based on each situation for presentation to an elementary level class.

1 *Example:* He's going to grow a beard when he leaves school.
  Situation: a pupil leaving school
  Use: expressing intention

2 *Example:* It's going to rain. Look at those clouds.
  Situation: It's a fine sunny morning. The seaside café owner is thinking about the rest of the day.
  Use: near future activities as a result of the present situation

3 *Example:* There was very little blossom this Spring. Apples are going to be scarce.
  Situation: There has been a very heavy snowfall.
  Use: expressing a feeling of certainty about the future.

D Mode of presentation

Having decided on the actual structure content and on a suitable situation for presentation, the teacher now needs to decide on his *mode of presentation*. John Haycraft in *An introduction to English language teaching* (pages 31-35) lists the following possibilities for presenting the present continuous:

1 *Model sentences* (accompanied by appropriate visuals).
  He's eating – She's telephoning – They're reading – He's sleeping – She's talking – They're writing etc. (*Compact English* Book 1, Judy Lugton, Nelson)

2 *Model sentences in dialogue form* (again accompanied by appropriate visuals).

Teacher:	Well, Kevin, what are you painting?
Kevin:	I'm painting a picture of my house.
Teacher:	Who's that?
Kevin:	That's my dad.
Teacher:	What's he doing?
Kevin:	He's cleaning his new car.

Teacher:	And is that you?
Kevin:	Yes that's me.
Teacher:	And what are you doing?
Kevin:	I'm helping too. I'm wiping the windows.

(**English Alive** Book 1, S. Nicholls *et al.*, Edward Arnold)

3 *Dialogue*

Father:	What are you doing up there?
Son:	Nothing.
Father:	Are you taking a bath?
Son:	No, I'm not.
Father:	Are you playing with the cat?
Son:	No.
Father:	You're eating, aren't you?
Son:	No, I'm not.
Father:	He isn't reading. His book's down here.
Mother:	Is he cleaning his room? Ask him.
Father:	Are you cleaning your room?
Son:	Yes, I am.

(*Action English* Book 1, Maricelle Meyer and Robert Sugg, Evans)

4 *Linked model sentences based on a situation.*

The Director is reading a report.
The Accountant is answering the telephone.
The Sales Manager is talking to a customer.
The Personnel Manager is writing letters.
The Production Manager is visiting the factory.
The Secretary is typing a letter.

(*Contemporary English* Pupil's Book 1, R. Rossner *et al.*, Macmillan)

5 *Classroom demonstration*
Many teacher's books or teacher's notes that accompany elementary level textbooks offer the teacher advice as to how he

can exploit the classroom situation to demonstrate the meaning of certain structures by performing actions in the classroom. Look at the following examples:

'The most useful verbs for presenting and practising the present progressive tense (what we have called the present continuous tense) are those which need some time to perform: writing, drawing, touching, holding and so on. Verbs such as "opening, closing, and putting" are only suitable if the actions are performed with several objects (e.g. "He is opening the windows") so that students have time to comment while the action is going on. Some teachers may prefer to introduce this tense with students performing actions in the classroom first.'

Active Context English Book 1 (Teacher's edition) page 63, Brinton *et al.*, Macmillan.

6 *A short text*
Jimmy is in the living room. He is writing his name in his notebook. Now he is drawing a picture in a book. It is Kate's book. It is not his book. Penny is in the kitchen. She is looking at a plate. She is holding it in her hand. It is dirty, She is washing it. She is working. Now the plate is clean. Kate is in the bedroom. She is not working. She is looking out of the window. Now she is reading a book ...etc.
(*Note:* the above text is in fact broken down into several smaller texts with appropriate visuals above each.)
(*Active Context English* Book 1, Brinton *et. al.*, Macmillan)

7 *Grammatical statements*
This is a mode of presentation that in a grammar-translation approach could have existed side-by-side with one or two model sentences or an entire paradigm. In other approaches it is often combined with one of the above modes, in order to confirm or underline the meaning. Look at the following example:

(Following on from a short text)
Study these ideas:
   ... I'm looking for an underground station.
   ... we are ... enjoying the Spanish sunshine.
   I'm sitting beside the swimming pool.

In each of these ideas the verb is in the *present continuous* tense. In unit eight we noted that this tense is often used with a time word to describe a future action. In the examples above it is used to describe something that is taking place while the speaker is speaking.
(*Starting English*, Joanna Gray, Cassell)

Activities

1 Now complete the following table with reference to the above examples of different modes of presentation:

Tick the appropriate column to show the mode of presentation:		
Form only	*Form + Meaning*	*Form + Meaning + Use*
1		
2		
3		
4		
5		
6		
7		

2 Now look at the elementary level textbook that is used in your school or institute and complete the following questionnaire.

(1) Does the material, in which the present continuous tense is first presented,
(a) Stand on its own as suitable presentation material *or*
(b) require supplementing on the part of the teacher?
Tick the appropriate box. (a) ☐ (b) ☐

(2) (To be answered if you ticked (b) in question 1.)
Does the supplementing entail:
(a) some form of pre-teaching of the structure before coming to the textbook material
(b) some form of visual support of the textbook material *or*
(c) some form of additional language material?
Tick the appropriate box. (a) ☐ (b) ☐ (c) ☐

(3) (To be answered if you ticked (a) in question 2.)
Which mode of presentation would you adopt for the pre-teaching of the structure? Write the number between 1 and 7 (according to the list above) that refers to your chosen mode. Use the box below.
☐

(4) (To be answered if you ticked (c) in question 2.)
What form would your additional language material take? Write the number between 1 and 7 that refers to your chosen form. Use the box below.
☐

(5) Does either your textbook material or your additional language material present examples of any of the communicative uses listed on page 163 (List B)?
YES ☐ NO ☐ If yes, list the example sentences with the definition of the use(s) next to them.

(6) If you feel you need to supplement the textbook with visual aids, give a brief description of the aids that would ideally be necessary. Indicate how they could help you convey (a) the meaning of the tense and/or (b) the use(s) that you are teaching.

(7) Now write out any example sentences/texts/dialogues that you may need, for either pre-teaching of the structure or as additional language material.

3 Now look back to *Activities* 3 on page 163 and decide on the mode of presentation for each of the two categories that you dealt with.

4 Take one of these and write out your presentation material according to the mode that you have decided on. Keep your material for a later exercise.

5 If possible, 'perform' this as a peer-teaching activity.

E Summary

So we might summarize the planning and preparation procedure for the structural content of the presentation stage as follows:

A. If the teacher is in a position to produce his own material.
1 Check what structure comes next on the syllabus, or on your own year or term plan of work.
2 Decide which aspects of the structure are to be taught in the initial lesson and which are to be left for later lessons.
   (a) Which grammatical meaning?
   (b) Which forms – all persons? Affirmative, negative and interrogative? Or only one or two of these?
   (c) (a) and (b) will, of course, depend on the 'complexity' of the structure and the ability of the class.
3 Decide on a situation that will make the meaning clear, and, if possible, incorporate a communicative use of the structure.
4 Decide on a mode of presentation.
5 Write the presentation material. (If possible have it checked by a native speaker, and if it is a dialogue try to have it recorded by native speakers.)
6 Gather together any necessary aids (possibly modifying the material to fit the aids available, if necessary).

B. If the teacher has to follow a prescribed textbook.
1 Check what main structure occurs in the next unit.
2 Check which aspects of the structure are introduced (see 2a/2b/3 above) and break down the unit into 'manageable teaching units', taking into consideration such factors as length of lesson, level of ability of class.
3 If necessary, and if possible, modify the material or add

supplementary material according to the criteria outlined in A. Do not be a slave to your textbook. No textbook is that good.

4 Decide on the mode of presentation most suitable to the textbook material.

5 Gather together any aids that will help you to exploit the textbook material.

C. If the teacher is using a textbook that is accompanied by a teacher's book or by teacher's notes.

The degree of guidance given by teacher's books or notes varies considerably. Some give detailed step-by-step instructions that are virtually ready-made lesson plans, while others just give suggestions to act as inspiration to teachers and put them on the right path or merely indicate potential pitfalls that the teacher should be careful to avoid.

Activity

Part 1

Try to get hold of the following textbooks: E. Rudd, *One,Two, Three, Go!* Teacher's Book (Hodder & Stoughton) Unit 7 move 1; E. Austen & P. Mugglestone, *Signpost*, Teacher's Book 2 (Nelson) – 7b Community Centre; E. Brinton *et al., Active Context English* Teacher's Book 1 (Macmillan) – Lesson 15; W. Fowler *et al., Incentive English* Teacher's Book 1 (Nelson) – unit 8. Read the extracts and complete the table. If you cannot get hold of any of these books, go straight to part 2 of the activity. Try to look at two books apart from your own.

Do the teacher's notes contain:	Extract 1	Extract 2	Extract 3	Extract 4	Your teacher's notes
A an indication of the form(s) of the structure to be taught					
B a definition of the meaning(s) of the structure to be taught					
C an explanation of the use of the structure to be taught					
D detailed step-by-step instructions for the presentation of the structure					
E suggestions for situations for practice of the structure					
F an indication of which vocabulary items to include					

	1	2	3	4	
G warnings not to do certain things that may confuse the learners					
H a prediction of problems that may arise					
I a description of techniques to overcome these problems					
J further language notes that may help the teacher develop his knowledge of the language					

Part 2
Now turn to your own teacher's book (or notes in a teacher's edition) for any one unit of your own choosing (it should of course be a unit that presents a new structure for the first time) and complete the fifth column ('Your teacher's notes') by writing YES or NO in the appropriate boxes.

Part 3
If any of the above categories (A – J) are not dealt with write out your own notes.
Where will you look for any information that may help you? (See *Recommended reading* at the end of the chapter.)

Part 4
Now answer the following supplementary questions about your teacher's book (or teacher's edition of the student's book).

A Is there a complete list of structures introduced in the order in which they occur?
B Is there also an alphabetical index of structures?
C If the answer to B is YES, does this alphabetical index indicate by number the units (or pages) in which the structure is presented, practised and revised?
D Does it contain an alphabetical list of vocabulary items introduced?
E If the answer to D is YES, does this alphabetical list indicate by number the units (or pages) in which the vocabulary items occur?
F Does this list also give the pronunciation of the new vocabulary items?
G If the answer to F is YES, is there also a key to phonetic symbols used?
H If the answer to G is NO, where are you going to look for the information?
I Is there any form of notional or functional cross-reference for the structures and vocabulary items contained in the units?

J If the answer to I is NO, where are you going to look for
information about the function(s) of the various structures?
K Is there a general introduction suggesting the methodological
approach to be adopted?
L Is there a key to the exercises contained in the student's book?

We have spent a long time on this section because we feel that the
initial presentation of new language items is vital. It is here that the
teacher usually succeeds or fails in achieving the objectives of the
lesson. We hope that by working through this section the teacher has
achieved the following:

1 a more critical awareness of the material he is using, both the
   students' material and the teachers' notes for guidance;
2 a deeper understanding of the complexities of the language items
   that he is teaching;
3 an extension of his range of techniques for presenting a new
   structure;
4 an awareness of the need for careful planning and preparation;
5 an idea of ways in which he can produce his own supplementary
   material for presentation of a new structure (this will be developed
   in the following sections).

The length of this section is not meant to indicate, however, that the
teacher should spend a long time in the classroom in presenting new
language items to the class. 'In general, your presentation should be
economical. Much more time should be spent on practice than on
presentation. Meaning and form should be made obvious quickly.
Otherwise your students will not understand what you want them to
practise.' (John Haycraft *An introduction to English language teaching*
page 32) There is no obvious way to achieve this ideal, and one
cannot be dogmatic about mode of presentation. No one way is more
economical than another, bearing in mind that over-emphasis on
brevity may hinder understanding. Economy must be seen in the
light of the structure itself. A teacher should ask himself the
question, 'What is the most economical way of presenting *this*
structure?' and the nature of the structure may suggest an obvious
mode of presentation. In addition, careful selection of language, of
examples of the new structure that are clear, vivid and precise,
contributes just as much to an economical presentation as the
employment of time-saving techniques and good classroom management and organization. This has been our main reason for such
detailed work on planning the choice of examples of a new structure.

Activity

Look at the material you prepared for an initial presentation of the
present continuous and answer the following questions:

1 Will it result in an economical presentation?

2 Are meaning and form made obvious quickly?

3 Are the examples included in your material clear, vivid and precise?

4 Is the material based on a rather complicated situation that would, itself, need a lot of time for presentation, or is the situation easily and quickly presented?

5 Estimate how many minutes your presentation of situation and examples of structure would take you.

6 If possible present your material as a peer-teaching activity and ask a colleague to check the timing.

7 Discuss the results with other teachers.

The lexical content

A Separate vocabulary presentation

For any lesson, not only for an RSA assessment lesson, the teacher has also to plan the vocabulary that he wishes to incorporate into the structure lesson. Before reading this section look at the discussion point.

Points for discussion

'The cardinal rule, when you're introducing a new point, is "one thing at a time". For example, don't complicate the teaching of a grammar point by introducing new or difficult vocabulary.' (Introduction to *One, Two, Three, Go!* Teacher's Book, E. Rudd, Hodder & Stoughton)

1 Do you agree or disagree with the above statement? Give reasons.

2 Select any unit from any textbook that you know and see if the material for presentation of a new structure adheres to the above 'cardinal rule'.

Many published textbooks do not adhere to this principle and the teacher may be faced with a text or dialogue that contains both a new structure and new vocabulary, and the two combined may present the learner with a very heavy learning load indeed. To help the learner here the teacher may need to extract certain vocabulary items, those whose meaning is not clear and cannot be deduced from the context, and pre-teach these items before moving on to the structure presentation. The teacher here has several techniques at his disposal for direct vocabulary presentation. See Chapter 2, pages 50-58 for a detailed presentation.

B Integrating structural and lexical content

The teacher who is planning his own material, however, can be more selective about the vocabulary he incorporates into his structure lesson. He can adhere to the above principle (the 'cardinal rule') and base his structure presentation around a situation that would involve known vocabulary. However, at the controlled practice stage of the lesson (the stage following the presentation of the structure) new vocabulary items can be fed into the drills (by use of flashcards and cue words). Ideally these two stages should be linked and the initial drill for practice would involve further examples based on the same situation that has been exploited for presentation. So when selecting a situation for presentation of a new structure, the teacher should not only make sure that the situation makes the meaning and the use of the new structure clear, but also that it is a situation which can be developed into practice, and not a situation that is too limiting. Furthermore, the situation should be such that enough examples can be found that contain known vocabulary and further examples (for the initial drill) that would extend the vocabulary area. A group of vocabulary items that are common to a situation, theme or topic form what is called a *lexical set*.

Example
At the grocer's

Grocer:	Good morning. Can I help you?
Customer:	Yes, please. I'd like a kilo of oranges please.
Grocer:	Here you are. Anything else?
Customer:	And half a kilo of lemons. How much is that?
Grocer:	That'll be 75p, please.

Having used the dialogue for presentation of 'I'd like' the teacher then cues the following drill to practise the structure. The vocabulary items progress from the known to the unknown, thus integrating vocabulary presentation and practice with structure practice.

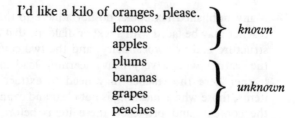

Activities

1 Now look back at the material you prepared for an initial presentation of the present continuous.

(a) Does your presentation situation contain what would be, in your opinion, known vocabulary only?

(b) Does it give scope for development into an initial drill practice? List further examples around which a drill could be made.

(c) Can you add further examples of vocabulary items of the same type to form a lexical set to incorporate into the controlled practice stage? Modify your list for 1b, if necessary.

2 Look at the following list of structures (LIST A) and the list of vocabulary areas (LIST B) and decide which vocabulary area would be suitable for a presentation and initial controlled practice drill for each structure (or use of structure) mentioned.

LIST A

1 There is ...(+ *noun* + *adv of place*)... talking about what is on in the town.

2 There is ...(+ *noun* + *adv of place*)... giving simple street directions.

3 There is ...(+ *noun* + *adv of place*)... simple description of a place.

4 Present continuous .... informing about a 3rd person's whereabouts.

5 Present continuous .... making an indirect request, something requires attention.

6 Present simple .... talking about daily routines.

7 'going to' future .... stating personal intentions.

LIST B

(a) rooms and furniture

(b) domestic appliances and other things found in the house

(c) jobs and their activities

(d) types of buildings

(e) things needed for a holiday

(f) types of films, plays and musical events

(g) household chores

3 Now take the vocabulary areas in list B and write out lexical sets of about 10 – 15 words for each area.

The situational content

What is a 'situation'?

In talking about the presentation of a new structure and in dealing with the integration of structure and vocabulary work, we have used the term 'situation'. We feel it is now time to look in more detail at the process of setting a situation for presentation purposes.

Before presenting the language patterns, whatever form they may be in, the teacher needs to set the situation. This is particularly so if the new patterns are incorporated into a dialogue. Experience has shown that the learning of new language items is hindered unless the learners have a full understanding of the situation. One way of achieving this is for the teacher to introduce the situation in the form of a 'mini-text' as an initial reading or listening activity (or possibly even in the mother tongue in certain cases). Although this should be as brief as possible, there are certain factors that need to be thought about to make the situation as clearly understandable as possible:

1 *Are the characters plausible? Will they appear realistic personalities that the students can recognize and possibly identify with?*
It will help here if the teacher begins by assigning names to the characters (instead of simply calling them 'A' or 'B'.) Then he should try to 'bring them alive'. A blackboard drawing or a magazine picture of the character helps a great deal to make them seem more real. But extra biographical details need to be added. The teacher could just give these. Alternatively, he could simply display the picture and invite the students to ask questions about the characters, to which he supplies the answers. This has the advantage that the students initiate the activity by asking questions and are therefore more motivated to learn the answers (the biographical details). It also gives them some extra practice in asking questions.

2 Define their *social roles* – Is John Smith a father talking to his son, or is he at work, and is a manager talking to his employee?

3 Indicate the *psychological roles* involved – Is John Smith in a superior or inferior position to the other speaker(s) or in a position of equality?

4 Describe the *setting* – Are they at a football match or in the office?

5 Say what they are talking about – the *topic*.

6 What is the *purpose* of the conversation? Again, this *may* be obvious from the dialogue itself, but in many cases it will not be clear to every student what the exact *use* of a particular form is. (Remember that a given form can have a variety of different uses.)

These six points are for the teacher's information and he, of course, would not use the above terms in presenting a situation to a class. Above all, the situation has to be made clear quickly and briefly so that the presentation of the language can be made as soon as possible. Quick blackboard sketches, or sticking pictures on the blackboard with Blu-Tack, with an accompanying brief commentary on the situation (in L_1 at a more elementary level) would be appropriate.

Example commentary (possibly to be given in L_1) used to situational-ize the presentation of 'was' and 'were'.

Richard and Paul are two 14-year-old boys. They are close friends. They live next door to each other, and they have been to a football match together. They are talking about the match as they leave the stadium. Their team, Manchester United, has just lost 5-0 and they are both angry. They are criticizing the team.

Richard: That was a bad match, Paul.
Paul: Oh, it was awful. Our team were hopeless.
Richard: Yes, but their forwards were good, weren't they?
Paul: Yes, not bad. But our goalkeeper was terrible.

The six points above are suggested as general guidelines for setting situations for presentation purposes. But the teacher should also think carefully about the students in his class, since this will affect his choice of situation. Here are some questions the teacher might ask himself about the example dialogue above:

Question	*Answer*
1 Is the situation familiar to the students or easy for them to imagine?	Yes, a football match is a familiar situation for most secondary learners, especially boys.
2 Do they have the necessary language to understand the situation quickly and easily?	Yes. *Criticizing* and *angry* might need to be explained or translated into L_1.
3 Will the situation make the form and meaning of the new structure quickly obvious?	*Was* and *were* do not pose any great problems as regards form. The singular/plural idea is obvious. The idea of 'past' is clear from the context.
4 Does the situation allow me to isolate the particular communicative *use* I am interested in?	Yes, *criticizing*, by using the verb *to be* in combination with certain adjectives.
5 Does the situation give rise to a reasonable number of examples for the first stage of practice, with known vocabulary only?	Assuming that these adjectives are known items, we have five examples of the new structure, three of *was* and two of *were*.
6 Can the situation be extended to a parallel one to provide more practice?	It would certainly be easy to transfer this situation to parallel ones such as criticizing a bad film or even a bad English lesson!
7 Does the situation give rise to possible vocabulary work – i.e. suggest a new lexical set which can be taught?	It includes a limited set of adjectives which express criticism. At a later stage, we could feed in a set of adjectives to express praise – *good, fantastic, marvellous*, etc.

Although we have spent some time describing the factors to be borne in mind when *choosing* a situation for presentation purposes, remember that this is all work to be done at the *planning* stage. The actual setting of the situation should not take longer than three minutes (unless some extra practice activity is included) and probably the whole presentation should take no longer than five to ten minutes.

Activities

1 Look back at the material you prepared for an initial presentation of the present continuous and ask yourself the same questions. Then rewrite your material if necessary.

2 Look at any one unit of your textbook and ask yourself the questions with reference to the situation in which a new structure is presented.

3 Of course the selection of a situation will depend very much on the type of learner for whom the material is intended. Look at the following situations for presentation and practice and decide for which type of learner they are suitable.
   (a) *Could ... ? (polite requests)*
       In the office. Boss and secretary.
   (b) *Would you like ... ? (invitation)*
       At a dinner party.
   (c) *Present continuous ... future arrangements*
       2 people (friends) trying to find a communal free day to have dinner.
   (d) *Can ... (ability)*
       A spaceman asking an Earthman about his abilities.
   (e) *Can ... (ability)*
       An interview for a job.
   (f) *Present simple ... daily routine*
       What a policeman does every day.
   (g) *Present simple ... general or scientific truths*
       The life cycle of a butterfly.
   (h) *Must ... obligation*
       Traffic regulations.
   (i) *Present perfect ... (e.g. Have you ever ... ?)*
       Talking about countries visited.
   (j) *Will ... ('neutral future')*
       A horoscope.
   (k) *Present simple passive*
       How paper is made.
   (l) *There is/are ... (pointing things out)*
       Looking over an old house with spiders, mice etc.
   (m) *Used to do*
       An old lady remembering her youth.
   (n) *Have got*
       Children at a party with balloons, paper hats etc.

4 List the above situations that are suitable for a 12-15 year-old secondary school learner.

5 Taking the same structures listed above devise situations suitable for young secondary school pupils in your country.

Integrating material

It was suggested at the end of section 2 (*The lexical content*) that a good situation would give rise to vocabulary work in the form of a lexical set and that this could be integrated into the structure practice. In some cases, however, certain structures demand certain vocabulary, or certain uses of the structure require this. The one cannot usually exist without the other.

Activities

1 Look at the following extract of material and underline the vocabulary and structure that go together.

'This is called a tin-opener. It is made of metal and it is used for opening tins.'

2 Various other structures tend to go naturally together with certain other lexical sets, which may not always be finite, and the actual individual words may depend on the situation, but in any situation they will be of the same type. Try to match the structures in list A with the vocabulary areas in list B.

LIST A
1 got
2 Present simple
3 I've never seen/read such a ...
4 Must (obligation)
5 Must (logical conclusion)
6 What a ... film! (etc.)
7 'the man/woman with'

LIST B
(a) Adjectives expressing criticism.
(b) Physical features.
(c) Laws/regulations.
(d) Personal possessions.
(e) Adjectives expressing praise.
(f) Adjectives describing a physical condition.
(g) Verbs expressing habits.

3 Can you think of any other possible natural combinations?

So far, we have looked at a semantic link between structure and vocabulary and seen that certain structures and vocabulary tend to go together. So the material used by the teacher could well incorporate both and the 'cardinal rule' mentioned above would not be adhered to. How could you present 'is made of' without the names of materials? How could you fully convey the concept behind the name of a material without using 'is made of'? 'This is wood', probably the only other possibility unless the teacher resorts to translation, risks inducing confusion with 'This is a piece of wood'.

This obviously applies to structures that are in a sense 'fixed phrases', just as certain colloquial expressions are, and the learning process is the same as for learning vocabulary items. A further example would be 'I was born' which has to be followed by an adverbial of place (the names of countries would be an obvious lexical set) and/or an adverbial of time, involving some form of precise date. It is somewhat nonsensical to produce 'I was born' in isolation! However this process is not limited to this type of 'fixed expression' structure. Vocabulary and structure presentation could be combined with certain tenses of the verb, provided the teacher can refer to an appropriate visual so that the meaning of his utterance is immediately clear. E.g.: He's *watering* the flowers/I was *having a nap* when the telephone rang.

A further aspect of integration in teaching materials is when a new structure is presented in context combined with a known structure so that the meaning of the item to be learnt is obvious from the context. This usually takes one of two forms: either the new structure is presented in *contrast* to a known structure (as in example 1 below) or the new structure is presented in combination with a '*synonymous' structure*, which in 'normal everyday English' would not be used and would be redundant as it expresses the same meaning as the other structure. But in teaching materials it acts as a clue to the meaning of the new structure (as in example 2 below).

Example 1
John usually drives to work, but today he is walking. His car is at the garage. (Here one assumes the present simple is known and the present continuous is being presented.)

Example 2
A: Excuse me, where's Mr Knott?
B: I'm not sure. He may be in his office, or he may be in the canteen. He sometimes has coffee at this time.
(Here the structure being presented is 'may' expressing possibility. Notice the uncertainty is conveyed by 'I'm not sure' and the existence of two possible alternatives is a further clue to the meaning of possibility.)

If the teacher is going to produce material for presentation of a new structure that makes form and meaning obvious quickly (as was suggested earlier in this chapter) then the existence of clues to help the learner is clearly desirable.

Activities

1 Let us assume we are dealing with a unit of work on present simple + adverb of manner (well/badly), then we may have a combination of sentences such as:

Kevin Keegan is a good footballer.
He plays football well.

Frank Sinatra is a good singer.
He sings well.
etc.

Notice how the first sentence expresses virtually the same
meaning as the second, containing the new structure, thus
guiding the learner towards an understanding of present simple +
adverb of manner. This type of material would also give rise to the
integrating of vocabulary work in the form of a *rule based set* (sing
– singer etc.)
Now you write a continuation of the above material, making sure
that the 'heroes' you use are known to your learners.

2 One use of the present perfect can be presented by contrast with
the simple past. Write out a series of model sentences that do this.

3 Look at any textbook(s) that you know and list the structures that
are presented by (a) contrast with another structure and (b)
combination with some form of 'synonymous' structure.

4 If your textbook(s) does/do not have this type of material, make a
list of structures that could be presented by incorporating clues in
the form of virtually synonymous structures. Give one example
sentence for each.

A further aspect of possible integration in teaching materials is to
combine a structure with other structures that naturally occur
together. The above procedure may be fine for presenting a new
item, but we must not forget that this will quite often involve
artificial classroom language, and the teacher needs to move on fairly
quickly to further practice in which structures are paired naturally
rather than unnaturally for pedagogical purposes. As Rod Wheeler
has pointed out, 'Such examples as "Today is Monday. Peter usually
goes to school on Mondays but today he is staying at home." present
the student with a piece of language in which the present continuous
and the simple present exist side by side, a pairing of structures that
does not have a very high frequency of occurrence in English.
Normally the use of one would imply, and in production exclude,
the other. "Peter's staying at home. (He's feeling ill.)" would be
more natural in the above situation. One can think of only rare
occasions in which one might say, as a response to a telephone
interruption at lunch, for example, "No, I can't see you now. I'm
having lunch. I always have lunch at this time." So would it not be
possible to revise, consolidate and extend the use of the present
continuous by presenting it in situations where it is paired with other
structures which are, in fact, its "natural companions" in English.'
(*Structure interaction – The present continuous and its companions* Rod
Wheeler ELTJ Vol.XXXV No.2 Jan 1981.)

Rounding off a lesson

A Key questions

It was suggested earlier in the chapter that a good piece of material for presentation of a new structure might contain clues to the meaning in the form of a contrasting structure or a 'synonymous' structure. This same principle might be applied in reverse to a stage of checking, at which point the teacher wants to know whether his learners have assimilated the meaning and/or use of the structure or not. He may do this quite informally at the end of the lesson by simply asking one or two 'key questions'. This may become clear if we look at one or two examples.

1 The teacher has just presented and practised the present continuous passive with such examples as 'My car is being repaired'. He wants to know whether his pupils have understood that the passive form is used because the important element is 'car' and that the person who is actually repairing the car is so unimportant that we do not know who it is exactly nor does it really matter. So if the following question and answer exchange takes place then he will know whether the meaning of the structure is clear or not.

> T: Where is my car?
> S: At a garage.
> T: *Who is repairing it?* (The key question)
> S: I don't know.
> (*Note:* If the pupil says, 'A mechanic' instead of 'I don't know', then the teacher needs to continue with a question such as, 'Well, do you know which mechanic?')

2 Now supposing the teacher has taught the structure exemplified by 'I was having a bath when the telephone rang.' and he needs to check that the time reference has been understood, then he could produce questions such as the following:

> (a) What happened? (The telephone rang.)
> (b) Where was he? (In the bath.)
> (c) Was he in the bath before the telephone rang? (Yes.)

Activities

Now see if you can produce some key questions for the checking stage of work on the following structures:

1 If I had known, I would've come earlier.

2 I was about to cross the road when I saw the car coming.

3 If I were rich, I'd buy a new car.

4 My car has been stolen.

5 My wife may be doing the shopping.

6 I used to get up earlier.

7 I am used to getting up early.

8 When I arrived at the airport the plane had already left.

B Summarizing

Another useful way of rounding off a lesson is to provide a short summary of what the pupils have been practising. This in effect will be a simplified grammatical statement. For example, if the new structure has been 'Would you like to come to the cinema with me?' functioning as an invitation, the teacher may finish by saying something like the following: 'What we have been doing today is learning how to invite people.' (If such a structure has been introduced into an early stage in the course maybe this summary could be given in the mother tongue.)

Activity

Could you think of possible simple explanations that could act as summaries of work on the following structures?

1 I may be going to London in the summer.

2 I'm seeing Peter tomorrow.

3 I've got used to driving on the left.

4 Could you tell me the times of the trains to London, please?

5 If I hadn't eaten so much last night, I wouldn't be feeling so ill this morning.

(You will probably notice that, from the structures selected for this activity, this is a technique more suited to intermediate level teaching.)

Written assignment

RSA Certificate for Overseas Teachers of English and other questions.

1 Devise a situation and a presentation dialogue to teach the structure contained in 'You can't sit on the grass.'

2 Suggest two different kinds of drill which you would use to teach the structure contained in 'I've been waiting for ages.' (*Certificate for Overseas Teachers of English*, June 1980)

3 The present simple tense is used for different purposes in English.
(a) State, with examples, the main uses of the present simple tense.
(b) Describe your initial presentation of one of these uses.

4 Take any structure that you are about to teach and write out a lesson plan for presentation, practice and rounding off the lesson.

Key to activities

Page 156
Initial discussion points. (The writer's opinion)

1 (a)√ (d)√ (e)√
2 (b)
3 (b)√ (e)√
4 In the classroom – 3 √

Page 158
Where are you phoning from? - (a)
What are you doing there? - (b)
I'm having a fortnight's holiday – (b)
How's it going? – (b)
I'm really enjoying myself – (b)
The sun's shining all the time – (b)
I'm going quite brown – (b)
I'm getting a very good tan – (b)
It's raining here – (b) or (a)?
I'm getting quite bored – (b)
Aren't you working? – (b)
I'm spending more time in the pub – (b)
I'm feeling low – (b)
I'm drinking a lot – (b)
You're always drinking too much – (e)
You're always complaining about that – (e)
When are you coming home? – (c)
I'm flying back on Saturday – (c)
I'm playing darts then – (c)
We're not finishing the match until 11 – (c)
Note: Having checked your answers what conclusions could you reach about the present continuous tense?

Page 161
Example 2
(a) The third person singular only is presented.
(b) Appropriate visuals.
(c) Add the visuals.
(d) They all describe what various members of the family are doing.
(e) In a house after dinner(?)
(f) None.

Page 163
1(b) 2(a) 3(e) 4(f) 5(d) 6(e) 7(a) 8(c) 9(d) 10(e) 11(b) 12(c)
13(f) 14(a) 15(f) 16(d) 17(b) 18(c)

Pages 163-5
The future
Part 1   Part 2
1(c) 2(a) 3(b)   1(b) 2(c) 3(a)

Part 3
(possible, suggested answers)
(1)B. I've already arranged with the garage to take it there this afternoon.
(2)B. I intend to take it to the garage this afternoon. I had already realized.
(3)B. I didn't know, but now you've told me, I promise to take it to the
garage this afternoon.

Part 4
1C 2A 3A 4A – A 5B 6A 7B (possibly C) 8B (possibly C) 9B
(possibly C) 10B 11A 12A 13A 14C 15B

Page 168
Form + meaning Nos. 1, 4, 5, 6, 7.
Form + meaning + use 2, 3

Pages 170-71

	Extract			
	1	**2**	**3**	**4**
A	Yes	Yes	Yes	Yes
B	No	Yes	No	Yes
C	Yes	Yes	No	Yes
D	Yes	No	No	No
E	No	Yes	No	Yes
F	Yes	No	No	No
G	Yes	No	Yes	No
H	No	No	Yes	Yes
I	No	No	Yes	Yes
J	No	Yes	Yes	Yes

Page 175
Activity 2
1(f) 2(d) 3(a) 4(g) 5(b) 6(c) 7(e)

Page 179
1 made of + metal (names of materials must be used)
2 1(d) 2(g) 3(e) or (a) 4(c) 5(f) 6(a) or (e) 7(b)

Pages 182-3
1 Did he know? Did he come earlier?
2 Did he see the car? Did he cross the road? Where was he when he saw the
car?
3 Is he rich? Can he buy a new car?
4 Who stole the car?
5 Is his wife shopping? Is he certain where she is and what she is doing?
6 (text would have made context clear)
What time does he get up now? What time did he get up before? Did he
always get up earlier before? Does he get up later now?
7 Does he get up early? How does he feel? Can he get up easily enough or
does he find it difficult?
8 Did the plane leave before he arrived at the airport?
Put these 2 events in the correct order. Number them 1 and 2.
The plane left. He arrived at the airport.

Page 183

1 *I may be going.* I'm not sure but it is possible.
2 *I'm seeing Peter tomorrow.* I have arranged to meet him. We have an appointment. He's expecting me.
3 *I've got used to driving on the left.* Driving on the left was difficult at first, but now I don't find it so difficult.
4 *Could you tell me the times of the trains to London, please?* This is a polite way of asking for information.
5 *If I hadn't eaten so much last night, I wouldn't be feeling so ill this morning.* He ate too much last night. Now he is feeling ill. He regrets the fact that he ate too much.

Bibliography

The structural content

A practical English grammar, Thompson and Martinet (O.U.P)
Teaching language as communication, H.G. Widdowson (O.U.P)
A learner's grammar of English, Norman Coe (Nelson)
A practical English grammar – Exercises 1, Thompson and Martinet (O.U.P)
An introduction to English language teaching, J. Haycraft (Longman)
Compact English Book 1, J. Lugton (Nelson)
English Alive Book 1, S. Nicholls *et al.* (Edward Arnold)
Action English Book 1, M. Meyer & R. Sugg (Evans)
Contemporary English Book 1, R. Rossner *et al.* (Macmillan)
Active Context English Book 1 (Teacher's Edition), E. Brinton *et al.* (Macmillan)
Starting English, J. Gray (Cassell)
One, Two, Three, Go! (Teacher's Book), E. Rudd (Hodder and Stoughton)
Signpost, Book 2 (Teacher's Book), E. Austen & P. Mugglestone (Nelson)
Incentive English, Book 1 (Teacher's Notes), W. Fowler *et al.* (Nelson)

The lexical content

One, Two, Three, Go! (Teacher's Book), E. Rudd (Hodder and Stoughton)
Active Context English, Book 2, E. Brinton *et al.* (Macmillan)

Integrating material

Structure interaction – The present continuous and its companions, Rod Wheeler in ELTJ Vol.35 No.2 Jan. 1981.

6 From controlled to free practice

In the previous chapter we looked at the complexities of the language that needs to be taught, and above all, we concentrated on the factors involved in the planning and preparation for the first stage of work on a new structure – the presentation stage. However, as was pointed out in the quotation from John Haycraft, 'much more time should be spent on practice than on presentation.' (*An introduction to English language teaching*, page 32.) Practice can take many different forms, and basically, when planning his work, the teacher needs to take into consideration the following stages:

Presentation
Controlled practice
Free practice (what Donn Byrne terms 'production' in *Teaching oral English*)
Checking that the structure has been learnt
Further practice – this could take the form of practice in further situations, or in combination with a later new structure, consolidation, revision or, if necessary, remedial work.

Controlled practice

This is the stage at which learners are given intensive practice in the new structure, but their production of the language is very carefully guided and controlled by the teacher, so that correct form and meaning are consolidated, and the possibility of error is reduced to a minimum. This traditionally takes the form of some kind of drill.

Activities

1 Reread the sections on drilling, Chapter 1, pages 15-30 and do the following exercise.

Look at the following types of drill and put a tick against the types that you think are suited to the early part of the controlled practice stage. In other words, which types of drill involve manipulation of the structure based on an immediate preceding model?

Clause combination drill
Mini-dialogue drill
Question drill
Expansion drill
Progressive substitution drill
Simple substitution drill
Variable substitution drill
Situational drill

2 Assuming that your initial drill is based on the same situation that has been exploited for presentation, and that one of the aims of the drill as the learners practise the structure is to feed in new lexis connected with that situation, select from the above list the type of drill that you would begin your controlled practice with. (It is assumed that the link between the presentation and the controlled practice stage has already been a 'listen and repeat' drill, as the learners repeat the model sentences, whether they have been presented in isolation or extracted for repetition from a dialogue or short text.) What would you need to cue the drill?

3 Imagine that you have presented 'some' and 'any' (with uncountables) with the following dialogue. Write out a simple substitution drill based on the same situation that could be your initial controlled practice drill after the presentation and repetition. What would you need to cue the drill?

Customer:	Excuse me, I'd like some brown bread, please.
Grocer:	I'm sorry. There isn't any brown bread. But I've got some white bread.
Customer:	OK. And I'd like some milk, please.
Grocer:	I'm afraid there isn't any fresh milk, but I've got some tinned milk.
Customer:	That's all right. And I'd like some Edam cheese as well, please.
Grocer:	I'm sorry there isn't any Edam cheese, but I've got some Cheddar cheese.
Customer:	That's all right. How much is that?
Grocer:	£1.65, please.

Point for discussion

Bearing in mind what you have read about situational presentation and initial practice, discuss the following. What does the writer mean by the statement in italics? Do you agree or disagree with this view?

'The structural method has often been combined with a situational presentation. According to this approach, the teacher (or textbook writer) selects a situation in which to present a given structure. At its best this approach is very successful; but at its worst, *it leads to some grotesque misalliances between structure and situation.*'

(Ronald V. White *Functional English* Teacher's Book 1, Nelson)

After you have discussed the above point read the following.

Although the presentation of a structure through a situation can give rise to presentation of more 'realistic' language examples, and although the exploitation of the same situation for initial controlled practice provides linking and continuity within the lesson as the teacher progresses smoothly from one stage to the next, too much work based on the same situation could result in 'grotesque misalliances between structure and situation', in other words, the learner would associate the structure with one situation only, or would come to the conclusion that in a particular situation there is a certain structure that has to be used. We are by no means advocating an abandoning of a situational approach as a result of this criticism, but the teacher needs to be well aware of the danger, and to overcome the first objection (that the learner would associate the structure with one situation only) the teacher needs to set up practice within *a variety of situations*. The learner is possibly incapable of transferring the structure to other situations unless the *process of transfer* is begun in the classroom by the teacher introducing material that transfers the structure to other situations.

What this implies is that after the initial drill, the teacher needs not only to change the activity (by using a different type of drill or a different form of cueing) but also to switch to another situation. This needs to be done gradually because, as we have pointed out, the learner would have difficulty in adapting the structure to another situation himself. He has not yet attained a sufficient understanding and mastery of the structure to do this. The first stage of transfer should be to another *similar situation*. By this we mean, very loosely, one that is connected by setting or topic to the original situation. Or it may be a variation on the original situation. For example, if the original situation has been 'Describing a house' for presenting 'There is/are' with such examples as 'There are three bedrooms in my house,' the process of *gradual transfer* may involve 'Description of the rooms' (e.g. 'There is a fridge in the kitchen.') or 'Description of the garden' (e.g. 'There are some lemon trees in the garden.').

Activities

1 Look again at *Activity* 3 on page 174 which was 'at the grocer's'. What other similar situations could you find? List them and write out a drill of any type.

2 Now try to think of two to three similar situations for presenting and practising (a) The present perfect continuous (b) Must (expressing obligation).

Contextualizing drills

The main problem with this approach is that the teacher needs to present a new situation for a drill quickly and economically. He should not interrupt the flow of the practice while he sets up a complex situation that requires a lot of explanation. He could do one of the following:

1 reveal to the class a visual (or series of visuals) that are immediately obvious;
2 present a table of information in the form of a handout or pre-written on the blackboard;
3 explain quickly (in L_1, if necessary) the situation.

Activities

1 What structures could you drill by using a series of flashcards consisting of items of food and drink? Write down the model sentence and cues for each structure.

2 Look at the following 'table of information' (it is a simplified diary page). What structures could be drilled from it? Write down the model sentence for each structure.

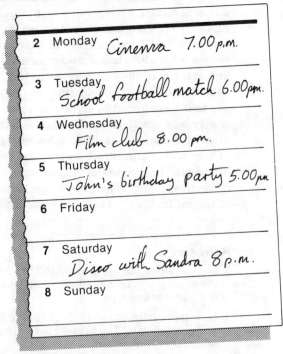

2	Monday	*Cinema 7.00 p.m.*
3	Tuesday	*School football match 6.00pm.*
4	Wednesday	*Film club 8.00 pm.*
5	Thursday	*John's birthday party 5.00pm*
6	Friday	
7	Saturday	*Disco with Sandra 8 p.m.*
8	Sunday	

3 How could you modify the above diary page to make the meaning of the following structures obvious from the given information – (a) present continuous (future arrangements) (b) future continuous (c) simple past?

Free practice

It is no exaggeration to say that most language produced by students in the classroom occurs under highly artificial conditions. Perhaps the biggest problem for the teacher is to bridge the gap between this artificial use of language and genuine use outside the classroom.

Many teachers assume that if they have managed to get their students to that level of competence where they can understand and correctly produce a given form, they have 'taught' that form. But really this is only half the process of teaching: the other and more difficult half is to provide students with an opportunity to *use* the language they have learnt in the classroom. In short, we must try to encourage our students to put their newly acquired language into action, and it is this process of language *activation* which we will be considering in the rest of this chapter.

A certain amount of oral work in class is going to be highly controlled. This will be necessary at an early stage for a number of reasons. The teacher has to check that the students have grasped the pattern correctly, together with its pronunciation. He has to correct errors which arise. He has to direct and manage the class while they are practising; and if it is a large class he may have to exercise a great deal of control to make sure that everybody is participating and learning. Teacher control can be analysed as follows:

1 The teacher *initiates and manages* the activity: i.e. he makes clear to the students what they have to do and then ensures that they are doing it correctly.
2 The teacher *corrects errors*. Of course, as we have seen in Chapter 4 this does not mean that he always supplies the correct forms himself: he may encourage students to correct each other or correct themselves, simply by challenging an incorrect response and possibly indicating the type or position of the error.
3 The teacher *talks* for about half the time; the students the other half. We can compare the proportion of teacher talking time (TTT) and student talking time (STT).
4 The teacher *controls the subject matter* of the talk, either by suggesting the words to be used in a drill, etc. or by writing up words on the blackboard; or by choosing a particular set of language-teaching materials – textbook, wall-picture, etc.

In completely *free practice* the opposite occurs. The teacher may initiate the activity, but will not intervene or manage it, unless it breaks down altogether. The teacher does not correct errors: students have to cope by themselves. The teacher does not talk at all: the students do all the talking. And finally the teacher does not control the subject matter apart from setting up the beginning of the activity. Ideally, students are free to say whatever they want; they choose the direction their conversation takes.

The transition from controlled to free practice can be illustrated like this:

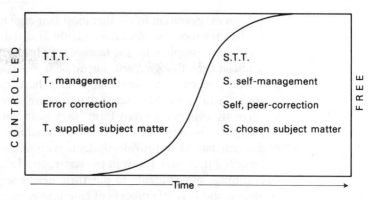

Making practice freer: the transitional stages

The transition from controlled to free work results from two changes of attitude on the part of the teacher. The first is to upset the teacher-student control pattern in the classroom by reorganizing the system of class management; the second is to change the type of activity from one which allows little or no choice on the part of the student to one which allows great freedom of choice.

A Class management: group-work and pair-work

The traditional class management pattern is called *lockstep*. Here the teacher is completely in control of every classroom interaction, whether T – S, S – T or S – S. The focus of attention is primarily on the teacher. This may be illustrated by the following diagram:

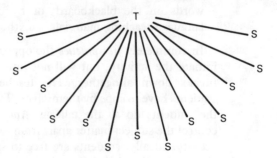

In *group-work*, students work simultaneously in groups of three or more, while the teacher circulates, provides assistance or encouragement where necessary, and checks that the task is carried out satisfactorily. This looks more like:

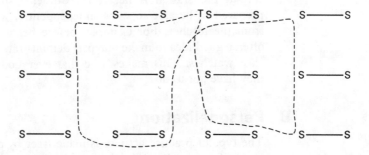

In *pair-work*, students work simultaneously in pairs. The teacher is available to help or sort out problems, but to do this type of activity the students must be sufficiently prepared to be able to work entirely by themselves. This can be illustrated like this:

Group-work is generally more *task-oriented*: that is, the students have a definite task to complete, and call the teacher when they have completed it. Usually it will take longer than pair-work, 10 minutes or more; and generally it is more suitable for intermediate level and upwards.

Examples of group-work are:

1 The group has to discuss and between them work out the answer to a number of questions about a text they have read or a tape they have listened to.
2 The group has to write up a story based on pictures, after the class as a whole has produced the story orally with suitable prompting from the teacher. One student (? the weakest) writes the story, while the others advise.

3 The group has to solve a problem or reach a collective decision on some matter. E.g.: They have to decide on how they would escape from a prison in a hostile country. (See *Notions in English* by Leo Jones, page 130, Cambridge University Press.) Or they have to agree on a programme of entertainment for the weekend which would suit all members of the group. (Here they are provided with a series of advertisements.) Or they have to decide what they would take with them on a camping expedition. (They are given a list of possible items, with the weight of each item. A limit is fixed as to how much each can carry.)

Pair-work may last for as little as two minutes and be simply an extension of controlled drilling which has been done lockstep. It often needs no special preparation or materials; and its main purpose is to increase STT, while also providing a change of activity for the sake of variety. Any drill work based on pictures or exercises in a textbook may be done in pairs. Further examples of pair-work are given later in this chapter.

One of the main advantages of group- and pair-work is that, since pairs or groups can work simultaneously, the amount of STT is enormously increased. However, in both types of class organization, careful preparation is necessary. Students should be sufficiently prepared to be able to work independently, with little or no help from the teacher. For example, before beginning pair-work, it is often a good idea to make one pair demonstrate while the rest of the class watches. This makes sure that everybody understands what they have got to do.

B Personalization

The type of practice activity is made freer by allowing the student *choice* of answer/direction. As we have seen, repetition and drill work offer the student only *one* choice: the 'correct' response. Freer work offers the student more than one choice or a variety of responses. The way the student responds is not arbitrary, but based on his opinion or experience or knowledge. Hence the student focuses more on meaning than on form or expression.

This step in the stages of practising a pattern is called *personalization*. In a sense, the earlier we personalize an activity, the better. The students stop performing like trained animals in a circus and start saying what they mean.

Here is an example:

DRILL FROM A PICTURE

Teacher: John likes collecting stamps.
            What about Mary?
Student: She likes listening to records.
Teacher: And Sam?

Student: He likes making model aeroplanes.
Teacher: (*Points to Tom in the picture.*)
Student: He likes playing football.

PERSONALIZATION STAGE

Teacher: (*Pointing at student*) Mario likes collecting stamps.
Mario: No.
Teacher: Oh? Well, he likes playing football.
Mario: Yes!
Teacher: (*Prompts other student*) Mario likes ...
Student: Mario likes playing football.
Teacher: Sofia. Do you like playing football?
Sofia: No.
Teacher: *No, I don't.* (*Gestures 'repeat'*)
Sofia: No, I don't.
Teacher: Do you like listening to records?
Sofia: Yes, I do.
Teacher: Good!
              Antonis. Do you like listening to records?
Antonis: Yes, I do.

Gradually the teacher shifts to S – S question and answer work. The
students are eventually enquiring about one another's interests,
hobbies, etc. As soon as the teacher is happy that the activity is
proceeding smoothly, he can switch to pair-work to increase the
amount of STT.

   When doing personalized practice activities, it is a good idea for
the teacher to carry out 'spot-checks' to make sure the students are
telling the truth, not simply responding correctly to please the
teacher. For example, in the activity above, the question 'Do you
like listening to records?' can be followed up occasionally by the
question: 'What's your favourite record, then?' This makes it clear
to the students that the teacher is asking genuine questions, not
simply carrying out a drill activity.

Exercise

The following are controlled practice activities. Explain how you
would personalize them:

1 What does Mr Black do?
   He works in a bank.
   What does Mary do?
   She's a hairdresser.

2 What was Mary doing when Mr Black got home?
   She was watching TV.
   What was Mrs Black doing?
   She was cooking the dinner.

C Extending the personalized drill: the dialogue frame

The dialogue frame is a highly versatile classroom technique which enables students to carry out a mini-conversation. In the initial stage, the 'conversation' is completely controlled: in fact, the entire exchange is memorized. In the second stage, the students substitute words or phrases in the original dialogue with alternatives provided. At this stage, it is really an extended drill. In the final stage, the practice is personalized and students genuinely converse and exchange information, although their conversation is limited to the patterns in the dialogue frame. The dialogue frame is an ideal way to practise two or more patterns in combination.

To make the technique clear, here is an example:

A: Have you ever been to *London*?
B: Yes I have.
A: Oh really? That's interesting. When did you go there?
B: About *two years ago*.
A: And what did you do there?
B: I *went to the zoo*.

Stage 1 The students repeat the lines of the dialogue chorally, in groups and individually. When all the students can reproduce it, they practise saying it in pairs.

Stage 2 The teacher writes up on the blackboard names of different *places* and various *activities* that can be done there. The students then practise in pairs substituting the italicized words in the dialogue.

Stage 3 The practice is now personalized. The teacher holds the conversation with one student and asks follow-up questions to emphasize that students must tell the truth. The teacher must write up places which the students are likely to have visited and the question of activities can be left completely open. The students then hold short conversations in pairs. At this final stage if the answer to the question is 'No, I haven't', A asks another question, and so on until he mentions a place that B has visited.

In this example, practice is still moderately controlled because there are only three spaces in the dialogue where substitution can occur. Practice can be made freer by introducing more variables.

This dialogue has six lines, but there is no reason why it should not be made longer, eight lines or more. It is also possible to design dialogue frames which take different directions depending on the choice taken at each stage, but these are quite complicated to set up and manage in class. Ideally the final line should be left open for a very free response. Good cues for final lines are Why and How questions.

Practical work

1 Here is a dialogue frame which can be personalized. Decide what stages you would follow in presenting this dialogue to your class and try it out on your students or other teachers.

A: Was your *brother* at home when you got in last night?
B: Yes, *he* was.
A: What was *he* doing?
B: *He* was *watch*ing *TV*.
A: Does *he* always *watch TV* in the evenings?
B: No, sometimes *he goes to the cinema*.

2 Imagine that the following dialogue occurs in your textbook.

A: Have you seen 'Jaws 2'?
B: No. Why do you ask?
A: Well, it's on at the Rialto. Do you want to see it?
B: That's a good idea.
A: Let's go this evening. There's a performance at 8.00.
B: All right. I'll meet you outside the cinema at 7.45.
A: Great! See you then.

How would you adapt this for use as a dialogue frame. To what extent can this practice be personalized? Outline the stages you would follow in using the dialogue frame with your class.

3 For further ideas on dialogue frames, look at the ways these are presented in the following books:

Contemporary English, Books 1-4, Rossner *et al.*, Macmillan
Functional English, Book 1, Ron White, Nelson.
Conversational exercises in everyday English, Books 1 and 2, Jerrom and Szkutnik, Longman.

D The situational drill

This is another teaching technique for making practice freer. Here is an example:

Situation (Cue): The phone's ringing.
Response: I'll answer it.

What might the responses be to the following situations?

1 The washing is outside and it starts to rain.
2 The window is open and your visitor says he's cold.
3 Your father can't understand something written in English.
4 A visitor tells you she's thirsty.
5 A visitor tells you he's got a headache.

Exercise

Continue the following language practice exercise by writing five different short situations to practise the same grammatical structure.

Situation: You left your bike in front of the cinema and went in. You
               have just come out and it is not there.
Response: My bike has been stolen.

**(RSA Certificate for Overseas Teachers of English, Language Paper,
June 1981)**

The basic principle that the teacher follows in the situational drill is
to set up a series of situations, but no longer feed in the required
structure. At this stage the learner should have acquired the form,
meaning and use of the structure so that he is able to transfer it to
new situations.

Language and communication

A Communication

Anyone who is familiar with recent books and articles on language
teaching will agree that the words *communication* and *communicative*
have tended to crop up with increasing frequency. Since this notion
is essential to the whole subject matter of this chapter we must
clarify it here.

Consider a teacher drilling language forms in an elementary
lesson. He has a wall-chart stuck to the blackboard depicting a
family. He is eliciting sentences from the class such as *Tom's shirt is
blue, Mr Carter's tie is red*. Once the pattern is established and the
lexis known, he can get students to produce the sentences by merely
pointing to parts of the picture. He then switches to a question-and-
answer drill. Again he points to the picture. Student A says *What
colour is Tom's shirt?* and Student B says *Blue*.

Let us analyse what is happening in this familiar type of classroom
activity:

1 The language *form* is established by standard drilling techniques,
   choral repetition and so on.
2 The students have to produce not only correctly formed sentences, but also true ones (according to the picture). They
   therefore have to think about *meaning:* the practice is meaningful.
3 However, no *communication* is taking place because (e.g.) in the
   question/answer drill both the asker and the answerer can see the
   picture. If it could be arranged that Student B can see the picture,
   while Student A cannot, the activity immediately becomes
   communicative because Student B is then genuinely communicat-
   ing some information to Student A. However, we need to do more

than this: we must provide *motivation* for Student A to ask the question; we must arrange it so that he *wants* to find out the answer.

Here is a way that we could achieve this. Tell the class that they are going to play a game. Divide them into pairs and make the members of each pair sit side by side, but facing in opposite directions.

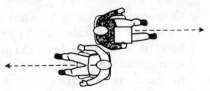

Stick the coloured wall-chart up at one end of the classroom so that only one member of each pair can see it. Provide the other half of the class (facing the blank wall) with uncoloured line drawings of the family in the wall-chart and coloured pencils. Tell them that they have got to colour their line drawings and ask their partners for the correct information using English only. The pair to complete the picture first is the winner.

Exercise

Think up similar communicative activities to promote more genuine language use of the following patterns. Describe the aids you would use and the instructions you would give:

1 *There are two chairs in the living-room.*
 There's a table in the hall. etc.

2 *Mary's eating an apple.*
 John's reading a book. etc.

3 *Do you like tennis/basketball/football?*
 Yes, I do. No, I don't.

B The information gap

The essential ingredient of a communicative activity is the element of unpredictability. For one reason or another, students do not know how their partners or other students are going to react to what they say or do. This makes the activity closer to real use of language.

The device used in the illustrative activity described above is termed the *information gap*: one student knows something that another does not. Only by bridging the gap, through the use of English, can the task be accomplished.

Although *information gap* is a reasonable term to use to describe this essential ingredient in communicative activities, we must remember that other things apart from factual information can be exchanged. We might induce our students to find out about each other's tastes, opinions or even their moods. For this reason, some teachers talk about *opinion gap*, *taste gap*, etc. These concepts will become clearer when more techniques have been introduced.

C The communicative interaction

Communication is a two-way process. When Speaker A says something to Speaker B, he expects some kind of reaction (not necessarily in words: he might get a gesture, a facial expression or a semi-verbal sound like 'Mm'). An interaction is what gets done when two speakers converse.

Dialogue	*Interaction*
A: Hey! Jack!	A greets B.
B: Hello, George. How are things?	B returns greeting.
A: Fine. Look, I'm sorry about last night.	A apologizes to B for X.
B: Oh, that's OK. Forget it.	B dismisses apology.

Some interactions follow a highly predictable pattern, especially when they are governed by social conventions. If A says 'Hello' to B, B will have to say 'Hello' or 'Hi' or something like that. When a person is introduced to another he says, 'How do you do?' and will expect back the same phrase or its equivalent, 'Pleased to meet you' or something similar. (West of the Atlantic he might encounter 'How are you doing?' or even 'How are you?'.) 'How are you?' normally evokes 'Fine' or some similar expression, even when the speaker feels far from fine! Again, 'Excuse me' said to attract the attention of a stranger would probably receive in reply 'Yes?'.

However, most interactions will follow unpredictable paths. In the dialogue above, when B says 'That's OK. Forget it', he might just as well have said 'Well, I should hope you are!', which is the equivalent of demanding further apology and explanation.

Exercises

1 Analyse the following dialogue in terms of its interactions:

A: Good afternoon.
B: Good afternoon, Madam.
A: I'd like to see the manager, please.
B: I'm afraid she's not here this afternoon. Can I help you?
A: It's this radio. I bought it here two days ago and now it doesn't work.

2 Make up two dialogues to fit the following interaction sequence. The first should represent a conversation between friends and the second between strangers.
A attracts B's attention. B acknowledges. A makes a request of B. B accedes to the request. A thanks B. B dismisses the thanks (disobligates A).

D Mood and emotion

The ability to express our feelings to others is an essential part of our linguistic repertoire; so it is also for the learner of foreign languages. Curiously enough, it is only in recent years that course writers, under the influence of analytic approaches to syllabus design, have begun to include in their materials means of expressing quite commonplace emotions such as *surprise, anger, pleasure, fear* and *contempt*. 'Negative' emotions such as *anger, displeasure, fear, contempt, disgust*, etc., have been particularly neglected. Some emotions such as *gratitude* are highly conventionalized and therefore always included in course materials. But it is still necessary to teach means of going beyond the everyday conventions to express sincere, strong feelings of gratitude. Some conventionalized emotions such as *sympathy* are terribly important to know, but are seldom found in course books.

Exercise

Choose *five* of the above emotions and write down three ways of expressing each. Try to make your three examples represent a range of speaker-hearer relationships extending from *formal* to *familiar*.

Apart from choice of words, intonation, gesture and facial expression play an important role in expressing the mood of the speaker. Intonation is clearly part of the language and within the language teacher's realm of duty. But many teachers argue that we should make a point of teaching foreign students the significance of gesture and facial expression. Features such as this, which are not strictly speaking linguistic, but play an important part in linguistic communication, are known as *paralinguistic* features. All of these features, including intonation, can express a message which runs parallel to that contained in the words alone. Sometimes this message can even conflict with the words themselves. For example, a wide intonation range indicates interest or a positive attiude; and a narrow range indicates the reverse. Consequently the phrase, 'That's interesting', said with narrow intonation range – i.e. in a slight monotone – expresses the opposite to what it says in words and constitutes a perfunctory remark rather than a serious comment.

Reading assignment

Now read *Teaching techniques for communicative English* by Jane Revell, Chapter 1.

Written assignment

Explain in your own words the difference between communicative practice and practice which is merely meaningful. Give examples to illustrate the points you make. (about 300 words)

E Communicative tasks in a structural syllabus

The following are suggestions as to how certain classroom techniques and activities that have been developed following recent trends in EFL methodology can be adapted to fit the 'free' practice stage of a more orthodox structure lesson. The idea is based around a form of simplified role-play that is, in effect, a *communicative drill*, done in pairs.

Activities

1 Look at the following exercise and say how the information gap is created.

LEISURE SURVEY
Work in pairs. Pupil A is an interviewer asking what people do in their spare time. He stops people in the street to ask them a few questions.
Pupil B is the passer-by.
Pupil A will use the Leisure Survey form. Ask questions beginning: 'Do you ever...?'
Pupil B answers:

No, never   Yes, very often
   hardly ever   every day/evening
   not very often   once a month
etc.

(*Act English* Peter Watcyn-Jones, Penguin)

(A fragment of the Leisure Survey form)

	ACTIVITY	HOW OFTEN
go	to the cinema	....
	to the theatre	....
	to a restaurant	....
	dancing	....
play	football	....
	tennis	....

2 Look at the following exercise and say how the information gap is created.

Group A:
Ask your partner the times of trains to five of these places. Write down what he tells you.

Manchester	Exeter ....
Durham	Cardiff ....
Leeds	Edinburgh ....
Liverpool	Oxford ....
Newcastle	Brighton ....

Group B:
Give your partner the information he asks for. They leave at...

Edinburgh – 5.35, 7.20, 8.36	Liverpool – 14.20, 16.35, 17.07
Leeds – 15.25, 16.05, 18.15	Newcastle – 9.42, 10.27, 11.08
Oxford – 9.47, 10.10, 11.21	Brighton – 13.06, 15.19, 17.17
Durham – 9.30, 12.15, 14.00	Manchester – 10.30, 11.45, 13.15
Cardiff – 8.17, 14.58, 21.08	Exeter – 10.49, 13.40, 17.08

(*Communicate I.* Morrow & Johnson, C.U.P.)

3 Activity 1 gave you in the instructions for the exercise the language that is to be used. Activity 2 does not do this. Can you suggest the structures that could be used in the exchange of information? (There are several possible ones all performing the same function – what is it?)

4 Both exercises asked one pupil/student to perform a simple writing task. Why should this be so in an oral exercise?

Having thought about and discussed point 4 read the following.

Both exercises create an information gap so that there can be a more realistic question and answer drill as information is actually passed from A to B (or vice-versa). Notice that the exercises are arranged in such a way that the person responding does not even know what question is coming. 'But this is not in itself enough to make student A listen and process. It is a necessary but not a sufficient condition...'. If the student is not asked to write anything down, 'he would have no reason to listen. He is not being asked to do anything with the information he has been given; hence he has no motivation for listening and processing.' It is the instruction, 'Write down what he tells you', that makes the exercise truly communicative. 'These words make (the exercise) conform to a principle important in communicative language teaching – the principle of getting the student to utilize in some way information given in the course of an exercise.' (All quotations from *Making drills communicative* by Keith Johnson in *Modern English Teacher* Vol. 7 No. 4.)

This process is adaptable to structure drills incorporated in a typical traditional syllabus. Attempt to produce such communicative drills in the following activities. (Remember that pupil A and pupil B must have different handouts.)

Activities

1 Take the use of the present continuous of 'Informing about a third person's whereabouts' and do three things: 1. Write out a situation where enquiring about a number of people would be relevant. 2. Write out a list of names together with the instructions for pupil A to produce the question, 'Where's X?'. 3. Write out the same list of names (in a different order) together with what they are doing (as the answer to 'Where's X?'). What would be your instructions to pupil A for the necessary, limited writing task?

2 Produce a leisure survey form suitable for your own learners.

3 Produce a diary page suitable for a communicative drill for production of the present continuous, used when talking about future arrangements. What could pupil B have as a sheet of instructions for this drill if pupil A has the completed diary page?

4 Produce (a) a partially completed street plan and (b) the complete street plan for a communicative drill based on 'There is/are' functioning as a simple way of giving street directions. What would pupil A ask if pupil B has the completed plan; what instructions would you write above the partially completed plan; what would be the simple writing task?

Further recommended reading

1 For a discussion of the principles behind making drills communicative see (a) *Making drills communicative* by Keith Johnson in *Modern English Teacher* Vol. 7 No. 4 and (b) *Making drills communicative: another opinion* by Dave Willis in *Modern English Teacher* Vol. 8 No. 1.

2 For textbook material that may act as inspiration see the following:

(a) *Communicate 1 and 2*, Morrow & Johnson, C.U.P.

(b) *Act English*, Watcyn-Jones, Penguin

(c) *Pair Work*, Watcyn-Jones, Penguin

(d) *Cue for a drill*, Harkess & Eastwood, O.U.P.

Reading assignment

Now read *Teaching techniques for communicative English*, Chapters 2-4, which gives a thorough discussion of the points raised here and suggests numerous communicative activities to be conducted in the class.

Some of these activities are more suitable for adults than children. If you teach children, select activities which would work well with your classes and think about adapting others to make them more suitable.

Exercise

Pick *one* communicative activity suggested in these chapters and prepare a lesson-plan for your own students based on this activity. Try this lesson out on your students. Discuss practical problems with other teachers.

Bibliography

Controlled practice
An introduction to English language teaching, J. Haycraft (Longman)
Teaching oral English, Donn Byrne (Longman)
Functional English Teacher's Book 1, R.V. White (Nelson)

Making practice freer: the transitional stages
Notions in English, Leo Jones (C.U.P.)
Contemporary English Books 1-4, Rossner *et al.* (Macmillan)
Functional English Book 1, R.V. White (Nelson)
Conversational exercises in everyday English Books 1 & 2, Jerrom & Szkutnik (Longman)

Language and communication
Teaching techniques for communicative English, J. Revell (Macmillan)

Communicative tasks in a structural syllabus
Act English, P. Watcyn-Jones (Penguin)
Communicate, K. Morrow & K. Johnson (C.U.P.)
Making drills communicative, K. Johnson in *Modern English Teacher* Vol 7 No 4
Making drills communicative – another opinion, D. Willis in *Modern English Teacher* Vol 8 No 1
Pair Work, P. Watcyn-Jones (Penguin)
Cue for a drill, S. Harkess & J. Eastwood (O.U.P.)

7 The teaching of pronunciation

A basic teaching strategy

We believe that the teaching of pronunciation is not an optional luxury to be left to advanced level studies of the language at university, although, of course, this would be the place to deal with the theory just as the theories of grammar etc. are studied at this level. But just as a student reaches university level with an active command of grammar structures and vocabulary so he should arrive with an active command of pronunciation. In other words, pronunciation should be an integral part of an English teaching programme from the early stages, just as the teaching of structures and vocabulary. However, one very basic question arises – 'What do we start with?' The standard works of reference, such as those by Gimson, Jones or O'Connor, follow an order that progresses from the smallest unit of speech (the phoneme) to combinations of phonemes (such as consonant clusters) to the word (word stress) and finally to connected speech, incorporating such features as sentence stress, rhythm and intonation. However, although this progress may be logical in terms of study of the theory, is it in fact the logical way to teach pronunciation to foreign learners?

Activity

Compare the textbook extract and the quotation below and think of the implications. (This is the initial lesson in a published textbook for absolute beginners.)

Lesson One: English Vowel Sounds.

/iː/	meat	a key	a bee	a tree
/ɪ/	a fish	a ship	six	a stick

(The lesson continues in the same way, giving four example words for each of the vowel sounds. Each word is accompanied by an appropriate picture.)

'I have found the most useful and stimulating order to be: first meaningful sentence stress within a context, accompanied by relevant expression i.e. basic intonation; second help with the difficult and important sounds.' (Brita Haycraft, *The teaching of pronunciation* page 4, Longman)

What conclusions have you reached? Which would you teach first –
(a) sounds (b) stress or (c) intonation?

Now read on.

'If other aspects of pronunciation are dealt with efficiently, then
sounds do not present such a problem.' (John Haycraft, *An
introduction to English language teaching* page 56.)

This certainly seems to be the case in many classrooms around the
world. Problems of sound formation often arise because of distorted,
exaggerated stress patterns. Many learners tend to produce utterances of the type, 'GIVE.IT.TO.HIM.' instead of, 'GIVE it to him'.
And unfortunately it is often the teacher who is the cause. When
presenting a structure orally, he tends to speak too slowly in order to
emphasize the individual elements that combine to form the
structure. Unfortunately this tendency of trying to make the form of
the structure easier makes the pronunciation more difficult. It is
quite often when the learner produces 'GIVE.IT.TO.HIM.' that he
has problems of correct sound production, producing /giːv/ /iːt/ and
/hiːm/ instead of /gɪv/ /ɪt/ and /hɪm/. Therefore the first point we
would like to emphasize is that the teacher should speak at a normal
speed and insist on the same from the student. This, of course, may
lead to a structure mistake, 'Give it him', as the 'to' (unstressed) may
not be perceived and therefore not produced. This can easily be
rectified by a *backchaining* technique – the learner repeating after the
teacher, 'him/to him/it to him/Give it to him.' This insistence on
normal speech may also lead to a staccato-like effect or speech that
sounds like a burst of machine-gun fire. Therefore straight imitation
of the teacher's natural speed is not enough. He needs to do more. It
is here that a teaching strategy similar to Brita Haycraft's 'initial
teaching method' may help. (See Brita Haycraft, *The teaching of
pronunciation*, pages 7-36.)

Brita Haycraft first of all suggests procedure for an *initial non-text
stage*, whereby learners do not see the written form of the language.
This procedure entails:

1 *Introducing stress*, by the use of common greetings and names.
2 *Introducing intonation*, by, again, the use of greetings + simple
  Yes/No questions that require a simple response of 'Yes' or 'No'
  with a falling tune, and other simple responses as the learner's
  knowledge of structure and vocabulary increases e.g., 'No, I'm
  `not', 'Yes, I `am', 'No, it `isn't', etc. All this time the teacher, of
  course, has been using a rising tune for the Yes/No questions but
  has not required the students to use it. This is subsequently
  introduced separately and then the two are mixed.
3 *Teaching the use of the whole voice range*, so that students do not
  produce a Low Fall, which sounds dull, monotonous and

uninterested. This can be done by setting up situations that require an enthusiastic ``Please' or ``Thank you' as a response.

This above procedure entails ideally restricting the teaching material to phrases of simple stress. Brita Haycraft has listed structures that can be taught to beginners with such examples.

The past and present tenses of the verbs – 'to be' and 'to have got'.
The present continuous tense.
The negative in short answers.
Plurals, the article.
There is/are.
Prepositions 'in' and 'on', etc. (See page 21.)

4 *Then introducing two adjacent stresses*, by teaching the adjective + noun.

Activity
Devise a series of examples with simple stress only for the above list of structures quoted from Brita Haycraft.

The merits of the 'initial teaching method' are that it focuses attention on areas that are essential to basic communication (such as the Fall or Rise as the difference between spoken questions and answers and the development of a polite, interested way of speaking); secondly it fits in well with a structural syllabus and exploitation of more traditional structural textbooks. (For example, 'It's a `PEN' always precedes 'It's a |BLUE `PEN', and initial presentation of the present continuous tense is often with intransitive verbs – therefore there is no object, which would mean a second stress – e.g. He's `running/She's `sleeping.) And thirdly, this method can be adapted to classes that are not beginners, using more developed vocabulary and structures.

Nevertheless, even with this systematic approach, problems with individual sounds will occur, but as they will have occurred as mistakes, then the strategy for dealing with individual sounds is one of *remedial teaching* and this can be considered as consisting of two separate approaches – (1) *Instant Remedial* and (2) *Planned Remedial*.

For instant remedial the strategy will divide into four parts: (1) imitation (2) demonstration (3) association (4) explanation. The teacher first of all draws attention to the 'offending' sound and pronounces it in isolation to be imitated by the learner(s). If this fails, he may then demonstrate how the sound is formed e.g. by telling his students to watch him carefully as he puts his tongue between his teeth to produce /θ/ or /ð/. However, certain sounds are not so easily made visible, so the teacher may adopt the process of association. 'If the /g/ of "Good" in "Good morning" proves difficult, the sound must be isolated, and attention can be drawn to its similarities with /b/ and /d/ on account of voicing, and with /k/ on account of its point of articulation.' (Paul Tench, *Pronunciation skills*, page 44, Macmillan.) Finally, explanation may help as the teacher explains (in the mother tongue, if necessary) how the sound is formed and gives instruction to the student(s) to move their tongue forward, round their lips more etc.

The teacher should of course not go into great phonetic detail in his explanation, but rather use layman's terms to convey the idea, much as he could do with grammatical explanations without using the terminology or metalanguage. *Ship or Sheep? An intermediate pronunciation course*, Ann Baker (C.U.P.) gives ideas how this can be done with reference to the consonant sounds.

Lack of space here does not enable us to go into the necessary details for each individual sound. Teachers requiring further information about specific sounds should consult one of the following:

1 *Pronunciation skills*, Paul Tench (Macmillan) Chapter 3, *Accuracy* (pages 47-58). This section deals with correction procedures for individual sounds in general. It is not limited to one specific nationality of learner.

2 *The teaching of pronunciation*, Brita Haycraft (Longman) pages 97-113. This section is very practically entitled *List of correction formulas for common persistent faults*, and that is exactly what it is – ready-made formulas for the teacher to put into practice. Her list is divided into columns – (1) sound (2) fault (3) nationality (4) cause of fault (5) quick teaching point – on the left-hand page, while on the right-hand page there are suggestions for drills for each case.

The nationalities of learner that she refers to specifically are: French, Italian, Spanish (including South American), German (including Swiss and Austrian), Scandinavian (including Swedish, Danish and Norwegian), Indian, Persian, Japanese and Chinese. This is a probably the most useful checklist and series of guidelines for teachers of learners of the above nationalities.

3 *Better English pronunciation*, J.D. O'Connor (C.U.P.) Appendix 1, *The difficulties of English pronunciation for speakers of Arabic, Cantonese, French, German, Hindi and Spanish* (pages 167-178). This is a more theoretical contrastive analysis that defines areas of difficulty but does not propose techniques for correction. However, they are useful checklists that indicate to the teacher the sounds and areas of stress that may need special attention.

4 *An introduction to the pronunciation of English*, A.C. Gimson (Edward Arnold) Chapter 7, *The English vowels* and Chapter 8, *The English consonants* deal with each sound individually. Included in the analysis of each there is a section entitled *Advice to foreign learners*, which points out areas of difficulty. There is also a useful inclusion of lists of pairs of words that can be used as the basis for remedial drills.

If, after this process of instant remedial work, the 'offending' sound is still proving difficult, then obviously there is the need for *planned remedial* work. The teacher should not continue to insist, but make a note of the problem and plan a short remedial drill for the following lesson. (This will be dealt with later in detail in the discussion of an *RSA Certificate for Overseas Teachers of English* examination question on pages 230 ff.)

We now turn our attention to classroom techniques and aids that will enable the teacher to put the above teaching strategy into practice.

Sounds

A Remedial work on individual sounds

Here the blackboard is possibly not such a useful aid, except for writing up certain specific minimal pair exercises.

It is probably easier for the teacher to demonstrate or explain the position of tongue, lips etc. than it is to draw a diagram of the mouth on the blackboard. It is not at all easy to draw this quickly and accurately. If the teacher feels that this is needed, then he would be better advised to use the published charts.

However, if the students have been introduced to the convention of the vowel chart, as devised by Daniel Jones, then this can be quickly drawn.

If you need to draw this quite often, then it is advisable to produce a more permanent template of stiff card that can be drawn round quickly. However, this aid may belong more to the lecturer of phonology addressing a group of trainee-teachers of English!

For non-specialist classes of learners, the teacher may use the blackboard for a system of *colour-coding* to indicate a sound that is represented by different spellings. In the following example list of words the italic letters would be written with coloured chalk (e.g. red) while the rest of the word would be written in white.

/ʌ/ *cut* – c*o*me – c*ou*ntry – bl*oo*d – d*oe*s

This coloured coding based on the use of coloured chalks (or felt tip pens on a whiteboard) may be particularly useful when the consideration of pronunciation work is integrated into other language work, for example during a unit of work on the simple past tense. The three possible pronunciations of the regular -ed ending /t/, /d/ and /ɪd/ can be represented by three different colours, and words can be written in three columns on the blackboard as follows: (We will say, for the sake of argument, that our colour coding is blue for /t/, red for /d/ and yellow for /ɪd/. The -ed ending is, of course, the item written in the appropriate colour, while everything else is written in normal white.)

Blue	*Red*	*Yellow*
jumped	saved	waited
washed	begged	folded
etc.		

As new verbs will be constantly introduced from now on in a course in the simple past tense, this colour coding can be used over and over again, as the teacher can indicate the pronunciation of the -ed ending by writing it in the appropriate colour.

(This same principle can be applied to other teaching points e.g. the plural – /s/ in book*s*, /z/ in pen*s* and /ɪz/ in hous*es*.)

The blackboard can also be used to draw objects that symbolize sounds, such as a (hissing) snake for /s/ and a (buzzing) bee for /z/. However, if the learners have constant difficulty with the /s/ – /z/ contrast, then these pictures are best drawn on stiff card to be used as flashcards for instant correction. (If the teacher cannot draw well, then, of course, magazine cut-outs could be used.)

B Types of exercise

See Ann Baker, *Tree or Three?* and *Ship or Sheep?*; M.D. Munro MacKenzie, *Modern English pronunciation practice*; Donn Byrne and Gordon Walsh, *Pronunciation practice* and Colin Mortimer, *Clusters* for types of exercises for specific problems. Examples are:

1 practice of individual sounds in isolated words, in short phrases and sentences, in dialogues;
2 practice of contrasting sounds in minimal pairs and in pairs of sentences; exercises contrasting three sounds in isolation and in context; contrasting more sounds, especially in a test exercise;
3 practice of combinations of sounds – clusters of consonants can be practised in isolated words, in minimal pairs and in context.

Stress

A Word stress

First of all let us look at what we mean by *word stress*.

1 A syllable can carry *primary* stress, that is to say strong stress. The syllable is longer, louder and said with more breath effort.

2 A syllable can be *unstressed*. In other words it is said very quickly, lightly and with very little breath effort.

3 A syllable can carry *secondary* stress. This syllable is said with more breath effort than 2 but less than 1.

Marking If you look into a good dictionary you will find that the stress pattern of a word is marked. The primary stress is marked with a high upright stroke ' before the syllable, the secondary stress is marked with a low upright stroke , before the syllable.

B Sentence stress

In a normal English sentence certain words are stressed and certain words are unstressed.

Normally stressed are *content* words – the words that are essential for conveying a message. These are nouns, verbs, adjectives, adverbs (most) and demonstratives.

Normally unstressed are the *form* words, the grammatical or structure words that result in a correct grammatical utterance even though these words are not essential to the communication of a message.

For example – in the following sentence:

'Janet has 'gone to the 'baker's,

Janet, gone, baker's are the content words and are therefore stressed. (The utterance as it stands communicates the message and would be readily understood – compare, for example, the language of telegrams that tends to use only content words – ARRIVING MONDAY. NEED CAR.)

has, to, the are form words not essential to the communication of the message and so are unstressed.

Activity

Mark the stressed words in the following sentences by placing an upright stroke before the stressed syllable.

1 I saw your brother yesterday.

2 Can I carry your suitcase?

3 Would you like a glass of beer?

4 Have you heard about John? He's going to New York tomorrow. He's flying on the Concorde.

5 I must be going. My wife's waiting for me at the corner of the street.

C Teaching stress

As with other aspects of pronunciation teaching, the first stage is pure *imitation*, repetition of the teacher's model in chorus and individually. Should there be difficulty with, say, 'Good morning' when it is repeated in its entirety, then the teacher can isolate the stressed syllable – MORN – , get that repeated a few times and then put the phrase together again for further repetition. So the process can be summarized as follows:

1 Repeat whole phrase.
2 Isolate and repeat stressed syllable only.
3 Repeat whole phrase.

The teacher may also wish to indicate the position of the stressed syllable in some way. It is here that he has several options open, dependent on the two most valuable aids to pronunciation teaching – the *blackboard* and *the use of gesture*.

1 Gestures

The teacher may do any of the following to indicate the stress pattern:
(a) thump the air when saying the stressed syllable
(b) make a downward stroke of the hand – marking the 'beat' like a conductor
(c) punch the palm of his other hand
(d) clap his hands
(e) bang his hand against something – e.g. the desk or the blackboard.
(*Note*: the dangers of (c), (d) and (e), however, are that the additional sound may distract from the sounds of the phrase. A *silent gesture* of some type is probably preferable.)

2 The blackboard

This is probably the most valuable aid for making pronunciation points visible to the class. The teacher can exploit the blackboard at both the initial non-text stage, when the written form of the language has not yet been introduced, and at the text stage. What he actually puts on the blackboard may vary.

Non-text stage
Without writing the word or phrase, the teacher can indicate the stress pattern by using symbols. There are several possibilities and it does not really matter which the teacher chooses provided that he is consistent.
(Taking 'Good morning' as an example)

(a)   — | —

(b)   ▫ □ ▫

(c)   ○ ○ ○

Text stage
(a) The above symbols (especially a and b) could be written above or below the phrase.

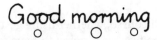

(b) The stressed syllable could be underlined.

Good <u>morning</u>

(c) The stressed syllable could be written in capital letters (though this is probably inadvisable in the case of learners who have a different script for the mother tongue and who have not yet mastered the Roman letters).

Good MORNing

(d) The stressed syllable could be written in a different coloured chalk.

However, once the written form has been introduced, there is a danger that the learner on seeing two words may separate the words when he says them, making a very slight pause between 'Good' and 'morning'. If this happens, though if it has been presented and practised orally first this should not occur, then the teacher can draw attention to the 'continuity' of the phrase and show how words are linked by drawing linking circles.

०–○–०

Activity

Choose one technique from *Gestures* and practise on your colleagues (or if you are reading this alone at home do it in front of a mirror) with the phrases listed below.

Then choose one blackboard technique from *Non-text stage* and one from *Text stage* and practise 'writing' (preferably on a blackboard or if you are at home on a piece of paper) the stress patterns of the following phrases:

1 Good evening.

2 Good afternoon.

3 Excuse me.

4 Cheerio.

5 I'd love to.

Of course, whether using gesture and/or symbols on the blackboard, the teacher is going to have to give the spoken model several times. How is he going to say it? A technique of *slight exaggeration* is probably advisable, as students' imitations always tend to fall short of the model. In the case of stress, this would entail *over-emphasizing* the stressed syllable(s), but the teacher must be careful not to pause either before or after the stressed syllable. 'Good morning' must still sound like a natural friendly greeting.

D Weak forms

Linked to the idea of sentence stress is that of weak forms. Certain of the unstressed words change their pronunciation from the way they are said when they are in isolation, and have a different phonetic form in the sentence or phrase. These are the following:

Prepositions – at, to, of, for, from
Auxiliary and modal verbs – be, been, am, is, are, was, were, have, has, had, do, does, shall, should, will, would, can, could, must
Pronouns – me, he, him, his, she, we, us, you, your, them
Others – who, that (as a relative pronoun), a, an, the, some, and, but, as, than, there, not.

Most of these words, when they are not in a stressed position, which is always at the end of a sentence and sometimes at the beginning, are said weakly and the vowel sound is usually reduced to schwah – /ə/.

Activity

Mark the stress in the following and practise saying them with the weak forms.

1	John's at home.	10	John has arrived.
2	A quarter to nine.	11	Where does this go?
3	A cup of tea.	12	I shall be there.
4	I bought a present for my wife.	13	I can speak English.
5	I come from England.	14	I must go.
6	I've been to France.	15	Did you see them?
7	I was here yesterday.	16	The book that I want.
8	We were leaving the house.	17	I'd like some potatoes.
9	They have seen it.	18	Bacon and eggs.

Here is an exercise to practise one weak form only – *of* /əv/.

Listen and repeat:
a glass of water – a bottle of beer – a tin of peas – a kilo of oranges – a block of flats, etc.

To practise several weak forms in unconnected phrases, see, for example, John Wright, *Speaking English*. Phrases can be read aloud by the teacher and repeated by the students. Short dialogues are a good way of practising several weak forms in context.

Written assignment

Plan two short drills which highlight and give practice on weak forms of common verbs such as *be, have, can*. (*R.S.A. Certificate for Overseas Teachers of English*, June 1981.)

E Sound linking

'One of the problems of English pronunciation is the way words run into one another. Without good sound linking and good stress, words become unmanageable chunks, and fluency is obstructed.' (John Haycraft, *An introduction to English language teaching*, page 60.)

The problem is exaggerated when the two words that run together end and begin respectively with the same consonant. E.g. 'I'm more than an hour late.'

Activity

Practise saying the following:

1 He isn't tall.

2 She's sorry.

3 We've varied the programme.

4 We're running in the same race tomorrow.

5 She's singing well.

6 Fred doesn't like tea.

7 I'd decided before I met Mary.

8 She'll leave it to the last minute.

This can be used with students as a 'listen and repeat' exercise.

Students may find problems with linking /r/, pronounced before vowels. For examples of exercises to deal with this and other linking problems, see Ann Baker, *Ship or Sheep* and Colin Mortimer, *Link-up*.

Activity

Devise three-line dialogues to practise sound-linking at intermediate level. See John Haycraft, *An introduction to English language teaching*, page 74.

Intonation

A Functions of intonation

Basically there are two functions of intonation:

1 It indicates grammatical meaning, in much the same way as punctuation does in the written language. For example:
(a) He lives in `London.
A full stop in the written language indicates that this is a statement. A falling intonation pattern indicates the same in the spoken form.

(b) He lives in ´London?
A question mark in the written language indicates that this is a question. A rising intonation pattern indicates the same in the spoken form.

(c) Do you come from ´London?

is the normal question form. There are clues to the meaning, such as the use of *do*, that show this, even if the intonation pattern is not produced correctly. BUT...

(d) You come from ´London?

is a perfectly acceptable way of asking the question in the spoken language. The clue *do* is no longer there. It is one of those words that have a weak form, and here it has become so weak that it has disappeared altogether. The intonation pattern would be the only clue left to suggest a statement or a question. In fact, because the intonation pattern gives the meaning, the *do* is redundant. It is not necessary, so it can be omitted.

We hope that these examples have clearly demonstrated the importance of intonation as *a means of conveying meaning* and as such that it should be part of a teaching programme and not the optional luxury that it often is.

Stress and intonation can also *change meaning*. Look at the following:

(a) I want to see your son `Harry. (The son is called Harry.)
(b) I want to see your ´son,| `Harry. (The speaker is talking to Harry, who has a son, whose name we do not know.)

(a) My brother who lives in `London| has just got `married. (I have more than one brother. It is the one who lives in London...)
(b) My `brother,| who lives in `London| has just got `married. (I have only one brother and he has just got married.)

(a) Mary said her `mother| had gone to the `cinema. (Mary's words are being reported. It is her mother who has gone to the cinema.)
(b) ´Mary,| said her ˇmother,| had gone to the `cinema. (Here it is Mary's mother who is talking and Mary is the one who had gone to the cinema.)

(a) My brother was born in `England. I was `two.
(b) My brother was born in `England. `I was too.
   (Here, of course, the contrasting written forms of *two* and *too* reveal the meaning, but in spoken language the differing stress and intonation patterns provide the only indication.)

(a) He lives in Luton. `Where? (i.e. in which part of Luton)
(b) He lives in Luton. ´Where? (I'm sorry I didn't catch the name of the town. Could you repeat it?)

(*Note:* this type of contrast is tested in the American TOEFL exam as follows:
    Listen: I 'thought you were `coming?
  Question: Did he come?)

2 Intonation can also indicate the speaker's *attitude*.
Look at the following examples:

(a) Really? may be an expression of great surprise, or of mild puzzlement, or merely a polite conversation-oiler, depending on the intonation pattern.

(b) What's your name? may show a great interest and desire to be friendly to the other person, or may simply be a request for information (made by a government official or policeman, for example). Again the intonation pattern would indicate which.

In some cases both grammatical meaning and attitude are conveyed by the intonation pattern alone.

Example: (I'd like a drink)
(a) You ´would?
(Simply a conversation-oiler, that has the additional function of asking for confirmation of the statement.)

(b) 'You `would.
(Here annoyance and criticism is conveyed. The implication is one of: 'Well, that's just typical of you. You always want a drink.')

From the above examples it should be clear that the *attitudinal* function of intonation is a complex area. It is made even more complex by the fact that standardization and classification is difficult, though not impossible, to accomplish, as the expression of feelings and attitudes are connected to the individual personality. And when teaching foreign learners there is an additional culturally-bound factor. It is near impossible to make an introverted student produce an exclamation of great surprise, when maybe he would not do such a thing in his mother tongue (e.g. certain Scandinavian students). Therefore we suggest that basically the practising teacher should concentrate on the use of intonation to convey grammatical meaning, perhaps limiting the attitudinal function to listening and recognizing at lower levels, and including only a limited amount of production at more advanced levels. The basic question that now needs to be answered is, *Which pattern for which type of utterance?*

There are four possible tune movements – two of them simple (moving in one direction only) and two of them compound (moving in two directions).

Simple   – falling (moving downwards)
              – rising (moving upwards)
Compound – falling then rising
              – rising then falling.

These four possible tune movements exist in six possible forms:

1 High Fall – a fall from a high level
2 Low Fall – a fall from a middle or lower level
3 High Rise – a rise from a middle or higher level
4 Low Rise – a rise from a low level
5 Fall-Rise – a fall from a high level and then a rise from a lower level
6 Rise-Fall – a rise from a low level then a fall from a higher level.

These tune movements are made on one syllable usually, and that is the last stressed syllable of an utterance, which is called the *nucleus*.

Shorter utterances usually consist of one word group, but longer utterances may be composed of two (or more) word groups. The division of such utterances into word groups is not difficult as this is usually indicated by a pause on the part of the speaker and in most cases corresponds to a grammatical division. Each word group from the point of view of intonation functions as a separate entitiy and the last stressed syllable of the word group is the nucleus.

From the above six tunes we suggest that the necessary minimum to be taught for production by the students are the following:

1 High Fall – statements, questions beginning with question words
2 High Rise – questions asking for something to be repeated or clarified
3 Low Rise – yes/no questions – lists (up to the last item) – conversation-oilers (encouraging the other person to go on)
4 Fall-Rise – corrections, polite contradictions.

Two tunes have been eliminated from the list of six – the Rise-Fall, because this is used mainly for expressing certain more exaggerated attitudes, such as great surprise or flattering admiration, and the Low Fall, which conveys the same meanings as the High Fall but not so politely!

Just as structures and vocabulary are graded in a teaching programme so can intonation be graded. To decide what comes first we need to ask ourselves the question, 'What are the learners doing with the language in the early stages?' Well, they are doing two things – 1. They are making statements (This is a `pen.) and they are asking questions of two types (What's `this? and, Is this a ‚pen?). So they need the High Fall for the statements and the questions with question words, and the Low Rise for Yes/No questions. Even if they never progress beyond these two patterns, they can do so many things in English with them.

B Teaching intonation

Again the use of gesture and the blackboard will help the teacher indicate the rising or falling pattern.

1   Gesture

A sweep of the arm from high to low will indicate the falling tune (vice-versa for the rise). Note, however, that the teacher should produce this gesture backwards – from right to left – as this will be the right way round – from left to right – for his students. However, this gesture can be somewhat vague, and gesturing from right to left while you mentally 'see' the utterance from left to right is difficult and does need a lot of practice. So it is possibly easier and more effective to use the blackboard. The gesture, however, can be useful since the teacher can indicate the rising or falling tune as he conducts a choral structure drill.

2   The blackboard

The non-text stage
1   The teacher draws two parallel lines on the blackboard; the top line represents a high pitch; the bottom line represents a low pitch. Then an arrow is drawn to indicate the direction of the intonation pattern. E.g. (for 'Good morning.')

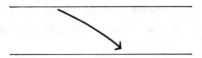

2   It is also possible to indicate both stress and intonation at the same time.
E.g. (for 'Who is it?')

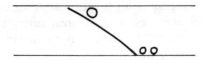

(*Note:* Once the convention of the lines and symbols has been established the lines can be dispensed with and only the symbols used.)

The text stage
Once the learners are able to read English (even if they were able to before, initial pronunciation work in a class of non-beginners should be oral only) the teacher can use *a sign system* over the text, either on the blackboard or on a stencilled handout with exercises for pronunciation work.
Brita Haycraft has pointed out the usefulness of such signs:

'they are a support for the students' memory; they can isolate stress and intonation... they are a neutral, common language, a code. Signs are there to help and therefore must be flexible. When students first begin, by merely looking at lines drawn on the blackboard (without words) they *hear* the sentence and imitate it. With the introduction of text, the teacher may write the stressed word or the whole sentence over the line, in different ways to suit the student to to get over the particular point he is making.' (*The teaching of pronunciation* page 38).

She then goes on to list several possible sign systems – see pages 38-39 for suggestions.

C Mood and attitude

Although we suggested earlier in the chapter that the teaching of intonation in the early stages should concentrate on the *grammatical* and not the attitudinal function, we by no means suggest that the teacher should accept a dull, monotonous, disinterested tone. We do want the foreign learner to sound polite, friendly and interested. The main difficulty here is usually one of shyness and embarrassment rather than inability to produce the required pattern. Therefore, in order to get the students to produce the necessary High Fall, instead of the dull Low Fall, the teacher needs to create the right atmosphere in the classroom to overcome the students' reticence. This can be done in several ways:

1 (as Brita Haycraft suggests) – *a game-like activity*, using realia to set up a situation that would illustrate the difference in attitude. The teacher gives each student a small coin and asks them to respond 'Thank you', at the same time drawing on the blackboard:

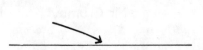

One student is then given a larger coin and encouraged to produce 'Thank you' on a slightly higher pitch, and so on with increasing amounts of money. The differences in pitch are illustrated on the blackboard:

(The teacher can use other objects, such as chocolate, depending on the age level and interests of the class.)
'Please' can be dealt with in a similar way – the teacher offering something and witholding unless the 'Please' is said with a high enough fall. (Brita Haycraft pages 15-16.)

2 *Mood cards* – two faces are drawn on cards, one indicating a bored, uninterested mood, like this:

the other a bright, lively, enthusiastic mood, like this:

and these, once introduced, act as aids to correction whenever the dull intonation pattern is produced. These drawings (like those above) can be very simple, or the more amusing cartoon-like drawing would be better.

For younger learners they could also be given names such as:

Mr Grumpy.   Mr Happy.

3 *Creating roles or enacting* – one way of overcoming shyness or embarrassment is to have the pupils or students adopt a role and act out a short sketch. For young beginners, this may quite simply entail having two pupils walking towards each other and producing greetings:

Mr Happy: `Hello.

Mr Grumpy: ˌHello.

or for more advanced learners (particularly adults) a more sophisticated contrast can be set up. The following short sketch could have two distinct scenarios:

(a) A bored, overworked immigration officer at an airport (role A) and a tired, hungry, bad-tempered traveller (role B).

(b) A handsome young man (role A) and an attractive foreign girl
(role B) in a disco. Obviously there will be a much greater degree
of friendliness and interest here, on both sides.

    A: What's your name?
    B: Monika Simonson.
    A: Where are you from?
    B: Sweden.
    A: What are you doing here?
    B: I'm on holiday.
    A: How long are you staying?
    B: Six weeks.

Once the two patterns have been enacted separately the teacher
may wish to put them together for contrast, using a dialogue for
acting out like the following:

A and B are invited to C's house. C is most welcoming. A is
delighted to be there, but B is reluctant and rude.

    C: How nice of you to come!
    A: ˈHello!
    B: ˌHello.
    C: Do come into the drawing room.
    A: ˈThank you!
    B: ˌOh. (only the Low Fall used)
    C: Do have some tea won't you?
    A: I'd ˈlove to.
    B: ˌOK.
    C: Indian or China?
    A: ˈIndian please.
    B: ˌChina.
    C: How about some scones?
    A: ˈDelicious.
    B: All ˌright.
    C: Don't you like scones?
    B: Not ˌmuch.
(See Brita Haycraft, pages 24-25.)

Notice in the above dialogue how other features combine with the
intonation to indicate B's attitude – his use of unenthusiastic,
non-committal replies, ˌOh, ˌOK, All ˌright, Not ˌmuch and the fact
that A uses enthusiastic language, I'd ˈlove to, Deˈlicious, and that
his early replies, ˈHello! and ˈThank you! are punctuated by an
exclamation mark. In fact after a few dialogues of this type for
practice this way of indicating attitude, particularly the use of the
exclamation mark, would probably be enough guidance for the
learners and the sign system could be dispensed with, except

perhaps as a reminder, if necessary, or as a correction device if the production by the learners is not satisfactory.

We hope that the above example dialogues have demonstrated clearly the vital importance of intonation as a part of correct social behaviour. Once the teacher has the basic idea the writing of such dialogues is not difficult. In order to find material at the level of his class, that is ready-made or can be adapted, the teacher may like to look at certain structurally-graded readers as a source of dialogues, particularly the Longman series or the Macmillan *Ranger* series.

D Types of exercise

It will be obvious from what has been said about a basic teaching strategy that intonation work is best dealt with as part of work on other materials. However, there are certain types of exercise that are specifically written for intonation practice. The best source for these exercises is specially written books, such as, *The intonation of colloquial English* by J.D. O'Connor and G.F. Arnold (Longman), and *Active intonation* by V.J. Cook (also Longman).

Integrated materials

There are two possible ways of integrating materials:

1 *Phonetic integration* – in other words, material can be specifically written that practises two aspects of pronunciation, usually one of three possible combinations:
   (a) Sound(s) + stress.
   (b) Sound(s) + intonation.
   (c) Stress + intonation.

2 Integration into other language work, particularly with structure. Examples of this:
   (a) It's a PEN – It's a PENcil – It's a PARcel etc.
   This practises the initial aspirated /p/ and a simple stress pattern.
   (b) Is it a pen? – Is it a pencil? – Is it a parcel? etc.
   This practises the initial aspirated /p/ and a rising intonation pattern.

Exercises and dialogues can be written specially to include examples of a particular sound, vowel or consonant, and to be read with a specific intonation. Thus suggestions, with a rising intonation pattern, can be contrasted with the falling pattern of commands. An example of the integration of structure and intonation would be an exercise on tag questions, where students would have to remember the falling intonation on the two parts of the utterance, e.g.:

She couldn't cook, could she?
(Note that this also practises the sound /ʊ/.)

This integration, which is possibly highly desirable, though not absolutely necessary at a lower level, becomes essential at an intermediate to advanced level, particularly if the teacher is using functional teaching materials. (This will be discussed in detail in Chapter 8, but I would just like to mention briefly certain pronunciation aspects here.)

Look at this following textbook extract:

Expressions of surprise...
You can say:
Whatever is it?
What on earth did you do that for?
Where on earth will you live?
Whatever are you doing?
Whatever did you eat?
Wherever are you going?
What on earth are you wearing?
What/where/how/why (on earth) (ever)...?

Now practise these expressions using the following ideas and responding according to the situation.
1. Your mother/wife/sister/girl-friend is wearing a strange hat.
2. It is 11 o'clock and your brother tells you he's going out.
3. Your wife/mother is cooking something that smells strange.
4. A friend tells you he has given up a very good job.
5. A friend tells you that he is going to spend some time abroad and he has very little money.
6. The postman gives you a parcel which is a very strange shape.
(From *Intermediate context English*, Sue Lake, Macmillan.)

In this exercise the intonation pattern is as vital to the meaning of the structure as is the form – *Whatever* or *What on earth*, etc. It would be next to useless to teach the form without the (very) High Fall intonation pattern or the emphatic stress on *ever* or *earth*. Here the integration is so absolute that separation is impossible. Exactly the same principle applied to the following extract:

Irene and Ernie are twins. They both like the same things, but Ernie expresses his feelings much more strongly than Irene. In the picture they are admiring a piece of sculpture. Here are some of the things they might be saying:

Irene	*Ernie*
Oh look. That one's not bad.	Just look at that sculpture!
	Isn't it amazing!
I think that's quite pretty.	I've never seen such a beautiful
Don't you?	piece of sculpture!

That's a rather clever idea,   What a brilliant idea!
    isn't it?
Mm. I like that. It's nice and   Now that's absolutely superb!
    simple.   It's so fantastically simple!
(From *Feelings*, Adrian Doff and Christopher Jones, C.U.P.)

Activities

1 Write a short dialogue with a shopping situation to present and practise one of the ways of asking for something in a shop – such as 'I'd like' or 'Can I have...?' or 'Could I have...?' – including items that would highlight the weak form of /əv/ e.g. a tin of peas, or a pair of shoes etc. Then write out a drill that would intensively practise this pronunciation point.

2 Write out a short dialogue that would highlight the falling intonation pattern of WH – questions. Take the situation of two strangers meeting.
A is asking B some personal questions. This would also be practice of the present simple.

3 Write out a question and answer drill containing examples of adjacent stress – e.g. 'It's a red pencil.' Be careful to avoid examples such as: 'Is it a blue pencil?/No, it's a red pencil,' as this changes the stress pattern, and includes emphatic stress, 'It's a *red* pencil' for the purposes of pointing out a contrast. This would be integrated into a lesson on what grammatical point?

Pronunciation games

See Chapter 2 for some suggestions. A game which can be used to practise a wide variety of language points is *bingo*. Teachers can devise their own *phonetic bingo* to practise the discrimination of English sounds. There also exists a published version of the game – *Sounds right*, by John and Marion Trim, C.U.P.

This published version is general, i.e. it contains examples of all the sounds. However, it is possible to produce adaptations that are in effect games of *mini-bingo* that concentrate on specific areas of difficulty.

(a) Mini-bingo for the vowels /æ/, / ʌ / and /ɑ:/

The students have cards with three or four of the following activities or objects depicted on them. The teacher reads out the words and the students cover the appropriate pictures if they have them on their cards:

cap – cup – hat – hut – heart – cat – cut – cart – track – truck – bag – bug – match – march – lamp – lump.

(b) Mini-bingo for numbers

The same principle applies and this is particularly useful for the contrast between the tens and teens which often causes problems. E.g. thirty and thirteen, forty and fourteen etc.

Other than forms of bingo the teacher can adapt existing vocabulary games so that they practise a particular pronunciation point. One well-known vocabulary game is 'I went to the (super)market.'

Teacher:	I went to the supermarket and I bought some eggs.
Student 1:	I went to the supermarket and I bought some eggs and some oranges.
Student 2:	I went to the supermarket and I bought some eggs, some oranges and some sugar etc.

Each student adds something to the list, and you must remember what the other students have said.

This game can be adapted so that specific sounds are practised. It might be a good idea to write a list of suitable words on the blackboard first – get your students to suggest them – and practise saying them. With a weaker class you could leave the list on the board during the game.

It is also possible to adapt certain of the more traditional guessing games – see W.R.Lee, *Language teaching games and contests*, 2nd Ed. O.U.P. Very commonly used in elementary level classrooms is this very simple guessing game: the teacher hides something in his bag/pocket/drawer etc. and the learners try to guess what it is by asking 'Is it a pen?' etc. The teacher can adapt this particularly for consonants by saying it begins with *p*, for example. To give himself more vocabulary to play with it might be better to use a picture. Learners then practise the initial aspirated /p/ intensively as they ask 'Is it a pen/pencil/pin/pear?'

Finally it is possible to turn simple recognition exercises into a game by simply dividing the class into two teams and introducing a competitive element by awarding points. Here is just one example, from Ann Baker's *Ship or Sheep?*

Having previously used exercises that practise the difference between a rising tone for a friendly suggestion and a falling tone for an unfriendly command, Ann Baker introduces the following as the final checking stage:

Competition – Friendly or unfriendly?
Divide the class into two teams.
The teacher reads the following sentences, with friendly or unfriendly intonation.
Students take turns to decide if he's friendly or unfriendly.
Score a point for each correct answer.

Put these socks in the box.	Don't wash these socks.
Put it on top of the clock.	Don't borrow Tom's watch.

Make the coffee hot.	Don't go to the wrong office.
Go to the hospital.	Don't go to the wrong restaurant.
See a doctor.	Buy some binoculars.

Devising pronunciation exercises

A 'Bit' and 'Beat'

'Some of your students have difficulty in discriminating between the vowel sounds in BIT and BEAT. Plan a short practice which would help them both to discriminate and to produce.'
(*RSA Certificate for Overseas Teachers of English Examination* June 1980)

We will look at this question in detail, not only in the hope that it will help candidates preparing for this (or another similar) examination, but also because this is a basic problem that will arise in classrooms all around the world. (If it is not this particular problem in contrasting sounds, then it will be other pairs that pose problems – see the list of questions on page 237.)

1 Recognition

When a teacher realizes that his students are making an error, then the first thing he has to do is analyse the cause of the error in more detail. In this particular case the fault probably lies in a confusion between the vowel /ɪ/ in BIT and the reduced form of the vowel /iː/ in BEAT, reduced in length because of the final voiceless consonant. The long form in BEAD would probably not be the cause of such a great problem. The result of this is that the students would tend to pronounce both BIT and BEAT as if they contained the same vowel /biːt/.

2 Discrimination

Following on from this awareness of the cause of the error, the teacher needs first of all to check that the learners are able to recognize the difference between the two sounds, to *discriminate*, by using one or more *sound discrimination drills*. Such a drill is devised by producing a list of *minimal pairs*, that is to say two words that differ only in one sound, with instructions, as in the following:

1 Indicate whether the following pairs of words are the same (if so write S) or different (if so write D):
(*Note:* the teacher reads the words to the class – the learners do not see the list.)
(a) bit – beat
(b) sit – sit
(c) sheep – sheep
(d) pick – peak
(e) peach – pitch
(f) leap – leap
(g) leak – lick

Although this error is more obvious in the lack of contrast between /ɪ/ and /iː/ in its reduced form, it is quite likely to occur also in the contrast between /ɪ/ and long /iː/ as in BID and BEAD. To spot the error the teacher would have to listen carefully to see if words such as live, give, bid are pronounced /liːv/, /giːv/, /biːd/. In which case he would need to produce a sound discrimination drill, containing pairs of words ending in a voiced consonant.

2 (Instructions as for 1)
(a) leave – live
(b) seen – sin
(c) bid – bid
(d) is – ease
(e) bin – bean
    etc.

If the error is occurring in both situations, which is often the case, then the teacher may wish to have two separate drills (as above) or produce only one which would be a combination or a mixture of 1 and 2.
    If the above drill has not produced good results, the teacher may need to use a further one, or he may wish to have a different type of drill for variation.

3 *Teacher:* I am going to read you groups of three words. Put a cross (X) in box 1, 2 or 3 to show whether the first, second or third word is different from the other two. If they are all the same put a cross (X) in the box marked O.

(a) leave – leave – live
(b) bin – bean – bin
(c) keep – keep – keep
(d) lick – lick – lick
(e) sheep – ship – ship
(f) is – ease – is

The completed student's paper looks like this:

	1	2	3	O
a			X	
b		X		
c				X
d				X
e	X			
f		X		

The student also needs to be able to recognize the sounds *in context*. It is often the case that students can recognize and produce the sound in isolation, but the difficulty returns when the word containing the sound occurs later in a sentence, leading to frustration on the part of the teacher. This can be anticipated by including in the practice *pairs of sentences*, as well as pairs of words.

The same procedure as for a sound discrimination drill with pairs of words can apply:

1 He's going to slip. / sleep.

2 He's drawing a picture of a ship. / sheep.

3 There were a lot of bins / beans in the shop.

4 They are going to live / leave together.

Note: Pairs of sentences are difficult to devise for three main reasons:
(a) Not many minimal pairs exist that belong to the same word class, e.g. two nouns, two verbs, etc.
(b) The sentences must be potentially ambiguous if mispronounced. In other words the context must be vague and must not provide a clue as to which word is being used. For this reason, the following sentences are unacceptable:

There's a *sheep* in the field. (ship?!)

I'm going on a *ship* tomorrow. (sheep?!)

(c) As well as lacking in contextual clues, pairs of sentences should also be lacking in grammatical clues. In other words there should be no variation in the sentence other than in the two contrasted words. For this reason the following pair is unacceptable:

I'd like a piece.

I'd like some peas.

Here although the context is sufficiently vague and does not provide any clue, the grammatical contrast between *a* and *some* indicates whether the word used is *piece* or *peas*.

However, despite the difficulties the teacher should attempt to produce pairs of sentences (or phrases) wherever possible. Donn Byrne and Gordon Walsh, in *Pronunciation practice* (Longman), have such pairs of sentences in each unit.

One objection raised to minimal pair discrimination drills is that they are too mechanical; they may contain vocabulary items that are unknown to the student, and at times, in order to make up a sufficient number of examples for a drill, the teacher includes unusual or uncommon words that the student might never otherwise meet and would certainly not need, for example in the following pairs, taken from a published pronunciation practice book:

sheen – shin

bream – brim

treacle – trickle

deem – dim

reel – rill.

However, although we would advise the teacher to avoid such uncommon words as far as possible, it may sometimes be necessary to correct the mechanics of the language mechanically.

It is sometimes possible to modify the drills to make them more meaningful by the use of pictures. This is particularly advisable for young learners.

Example:
The following pairs of words are accompanied by the appropriate pictures:

ship – sheep

chick – cheek

pitch – peach (a picture of a football pitch, for example)

meal – mill

bean – bin.

The teacher pronounces one word from each pair and the students point to the appropriate picture. It would also be possible to have *action pictures* to indicate the meaning of certain pairs of sentences. e.g.

He's going to $\begin{matrix} \text{slip.} \\ \text{sleep.} \end{matrix}$

Published pronunciation materials that adopt this more meaningful visual approach are *Tree or Three?* and *Ship or Sheep?*, both by Ann Baker, and *English pronunciation illustrated* by John L.M. Trim. (All three are published by C.U.P.)

3 Production

Following on from recognition or discrimination drills the teacher now has to devise a series of exercises or drills for the production of the sounds.

Stage 1. Keep the sounds separate!

Exercise 1
The teacher reads the following list of words, then each word separately, with the students repeating after his model.

feet – tree – leaf – piece – key – sheep – cheap – bead.

Exercise 2.
(Same procedure as for 1)

sit – bit – list – ship – chick – symbol – pretty – build.

(For more advanced classes the teacher would include other vocabulary items, particularly more polysyllabic words e.g. machine, policeman. But initially it is probably best to avoid them because of the additional word stress difficulty.)

Stage 2. Put the sounds together!

Exercise 3.
The teacher reads each of the following pairs of words to the class and they repeat after his model.

feet – fit	bead – bid	sheep – ship
leave – live	ease – is	reach – rich

Note: The above three exercises should probably be done twice – once orally only and secondly with the students looking at the written words. For this reason the teacher should include words that contain different spellings of the sound, so that he does not create the false impression that there is a one-to-one equivalent between spelling and sound. From this point of view, exercise 3 is by no means ideal as the sound /ɪ/ is represented only by the letter *i*. However, pairs of words are not available where the word containing the /ɪ/ sound is spelt other than with an *i*. For certain other sound contrasts this is possible, and the teacher must be careful to include such examples. Here are two:

1 *Contrasting /ɔ:/ and /əʊ/.*
   call – coal
   called – cold
   tore – tow
   door – dough
   flaw – flow
   torn – tone
   etc.

2 *Contrasting /eɪ/ and /aɪ/.*
   tail – tile
   day – die
   pay – pie
   tray – try
   fate – fight

rate – write
gay – guy
freight – fright
paint – pint
etc.

Stage 3
Production of the sounds in context, but initially separated.

Exercise 4
(Procedure as for previous exercises.)
    A green bean.
    Pete needs a key.
    A cheese sandwich, please, Peter.
    etc.

Exercise 5
(Same procedure.)
    Its a big ship.
    Is it a little bin?
    He'll miss the ship.
    etc.

Stage 4
Production of the sounds in context, but containing both sounds.

Exercise 6
    Eat it quickly.
    It isn't easy to speak English.
    Isn't this cheese bitter.
    etc.

B 'Sin' and 'Thin'

'Some of your students have difficulty in discriminating between the
consonant sounds in SIN and THIN. Plan a 10-minute practice
which would help them both to discriminate and to produce.'
(*RSA Certificates in Teaching of English as a Second or Foreign
Language* 1979 Booklet of Regulations)

1 Analysis of error

For consonants the same procedure is followed as for vowels, but
with one main difference, which is discussed first here.

Whereas a vowel occurs in medial position in a syllable (b*ea*t), or
in final position in a word, or occasionally as an entire syllable on its
own (*a*sleep), a consonant can occur in initial, medial or final
position in a word or as part of a cluster. Therefore the teacher needs
to note very carefully where the error occurs. If it occurs in a cluster
then the 'offending' cluster is best dealt with as an entity and not as a

combination of individual consonants. Some errors typically occur in one position only, since the actual sound may vary slightly from one position to another. For example, the learner may pronounce the unaspirated /p/ in medial position (*upper, capable*) or final position (*lip, keep*) quite correctly but may not produce the aspiration in initial position in words such as *pin, peach* etc., thus inviting confusion with *bin, beach* etc. Therefore in this case it would be the sound in initial position only that would need to be practised. With other consonants, however, the error may occur in all three positions. Looking at this question in particular, we would probably find that the error is the production of /θ/ as /s/ in initial, medial and final positions. Therefore the teacher needs to include exercises that practise the contrast in *all positions*.

2   Stage 1 Discrimination drills

Exercise 1
Indicate whether the following words are the same or different.
(a) sing – thing
     sick – sick
Now you continue this exercise.
(b) mouse – mouth
Now you continue.

Exercise 2
You devise a same or different exercise using groups of three words as on page 232.

Exercise 3
Can you devise (or find in published materials) pairs of sentences?

Exercise 4
Devise a word-picture matching exercise like the one on page 234.

3   Stage 2. Production

Exercise 1
A. Write out a list of words with /θ/ in (a) initial (b) medial and (c) final positions.
B. Write out a list of words with /s/ in (a) initial (b) medial and (c) final positions.

Exercise 2
Write out pairs of words for reading by the teacher and repetition by the students to practise the contrast between /θ/ and /s/ in all three positions. (*Note*: with the exception of possibly only *ethics – Essex* you will not find *exact pairs* for medial position – produce a few *approximate pairs* such as *lethal – losses*.)

Exercise 3
Try to find short phrases or sentences that practise the two sounds in context. (Remember to keep them separate at this stage.)

Exercise 4
As for exercise 3 but this time containing a mixture of the two sounds. (Avoid clusters.)

4   Supplementary questions.

1 Some of your students have difficulty in discriminating between the pairs of sounds listed below. Plan a 10-minute practice that would help them both to discriminate and produce.

(a) the vowel sounds in WET and WAIT
(b) the vowel sounds in CAP and CUP
(c) the consonant sounds in WINE and VINE
(d) the consonant sounds in COLD and GOLD

2 Identify two common pronunciation errors amongst your own learners (other than examples already dealt with) and devise similar discrimination and production sessions.

Bibliography

A   Published pronunciation practice materials

From the many books of pronunciation practice material that exist on the market, we have selected a few. It is very much a personal choice.

1 *Tree or Three?* Ann Baker, C.U.P.
This is subtitled *An elementary pronunciation course,* and is just that for two reasons:
(a) The structures and vocabulary used in the exercises are those that are typically found in elementary level textbooks.
(b) The pronunciation points themselves are elementary. It concentrates on sounds and basic stress and intonation patterns.
The exercises are varied and interesting. One unit generally contains a visual explanation of how the sound is formed, minimal pairs (which are made meaningful by the accompanying visuals), pairs of sentences, and a variety of free practice exercises such as dialogue production from visual stimuli, game-like activities, etc. Basic stress and intonation patterns are integrated into the exercises on the sounds, but at a later stage after the sounds have been intensively practised.

2 *Ship or Sheep?* Ann Baker, C.U.P.

This is subtitled *An intermediate pronunciation course* and is similar in form and content to its elementary companion – *Tree or Three?*, the difference being that this time the sounds are explained in English but in a way that the student can understand; specialist phonological terminology is avoided; the structures and vocabulary used are intermediate level; and many exercises are integrated in the sense that they practise specific sounds, stress and intonation patterns together.

The above two books could be used as a complete course in pronunciation, the student working through them in a linear sequence, or the teacher can select material from them for specific areas of difficulty.

3 *Pronunciation practice*, Donn Byrne and Gordon Walsh, Longman.

This consists of a teacher's book and a student's workbook. The material consists of diagnostic and perception tests and a variety of sound discrimination and production exercises. There are also units with stress, rhythm and intonation exercises plus a very useful appendix which gives a theoretical outline for the teacher.

4 On specific areas of pronunciation there is a very useful series of small books by Colin Mortimer, published by C.U.P.

(a) *Clusters* (b) *Contractions* (c) *Weak forms* (d) *Link-up*.

5 On sentence stress there is *Living English speech*, W. Stannard Allen, Longman. This also contains exercises on basic intonation,

6 *Speaking English*, John Wright, Books 1 and 2, O.U.P.

Book 1 consists of *Speech practice materials for intermediate and advanced learners* and contains material on sounds, syllable stress, weak forms (a really excellent section) and intonation, as well as various miscellaneous drills on clusters and other specific problems. Book 2 is sub-titled *drills and dialogues* and consists of material that integrates the material dealt with in Book 1.

7 On intonation there are the following:

(a) *Active intonation*, V.J. Cook, Longman. This consists of drills and dialogues that practise specific intonation patterns.

(b) *Intonation of colloquial English*, J.D. O'Connor and G.F. Arnold, published by Longman. This is a book of drills for the advanced student and 'for first-year university students of phonetics.' The theoretical introduction is highly recommended to teachers who wish to learn more of the theory of intonation.

B   Other books mentioned in this chapter

A basic teaching strategy

An introduction to the pronunciation of English, A.C. Gimson (Edward Arnold)

The pronunciation of English, Daniel Jones (C.U.P.)

Better English pronunciation, J.D. O'Connor (C.U.P.)
The teaching of pronunciation, Brita Haycraft (Longman)
An introduction to English language teaching, John Haycraft (Longman)
Pronunciation skills, Paul Tench (Macmillan)

Sounds
Modern English pronunciation practice, M.D. Munro MacKenzie (Longman)

Stress
An introduction to English language teaching, John Haycraft (Longman)

Intonation
The teaching of pronunciation, Brita Haycraft (Longman)

Integrated materials
Intermediate context English, S. Lake (Macmillan)
Feelings, A. Doff and C. Jones (C.U.P.)

Pronunciation games
Sounds right, J. and M. Trim (C.U.P.)
Language teaching games and contests, 2nd Ed, W.R. Lee (O.U.P.)

Devising pronunciation exercises
English pronunciation illustrated, J.L.M. Trim (C.U.P.)

8 Recent approaches

In Chapter 1 (pages 10-12) we introduced the principal of *structural grading*. Many textbooks are structurally graded: that is, the structural, lexical and phonological items are arranged in such a way as to help the students to learn them most effectively. These three types of item are aspects of language *form*. The form of a language is the actual words (written) and sounds (spoken) of which it is composed.

In Chapter 5 (pages 155-165) we demonstrated that a given form or a structural pattern can have a variety of uses and recommended that the teacher introducing a certain pattern should decide which use or uses of that form should be focused on during the presentation and controlled practice stages.

In Chapter 6 (pages 198 – 205) we emphasized the communicative role of language and recommended that practice in the classroom should be brought as close to genuine communication as possible.

Many textbooks nowadays are described by their authors as *functional-notional* or *communicative*; these terms are contrasted with *structural* or *grammatical*, and represent a powerful trend in modern EFL teaching. The former type of textbook is (or should be) organized according to radically different principles from those upon which structural courses are organized.

The practising teacher should be familiar with the underlying principles of functional-notional or communicative courses. Even if his prescribed textbook is clearly structural, he may be called upon one day to teach from a different type of textbook; and in any case he should be aware of recent trends in EFL course design.

This chapter, then, is designed to answer two questions:

1 What is a functional-notional course and how does it differ from a structural course?
2 What is meant by the communicative approach to teaching foreign languages?

Functional-notional courses

The designer of any language course has to begin by doing two things: first he must choose what items or aspects of the language are to be included in the course materials; then he has to arrange these pieces of material into the best possible order to ensure successful learning. The former process is called *selection*; the latter, *grading*. The final arrangement is the language *syllabus*.

As we have seen, structural grading consists mainly of arranging the structural items or patterns into a suitable order. The resulting syllabus is known as a *structural* or *grammatical* syllabus and can be represented by a *list* of language forms in a certain order.

A *functional-notional* syllabus is also an arrangement of 'pieces' of language, but these pieces are not language forms: they are *functions* and *notions*.

In any language there are many different ways of expressing the same thought. This may seem rather obvious, but the implications of this fact about language are important. We have already discussed in Chapter 5 the relation between language *form* and language *use*. It is clear that these two aspects of language are not directly related in every case. The statement, *That's John's car*, could be used in a variety of contexts, each representing a totally different type of interaction. It could be a simple identification of who the car belongs to. On the other hand, it could be a warning equivalent to: *That's not your car: it's John's*. Again, it could be a request for the hearer to open the front door because the expected guest, John, had arrived. Obviously, stress and intonation are of crucial importance here, also.

It is clear that a given language form cannot immediately be identified as having a particular use, without reference to the circumstances in which it occurs. At the same time, we cannot avoid the fact that, in a given set of circumstances, some forms of expression are appropriate while others are not. The following exercise is designed to make this point clear.

Exercise

Match the following list of forms *requesting permission* to a particular set of circumstances by writing A, B or C against each as appropriate. You may put more than one letter against each example if you wish.

Circumstances A You are a guest at a cocktail party and have only met your host on one previous occasion. You are speaking to him now.

Circumstances B You are at home with some friends, watching a programme on television.

Circumstances C You are attending a meeting with your colleagues.

Language forms

1 Shall I open the window? It's rather stuffy in here.
2 I wonder if I might open the window a bit.
3 Let's open the window, shall we?
4 If nobody objects, I'll open the window.
5 Do you think it might be a good idea if I opened the window?
6 I'm sorry, but I'm going to open the window.
7 Would you mind awfully if I opened the window?
8 May I? (said while opening the window)
9 I suggest I open the window.
10 I'm opening the window. OK?

The factor relevant here is *appropriacy*. In certain circumstances, some forms are more appropriate than others. In the examples above, the main consideration is the relationship between the speakers: who is speaking to whom. But other considerations may also influence a speaker's choice of words. For example, *where* does the interaction take place? What is the *topic* under discussion? Are there any special *conventions* determined by the circumstances or the medium of communication (e.g. telephone, letter, telegram, radio)?

Clearly, when designing a course, the writer must regard the teaching of appropriacy as as important as the teaching of language forms.

In the preceding exercise, the language forms (1 – 10) are, as we have see, appropriate to different circumstances, but they are all examples of the same category of language *use*, which we might describe as *requesting permission*.

Requesting permission is an example of a language *function* (the full term is *communicative function*). These are quite simply things we *do* with language. Further examples of functions will help to make this idea clear:

Requesting	Enquiring	Suggesting	Warning
Greeting	Describing	Agreeing	Promising
Apologizing	Reporting	Advising	Showing surprise
etc.			

David Wilkins is generally agreed to be the originator of the idea of developing a functional-notional syllabus. In his book, *Notional syllabuses*, he describes the process of designing such a syllabus as follows:

'Instead of asking how speakers of the language express themselves or when and where they use the language, we ask what it is they communicate through language. We are then able to organize language teaching in terms of the content rather than the form of the language.' (page 18)

Exercise

Describe the following utterances in terms of (a) their grammatical form and (b) their communicative function:

1 Can you tell me where the post office is?
2 Of course, he may not pass the exam.
3 Don't do that again.
4 Please don't do that again.
5 If I were you, I'd sell it.
6 If you eat any, I'll smack you.
7 If you eat some, I'll give you sixpence.
8 Why don't we go to the cinema?
9 I won't have that man in my house again.
10 You may not play football again this term.

	Form	Function
1	Indirect question	Requesting
2		Expressing doubt
3	Negative imperative	
4		
5		
6		
7		
8		
9		
10		

Functions are clear examples of pieces of 'language content'. Basically, a function is a label attached to a sentence saying what it *does*. But within any such sentence there may be other units of content, which we might call *concepts*, although they are often, confusingly, referred to as *notions*. Examples of these are the concepts of *time, space, quantity, motion,* etc. In practice, unlike functions, these concepts are closely linked to the structure and lexis of a language. But not entirely. The preposition *in*, for example, is used both to express *time* and *space*: e.g. *in the evening* and *in bed*. We should finally add a very important set of concepts representing the speaker's attitude to what he says. (Wilkins calls this modal meaning.) The sentences:

Our team may win.
Our team will win.
Our team must win.

represent a scale of *uncertainty – certainty*, and there are many other linguistic forms which are used to express the speaker's position on this scale. Apart from *certainty/uncertainty*, we have concepts such as *obligation* and *intention*. In practice, these categories overlap with communicative functions.

Organization

How might the course designer organize these pieces of linguistic content into a syllabus?

First, functions are much easier to arrange than concepts or notions. Most existing courses of this kind place emphasis on the communicative functions of language and they tend to be described as *functional* or *functional-notional* courses.

Secondly, all functional-notional courses have a strong *situational* element. Obviously functions have to be presented in the language materials contextualized in situations. But some situations, such as using the telephone, have strict conventions which govern the language forms used. Consequently, functional-notional courses often contain units which are, strictly speaking, situational, entitled 'Using the telephone', 'Asking the way', 'Making transport enquiries', etc.

A general scheme for combining the necessary elements of a notional course might be as follows:

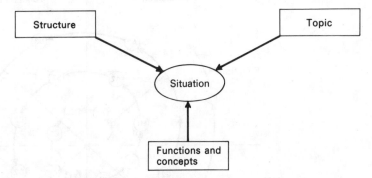

The *topic* element will include provision for a suitable range of lexical items. The situation chosen for presentation purposes will make clear the special reference or appropriacy of the forms chosen to express the functions in question.

Activity

Examine several different functional-notional course books and try to see how the writer(s) have arranged the material so as to incorporate the features referred to above.

Here is a list of some of the functional-notional course books available at the date of writing:

The *Strategies* series, Abbs *et al.* (Longman)
Over to you, Roy Boardman (C.U.P.)
Vital English, Morgan and Percil (Macmillan)
Functional English, Ronald White (Nelson)

Impact, Watcyn-Jones (Penguin)
Functions of English and
Notions in English, Leo Jones (C.U.P.)
Approaches and
Communicate, Johnson and Morrow (C.U.P.)

For children and juniors:
Crescent English Course, T. O'Neill and P. Snow (ELTA/OUP)
Kaleidoscope (University of York and Macmillan Education)

Plan lessons based on this material and, if possible, try them out on a suitable class of students.

Finally, instead of a linear arrangement of items, a *spiral* arrangement is envisaged. Obviously, in a particular unit on (e.g.) *requesting* not *all* the available forms of expression will be introduced. Instead, these should be built up gradually over the course.

The following pattern represents the spiral arrangement:

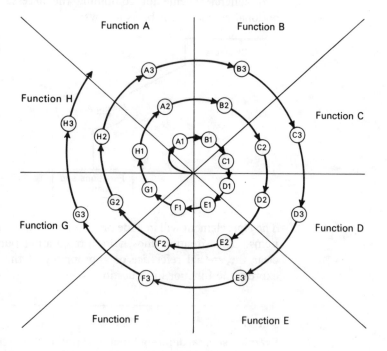

This model is a simplification: there are only eight functions included. But it gives us the general principle. The number of forms of expression for a given function (or notion) should be gradually increased and built up as the course proceeds.

Advantages and disadvantages of notional syllabus design

The main advantages of a notional syllabus usually cited are these:

Clearly, knowledge of structure and lexis (grammatical competence) is not enough to ensure that the student will be able to communicate effectively when required to do so in any given set of circumstances. A functional-notional syllabus, if well designed, can overcome this problem. In particular, it can make the student sensitive to the need for appropriate language in a given situation. Generally, such a syllabus will focus on the more important goal of *using the language for a purpose*.

Because of its obvious value in providing language which is relevant to the learner's needs, the functional-notional syllabus should enormously enhance motivation. Instead of learning to manipulate language items in a vacuum, the student will be able to recognize the value of the language he learns.

Finally, functional-notional syllabuses are especially suitable for *specialist* courses: E.g. *English for scientists*, *English for doctors*, *English for airline pilots*, etc. We will be examining specialist courses later.

We must also mention certain possible disadvantages of the functional-notional approach to course design.

Students must inevitably learn the grammar of the language at some stage. We cannot, therefore, totally abandon the principles and procedures of grammatical methods of teaching: we will still have to *drill* structures and organize the linguistic items into a suitable form of grading.

By aiming at communicational effectiveness, we have made our aims much more ambitious. We are now aiming at subtler uses of language. This makes the task of both student and teacher much harder. It could be argued that it might be simpler to aim at more accessible objectives and simply provide our students with the minimum equipment (i.e. basic grammar and lexis) to enable them to cope with most communication tasks, however inappropriate their language might be. (Here, the amount of teaching time available becomes of crucial importance.)

In some ways, the functional-notional syllabus might be very confusing for our students. Whereas before they could concentrate on the forms of the language, now they may encounter many different forms under the same heading.

All the above points have led many teachers and course writers to consider the functional-notional syllabus more suitable for the intermediate student, who has already covered the basic grammatical syllabus.

It might be worth pointing out at this stage that the argument that a functional-notional syllabus could be confusing for the student because of the variety of language forms introduced under one heading has another side to it: that *similarities* of language form can also be very misleading and confusing. Confusion can result both from the structural and the notional arrangement of language items; it is difficult to say which is most harmful. For example, it is possible to imagine a student taught by structural-situational methods encountering in the target country the question: 'Have you got a cigarette?', not recognizing it as a request and replying, 'Yes, I have. Haven't you?'

Exercises

1 Summarize, in note form, the advantages and disadvantages of using a notional syllabus.

2 Make a list of the teaching situations where (a) the grammatical syllabus and (b) the notional syllabus would be preferable.

3 Answer the following question in about 300 words:
   Nowadays both functional-notional and structural course books are available to teachers of EFL. Bearing in mind practical and other considerations, what are the advantages of using each type of course book? Describe circumstances which favour one type of course book over the other.

Specialist courses

When organizing a specialist course such as one for scientists, doctors, engineers etc., the *topic* aspect becomes very important. This will produce a special range of lexis relating to the specialization in question and also a special emphasis on certain particularly useful structural items. For example in scientific writing, the passive verb forms are particularly suitable. E.g. 'The test-tube was shaken for five minutes.' 'Molten metal is poured into the mould.' And so on.

Point for discussion

Which types of language apart from scientific writing have a strong preference or need for passive verb forms?

However, there is a particular advantage in organizing specialist courses according to a functional-notional framework. Any given specialist will inevitably have to perform certain specific functions with the language. If these can be isolated, the course writer can economize enormously by concentrating on those functions of the language. This makes the course easier for both the teacher and the student.

Reading assignment

Now read *Notional syllabuses* by D.A. Wilkins, pages 1 – 20 and 55 – 57, which provides a detailed discussion of the issues raised in this chapter.

The communicative approach to language teaching

Until recently the well established procedure for teaching a new pattern has been as detailed in Chapter 6:

1 Presentation
2 Controlled practice
3 Free practice (or production)

As explained in Chapter 6, the teaching policy changes at each of these stages.

At the *presentation stage*, the teacher is firmly in control and doing most (if not all) the talking. There is no possibility of error, because the student is not invited to speak.

At the *controlled practice* stage, the teacher remains in control. The possibility of errors has been reduced to a minimum, but, when they occur, the teacher corrects them until the class produces the forms correctly, meaningfully and consistently. At this stage, STT is equal to or greater than TTT.

At the *free practice* stage, the teacher relaxes control. Mistakes will occur, but students will correct each other or themselves when challenged. STT will be much greater than TTT and the teacher will only intervene if serious problems arise.

In reality there is no abrupt shift from one stage to another. There may be a change of the context for practice when shifting from the controlled to the free practice stage, although a good teacher may smooth this transition by providing some thematic coherence in the form of a link in subject matter between the two stages. Alternatively, the free practice stage may occur in a later lesson altogether: there is no law which dictates that all three stages should occur in the same lesson. As to the shift from presentation to controlled practice, any experienced teacher will agree that it is practically impossible to separate these stages: one will flow inevitably into the other.

The analysis of the teaching process as separated into three distinct stages is therefore more of a theoretical analysis than an exact description of what happens in the classroom. It is something for the teacher to think about when planning a lesson, rather than a procedure to follow. In practice, the three stages are moulded together into a pattern which represents a smooth transition from total teacher control to nil teacher control; the process is a *continuum* rather than three stages linked together.

At what stage, then, should *communicative* language practice be fitted into the teaching process described above? The most obvious suggestion would be to add it after the free practice stage. Once students have been encouraged to produce the new pattern freely and meaningfully, it would be reasonable to introduce a practice activity which gives students a motive and provides them with an opportunity to *use their newly acquired language for a purpose*.

The whole teaching process described so far can be summarized by means of the following diagram:

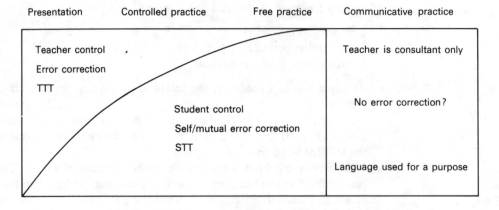

Presentation	Controlled practice	Free practice	Communicative practice
Teacher control Error correction TTT	Student control Self/mutual error correction STT		Teacher is consultant only No error correction? Language used for a purpose

Exercise

Choose one of the following patterns and plan an activity suitable for each of the four stages described above – presentation, controlled practice, free practice, communicative practice:

1 We're having a party on Saturday.
2 Can you tell me where the bus station is?
3 These shoes are too small.

Try your planned activities out on a suitable class.

We have seen that there has been a shift in emphasis in recent years from teaching language forms to teaching language functions. Many teachers and writers nowadays feel that this is not enough, but that the whole methodology should be made communicative, which will, in turn, change the shape of the classroom lesson.

Christopher Brumfit, one of the first to propose a change towards a communicative approach to ELT *methodology*, says this:

'The question for the teacher is: How close can my teaching take pupils to their anticipated language needs in the outside world? ... How much opportunity am I giving members of my class to talk as individuals to each other, using as much English as they can, to say things which they have decided to say and which are as far as possible in response to what has been said before – practice for fluency rather than accuracy?' (From *Teaching pupils how to acquire language*, article in *Problems and principles in English teaching*, page 125.)

If communicative teaching is teaching language for a purpose, then the sense of purpose needs to play a prominent part in the process of presentation and practice. Instead of teaching forms with their meanings and then going on to practise their uses, we might begin with the *use* and proceed to teach examples of the forms our students require. This type of procedure might be termed *communicative presentation and practice*.

To take a simple example, let us consider a concept rather than a function. Suppose the teacher is required to teach patterns like:

It is made of wood.
They are made of plastic, etc.

Of course, he could easily do this by following the conventional sequence of presentation, controlled and free practice. But just suppose he did it like this:

First, the teacher points at every wooden object in the classroom: the blackboard, desk, chairs, pencils, etc. He invites students to say something about these objects. They volunteer statements such as:

It's a blackboard.   They're chairs.   That's a pencil.

Then the teacher points out to the class that all these objects are the same in some way and asks what this is. Soon they will hit on the fact that they are all wooden and demand the lexical item *wood*. The teacher produces a piece of wood and teaches them this word. He then invites them again to describe the feature the various objects share in common. He may get a number of erroneous statements like:

They are wood.
They are from wood, etc.

He allows students to continue their unsuccessful attempts until a slight sense of tension or frustration is built up. He then *gives* the students the pattern:

> *They are made of wood.*
> *It is made of wood*, etc.

What is the advantage of this technique over the conventional one where the teacher *begins* by supplying the new language?

The main advantage is that, by employing these strategies, the teacher has built up a sense of *need* in the student for the new language item. When the item is supplied, the student feels a sense of relief; the meaning and use of the item is firmly conveyed and the form is strongly imprinted. The teacher can then go on to practise the pattern in the normal way.

Exercise

Think up similar techniques for presenting the following forms/concepts:

1 *bigger, hotter, thinner* (comparatives)
2 *too difficult, too hot*

The same type of procedure can be applied most effectively to the teaching of language functions. The procedure to be followed here would be like this:

1 The teacher sets up a communicative activity which demands ability to express the function(s) to be taught. At this stage, the teacher does not supply the language forms which the students require for expression of this function. Instead, the students have to cope with whatever language resources they have available. In performing this task they will inevitably produce errors, mistakes and much inappropriate language.
2 The teacher introduces the required language form(s) and does sufficient drilling to achieve a reasonable degree of fluency. Since a model interaction might be the best way to introduce these forms, a suitable way to do this would be to play a taped dialogue illustrating use of the forms and functions to be presented.
3 The teacher gives students a fresh communication task so as to provide them with an opportunity and motive to use the language forms they have learnt. If serious errors occur, the teacher goes back to the drilling stage again.

Activity

Look back again at fragment D in Chapter 1 (pages 8-9) and discuss to what extent the teacher has employed this communicative presentation strategy.

This procedure can be summarized as follows:

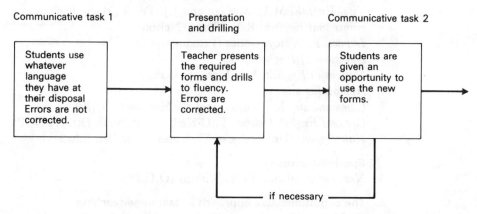

Communicative task 1

Students use whatever language they have at their disposal Errors are not corrected.

Presentation and drilling

Teacher presents the required forms and drills to fluency. Errors are corrected.

Communicative task 2

Students are given an opportunity to use the new forms.

if necessary

Exercise

Plan a communicative presentation and practice of the following interaction pattern:

    A invites B to (go to the cinema, watch a football match, etc.)
    B accepts or declines
    They make arrangements to meet or postpone the engagement to
    a later occasion, as appropriate.

In planning this lesson, first decide what the relationship between the speakers is. How well do they know one another? Second, make a short list of language forms which are suitable to use in the circumstances. Finally, prepare the aids you will need for the first communication task, the drill stage and the second communication task.

Try the lesson out on a suitable group of students.

Reading assignment

'Teaching pupils how to acquire language', article by Christopher Brumfit in *Problems and principles in English teaching*, pages 122 – 129, Pergamon Press.

Bibliography

Functional-notional courses
Notional syllabuses, D.A. Wilkins (O.U.P.)

Organization
The *Strategies* series, B. Abbs *et al.* (Longman)
Over to you, Roy Boardman (C.U.P.)
Vital English, M.L. Morgan and J.J. Percil (Macmillan)
Functional English, R.V. White (Nelson)
Impact, P. Watcyn-Jones (Penguin)
Functions of English and
Notions in English, Leo Jones (C.U.P.)
Approaches and
Communicate, K. Johnson and K. Morrow (C.U.P.)
Crescent English Course, T. O'Neill and P. Snow (ELTA/OUP)
Kaleidoscope (University of York and Macmillan Education)

Specialist courses
Notional syllabuses, D.A. Wilkins (O.U.P.)

The communicative approach to language teaching
Problems and principles in English teaching, C.J. Brumfit (Pergamon)

9 Testing

In one sense, the EFL learner faces some kind of test each time he uses the language; it is equally true that he faces some degree of subsequent assessment. Because of this constant test presence, there is not always an obvious difference between test and practice material. Looking back over sections of this book, you will notice that many of the suggested activities appear to be set out as tests. For instance, what do you think is the purpose of our questions on pages 4–5? The word *purpose* gives us our clue in attempting to distinguish between exercises and tests, and prompts us to ask ourselves why we test our students' language anyway.

Well, why do we? Fill in this questionnaire by putting a tick against any of the test purposes which apply to any of your courses.

Identification of problem areas for remedial attention. ☐
Giving each student a course grade. ☐
Assessment of your own effectiveness as a teacher. ☐
Checking on general progress and obtaining feedback. ☐
Course or syllabus evaluation. ☐
Preparation for public examinations. ☐
Institutional requirement for student promotion. ☐
Measuring what a student knows. ☐
Identification of levels for later group-work. ☐
Reinforcement of learning and student motivation. ☐
Any other purposes. *List them below.* ☐

Points for discussion

Which purpose do you consider the most useful and which the least useful? Give reasons.

In this manual we are not concerned with the theory of language testing, nor are we concerned with tests as commercially-produced measuring instruments. Reference to complex statistical techniques would be inappropriate here since we are concerned with a different kind of test – a test which is devised by the teacher himself for a very specific purpose. Returning, then, to the questionnaire and its discussion question, we would choose the checking of progress and the reinforcement of learning as the most useful test purposes, but concede that teachers very often have to make use of test material in order to give their students a course grade. We view testing as essentially a constructive and practical teaching strategy giving learners useful opportunities for the discussion of language choices. This view does not, however, disregard the use of tests in a formal situation for the purposes of assessment. In other words, the same test can be used formally for assessment and then exploited fully for language development purposes.

Point for discussion

'Both testing and teaching are so clearly interrelated that it is virtually impossible to work in either field without being constantly concerned with the other.' (J.B. Heaton, *Writing English tests*, Longman.)

If we concentrate now on teacher-produced tests, we still have a very wide range of possibilities. We shall examine a cross-section of them, discuss their aims, question their usefulness and construct a few samples of our own.

Traditional tests

These are closely related to the grammar-translation method in language teaching, at least in the early stages. (It might be useful for you to read again the brief section on this teaching method on pages 32–33.)

Example 1   Convert the following statement into a past tense question:
'She speaks English very well.'

Example 2   List the principal parts of the following verbs:
go, awake, buy, lay, etc.

Example 3   Write sentences containing the following words:
shrewd, diligent, antique, etc.

Example 4   Translate the following passage into English:
(*A short passage in the students' first language.*)

These tests also include a great deal of free composition and reading comprehension, very similar to what is used in first-language testing.

Example 5   Write a composition of about 150-200 words on 'The advantages and disadvantages of air-travel'.

Example 6   A passage for dictation.

Example 7   A passage to test reading comprehension.
Questions based on it might well include asking for definitions:
What is the meaning of the following words:
monitor, concede, strategy, etc.

Activities

Discuss the following questions with reference to the same examples.

Example 1   What value, if any, does this kind of grammatical conversion test have? Would it have any value as an oral exercise? If you were to use this kind of test involving two conversion steps, which step (or transformation) would you encourage your students to attempt first? Does it matter?

Example 2   To what extent does the learning of grammatial lists and subsequent testing help to eliminate an error such as – 'She didn't went there.'?

Example 3   Comment on this type of vocabulary testing where the words have no context.

Example 4   Is translation a valid and useful test? If so, how would you qualify your agreement?

Example 5   (a) Allowing for alternative topics in an examination, comment on this one.
(b) If you were to give this composition topic to your students, what stage would they be at?
(c) What assessment problems might you have?

Example 6   (a) Discuss the use of dictation based on an unseen passage.
(b) Read Donn Byrne's book, *Teaching oral English*, Longman 1976, pages 17 to 19, and attempt discussion question 4.

Example 7   What other methods could be used to test comprehension of these words? What are the disadvantages of this traditional test?

Objective tests

When you discussed problems of assessment related to the composition on air travel (Example 5c), you may well have commented on the notorious unreliability of subjective marking. We can accept the value of composition writing as a language exercise – especially if it encourages such things as reports and letters at the expense of traditional essays – and yet have misgivings about it as a formal test. It was largely dissatisfaction with this type of subjective assessment that led to the development of objective tests. It is worth noting, however, that many of the traditional grammar tests were also objective as far as their marking was concerned; whatever views we might have on the desirability of the kind of test illustrated in example 2, we are not likely to disagree on the correct answer.

Activity

Examine the following test examples and then discuss the questions relating to them.

Example 8   Give the following sentence an appropriate ending, using not more than eight words:
She didn't go to the party because ...

Example 9   Change the following statement into a question:
She works in a library.

Example 10   Insert the correct form of the verb in brackets:
If he (go) too, would you go?

Example 11   Tick the correct sentence:
(a) Works she in a library?
(b) Do she work in a library?
(c) Does she work in a library?
(d) Does she works in a library?

Example 12   Tick the correct form of the verb:
If he
will go
went
go
going
too, would you go?

1 Two types of objective test have been illustrated. What is the main difference? Is one type more truly objective than the other?

2 Comment on example 8. What assessment problems might there be?

3 Compare examples 10 and 12. What are their advantages and disadvantages?

4 In example 11 (as in 12) students are presented with three incorrect forms. To what extent can this be justified?

Some objective tests are obviously open-ended then, and others multiple choice. We shall now examine the latter type in more detail.

Multiple choice items

In this type of objective test the student chooses from a range of answers provided. As all the student has to do is indicate what he believes to be the correct answer, the test is simple to complete and easy to mark. If properly designed the test has only one correct answer, and, consequently, the element of subjectivity in marking is eliminated.

Let us examine a typical test item and introduce the basic terms.

Example 13   Jane arrived ... Saturday.
     (a) in   (b) on   (c) at   (d) to

This is the simplest form of grammatical test and is highly specific in that it is concerned only with the use of the correct preposition. It focuses on one single, or *discrete*, feature of the grammar.
The sentence frame, 'Jane arrived ... Saturday' is the *stem*.
The four prepositions are the *options*.
The correct option (b) is the *key* and the incorrect ones are the *distractors*.
Note that in this example each option is frequently found after the verb *arrive*. We could, for instance, just as easily find a context for *arrive to* ... as for *arrive on* ... . Each *verb + preposition* sequence is grammatically acceptable and occurs in its own pattern. Many multiple choice tests, however, make use of distractors that are *ungrammatical in themselves*. Example 11 illustrated this, and so does our next example:

Example 14   The mechanic ...... said it was the clutch.
     (a) whom he went   (b) to that he went
     (c) that he went to   (d) to whom he went to

Activity

Does this further example support your response to question 4 or prompt you to modify it?
Is it expecting too much that each distractor should be itself grammatically acceptable?

Suggest other distractors for example 14.

Most multiple choice tests present the learner with items that have no wider context. He is given no information about the speakers or the situation and, consequently, finds it difficult to decide on what is appropriate. Many of the traditional 'rules' of grammar may be relaxed very considerably in informal situations. We have found evidence to suggest that very able students find multiple choice items difficult because they are familiar enough with the language to find possible contexts for many of the distractors. We shall later in this section be examining tests that have a limited context and attempt to be communicative.

Activities

Look at the following example and attempt the discussion questions:

Example 15   How's John's sister?
(a) This is her.   (b) She's fine.
(c) That's she.   (d) She's good.

The test designer probably has the girl's health in mind, and option (b) as correct. But are there other situations that would allow option (d)? Is (d) a valid distractor?

Example 16   I put the milk ...... back in the fridge.
(a) holder   (b) flask   (c) jug   (d) vase

This is obviously intended as a vocabulary test using options that can all be associated with liquids.
Comment on the distractors.

Example 17   She chose some very pretty ... paper for the present.
(a) packing   (b) wrapping
(c) covering   (d) involving

Again comment on the distractors. Are they equally wrong? In most tests of this kind options are either entirely right or entirely wrong. Discuss a more discriminating marking system.

Example 18   I can always count ... my assistant.
(a) on   (b) by   (c) for   (d) with

The test designer here is concerned with the use of 'count on' as a phrasal verb (meaning something like 'trust' in this context) but is he ignoring the literal use of 'count' followed by various prepositions? Does it matter?

Example 19   My mother had me ... the house.
(a) to clean   (b) clean   (c) cleaning   (d) cleaned

Can you think of a context that might prompt the use of option (a)? What difference in meaning, if any, is there between options (b) and (c)?

We have presented these test examples to illustrate some of the problems and difficulties the test designer has to face. It is not easy to produce good test items with reasonable distractors; it is dangerously easy to produce bad ones. Elisabeth Ingram has some useful advice:

> The standard advice given to budding test constructors is to write a test first with open-ended items, give it to a group of people of the sort he wishes to test ultimately, and then use the wrong answers he gets *which are common and plausible* as distractors for the same items written in a multiple-choice format. (our italics)

Reading assignment

Read the chapter that this advice has been taken from.
Elisabeth Ingram, *Language Testing*, chapter 11 in J.P.B. Allen and
S. Pit Corder (eds) *Techniques in applied linguistics*, vol. 3 of the
Edinburgh course in applied linguistics, O.U.P. 1974.

Follow-up assignment

The obvious follow-up is to attempt to follow her advice. But for the
present let us assume that a number of wrong answers have already
been obtained in response to the open-ended test.
Test stem: The teacher ... me what to do;
Wrong answers: explained; suggested; saw; made; telling to;
wanted to describe; spoke; clears; know; said.
Construct a multiple choice item by introducing a key and choosing
three plausible distractors.
Discuss your choices with other members of the group.

We have already implied that wild and implausible distractors are
dangerous instruments to use in language teaching, whether that
teaching happens to be called testing or not. All too often, traditional
multiple choice tests throw students into a confusing maze of
unlikely error, into a situation where far more language is wrong
than is right. Let us then consider briefly a technique by which we
reverse the traditional approach, by which we encourage the more
natural activity of eliminating error. In other words, the test
becomes a *correction* test containing a single distractor.

Example 20   The teacher ...... me what to do.
  (a) told   (b) explained to
  (c) suggested to (d) said

Example 21   I can always ...... my assistant.
  (a) count on   (b) rely on
  (c) depend on   (d) trust on

Example 22   How's John's sister?
  (a) She's fine.   (b) She's good at English.
  (c) Not bad.   (d) Not so good.

Example 23   I ...... an old friend yesterday.
  (a) ran across   (b) bumped into
  (c) met   (d) came along

Example 24   He's eating a big ...... because he's hungry.
  (a) food   (b) sandwich
  (c) meal   (d) dinner

Example 25   At the frontier I saw many ...... with tanks.
  (a) guards   (b) troops
  (c) soldiers   (d) warriors

Questions for discussion

1 To what extent would you agree that this is a more natural exercise?

2 Is it more difficult to find three plausible keys than distractors?

3 Having eliminated the distractor, how would you use the remaining material?

4 Example 25 anticipates a later section of this chapter. How is it different? Can you put the distractor into a sentence so that the context is appropriate?

So far all the multiple choice tests that we have discussed have relied upon single and unrelated sentences that fail to provide a useful context. It is possible, of course, to have test items embedded in a text so that there is a degree of continuity and progression. The following example is obviously taken from a school situation where the writer is reporting a teacher's reaction to some pupils arriving late.

Example 26

The teacher
pointed out
said
told
stated
that quite a number

of pupils had
arrived
reached
got there
turned up
much too late. He wondered

if they were
anxious
interested
keen
prepared
to take part and asked ...

Often in this kind of test the teacher is left with material which can illustrate differences of formality. The test item is converted into a small but very usable substitution set to allow students to focus on contrasts such as 'encounter/meet/bump into' or 'residence/house/place'.

Discrete item tests

You might find it useful at this stage to skim through once again the section on the behaviourist view of language learning. (See pages 15-19). As we have seen, behaviourists regard the process of learning a language as one of habit formation. They view language as a complex network of habits, which can be built up step by step. Many language tests are intended to examine these steps individually because language is viewed as an aggregate of skills. Thus we can have tests that are linked specifically to the four traditional language skills and to very detailed features within them. We shall now examine a few of these discrete item tests and, again, many of them will be of the multiple choice type.

A Listening tests

We must make an immediate distinction between pure listening tests, or hearing tests, and listening comprehension tests. We shall begin with the former. Many students have difficulty in hearing certain English sounds or in discriminating between them. Sounds in certain weakened syllables can be a serious problem at times. Take, for instance, the weakened (or shortened) auxiliary verbs in these sentences: I'*m* meeting her tomorrow; She'*d* do it; You'*ve* finished. It is not surprising that many learners go through a stage of saying 'I meeting' because this is what they think they hear. Then, depending on the learner's mother tongue, there exist many problems related to hearing differences between certain vowels or consonants. In Chapter 4 we saw quite clearly that different languages have different systems and that this basic difference leads to error. Putting students in a test situation forces them to concentrate on problem areas in the target language and make more deliberate choices within them. Thus, one reason for testing is not so much to discover error as to bring predictable errors to the surface for remedial attention.

Point for discussion

We began the section on discrete item tests by referring to the testing of separate language habits and skills and went on to suggest that students would profit from an examination and discussion of their errors.
To what extent are we using both behaviourist and mentalist approaches?

The simplest type of listening test requires the student to recognize different phonemes. You were introduced to the term *minimal pairs* in Chapter 7 and these can be incorporated into a test item.

Example 27   Students listen to four words and mark the ones that are the same:

(a) cat   (b) cat   (c) cut   (d) cat

Example 28   Students listen to a whole sentence and mark the missing word in their test frame:

They could just see the ......

(a) sheep   (b) ship   (c) shop   (d) shape

Example 29   The test may go beyond minimal pairs:

She went to America when she was ......

(a) four   (b) forced to   (c) forty   (d) fourteen

Other listening tests focus on stress and intonation. We suggest that you skim through the sections on word stress, sentence stress and intonation in Chapter 7 because we shall relate our few examples to that material.

Word stress Students listen to polysyllabic words read by the teacher and mark the main stressed syllable on their test paper. Chapter 7 suggests several ways of marking stress – see page 215.

Example 30   progress   photography   interesting   familiar

Sentence stress Initially, short sentences should be used but later students can mark the stressed syllables in a short passage. This latter technique might be called stress dictation.

Example 31   Well, I must be going, it's getting late.

Having just mentioned dictation, it might be appropriate here to note that it can be used as a discrete item test. It is possible to give students a dictation from which certain weakened syllables have been deleted. Their task is to listen carefully and fill in the blanks:

Example 32   *I'll* be with you in a minute. *I've* finished my work now and *I'm* just clearing up. By the way, John and Kate called and said *they're* going to Spain next week. They said to tell you *they'll* be calling to see if *you're* all right after your accident.

(The italics indicate the blanks on the students' test paper.)

Intonation The simplest intonation test is one that requires students to identify and mark the last stressed syllable in an utterance and indicate whether it is rising or falling.

Example 33   The door needs repairing.

Example 34   Have you finished?

Once we take the test beyond recognizing stress and direction we can begin to look at the speaker's meaning and attitude, and we shall comment on this later.

We now move on to what might more accurately be called listening comprehension. You have already examined a few listening activities and done a certain amount of reading (*Isolating the listening skill*, page 85). Street maps, such as the one on page 87, can provide a great deal of useful listening comprehension. Younger students enjoy an activity ('test' if you prefer) called 'taking a pencil for a walk'. The teacher dictates directions and students mark the route with their pencils. The route can, of course, be circuitous and end up at the start!

Traditional listening comprehension tests have a great deal in common with reading comprehension. Indeed, the reading of a passage is often an initial step before the listening. Students listen to a text, or part of a text if lengthy, and answer questions based on it. Again, many such tests use the multiple choice format.

Example 35   John told Richard to come over and stand behind William,/ while he went and shut the front door./ He did not want either of them to know that Mary was hiding under the table.

Choose either (a), (b), (c) or (d) as the best answer to the following questions:

1 Who was told to come over?
  (a) John   (b) William   (c) Richard   (d) Mary

2 Where did Richard have to stand?
  (a) behind William   (b) in front of the table
  (c) over the door   (d) under the table

3 Who went and shut the door?
  (a) John   (b) Richard   (c) William   (d) Mary

4 Where was Mary hiding?
  (a) under the table   (b) behind John
  (c) in front of William   (d) behind the door

This example of a simple listening comprehension test based on a short text is taken from M. H. Combe Martin, *Listening and comprehending*, Macmillan 1970. The book contains a collection of texts at two levels and very helpful notes for the teacher on reading aloud.

Activities

1 Devise a listening test item, similar to either example 28 or 29, for an area of difficulty experienced by your students.

2 Devise a word stress test for six polysyllabic words that cause problems for your students. Make sure that you give an example followed by clear instructions for marking the stressed syllables.

3 Work out a format for testing your students' ability to recognize different patterns of sentence stress. Use the following model:

Jane's grandmother bought her a new dress for Christmas.

4 The following passage for reading aloud (and marked approp:iately) is again taken from Combe Martin's book. Suggest suitable questions at about the same level as example 35.

There is only one way to make a good cup of tea,/ my old aunt told me./ I was about fourteen years old when she first enlightened me / and I think she must have repeated her instructions a hundred times./ Make sure the kettle is boiling;/ heat the tea pot first / and then put in one teaspoonful of tea per person and one for the pot.

Now compare your four questions with those on page 4 of *Listening and comprehending*.

5 Outline how you would use selected listening tests (not listening comprehension) as material for a language game or competition.

Further reading: J.B. Heaton, *Writing English language tests*, Longman 1975, pages 57-82.

B Reading comprehension tests

You have already considered a variety of comprehension activities linked to the development of students' reading skills. We suggest that you now skim through pages 41-44 again since we shall be using the same text to illustrate different levels of testing.

But before we look at a text and use it as test material, we ought to refer briefly to one classification of reading comprehension skills that has been widely used. The *Barrett Taxonomy* of skills recognizes five levels of comprehension.

1 *Literal*
Literal comprehension focuses on information which is explicitly stated in the text. As has already been shown, there is the danger that this need not involve true understanding at all; it can be no more than a demand for the mechanical repetition of what is plainly in the text.

2 *Reorganization*
At this level, the student has to organize for himself some of the information explicitly expressed. He may have to summarize information or handle it in a different sequence. For instance, if he has been told that B happened *after* A, he may be asked what happened *before* B.

3 *Inferential*

Here the student is required to go beyond the immediate text. He has to make use of his own experience and intuition, and possibly predict outcomes. A question set at this level might begin something like this: 'From what you have read do you think that Mr. Smith really wants to sell the house, or is he possibly being forced into it?'

4 *Evaluative*

This level of response requires the student to make judgements. These may require him to make use of his own knowledge of a particular subject. An appropriate question might begin: 'To what extent do you think the writer has provided adequate support for his conclusion that ...?'

5 *Appreciative*

At this advanced level of response to a text the student has to be emotionally and aesthetically sensitive to what he is reading. It also requires some appreciation of literary techniques.

It will not have escaped you that one category blends into another; they are not intended to be separate and unrelated levels but, rather, convenient stages along a cline from very easy to very difficult. It will also not have escaped you that level 5 is almost certainly beyond what is normally considered to be the scope of TEFL. However, many overseas candidates do sit for English examinations that demand very high standards of reading comprehension.

Barrett's five stages can for practical purposes be reduced to three wider categories – to *literal comprehension*, *inferential* and *evaluative*. We shall make use of this simpler classification and illustrate it with a range of different types of questions based on Text 1 on page 42.

1 *Literal*

Example 36 (a)   Why does everybody know Gregory?

Example 36 (b)   Everybody knows Gregory because
  (1) he is a pop star.
  (2) he is a newsreader.
  (3) he lives in their street.
  (4) he likes everybody.

Example 36 (c)   Does everybody recognize Gregory?

Example 36 (d)   Gregory is known by everybody.
  TRUE ☐   FALSE ☐

2 *Inferential*

Example 37 (a)   Gregory is likely to lose his job because
  (1) he is not as popular as he used to be.

(2) he has become very conceited.

(3) television companies prefer younger people.

(4) he is unmarried.

Example 37 (b)   Gregory will probably have to resign as news-reader because he does not appear to have sufficient strength of character to stand up to his boss.

Agree or disagree with this statement in about thirty words.

3 *Evaluative*

Example 38 (a)   To what extent does the passage lead one to believe that television work is a 'cut-throat' type of profession with little regard for personal feelings or loyalty?

Example 38 (b)   Popular appeal is more important than professional ability in a competitive situation where different televison companies are struggling for supremacy.

TRUE □   FALSE □

Points for discussion

1 To what extent is Example 36 (a) a useful test item?

2 Is Example 36 (b) really any better? Does the small degree of reorganization (use of the new noun 'newsreader') make much difference? Comment on the distractors.

3 There is also reorganization in Example 36 (c). What is it in grammatical terms?
What are the disadvantages of true/false test items?

4 In what way does Example 37 (a) make use of a rather different multiple choice approach?

5 Comment on Example 37 (b) as an open-ended test item. Does this type of test have advantages? Is it still objective?

6 To what extent do Examples 37 satisfy criteria for the inferential category of reading comprehension?

7 Do you agree that there is sufficient information in this short text to justify questions at the evaluative level? If so, can you suggest others?

8 Can you justify using a simple true/false format at this level?

Activities

1 Construct a set of three multiple choice test items at the literal stage based on Text 2 on pages 45-6.

2 'Flight BA121 to London Heathrow is now boarding.'
The use of the verb *board* in this context is a good example of

current idiomatic English. Design a test item to test a learner's understanding of it.

You might like to discuss the grammar of this usage.

One example is 'Houses are building', and another might be 'Tickets are selling'. Is this possibly an area of language change?

3 Suggest a set of three questions to test inferential comprehension.

4 Construct a multiple choice test item for the meaning of *set off*.

There are many other reading tests, and we shall be later looking at tests of a more general or global nature, tests related to the learner's experience of the language as shown by his ability to anticipate and predict.

Reading assignment

J.B. Heaton, *Writing English language tests*, pages 103 – 125.

C Tests of writing skills

The more we examine tests of separate language skills, the more we come to realize that they in fact make considerable demands on other skills. Example 37 (b), although ostensibly testing the learner's understanding of what is inferred in a text, is also a test of his ability to write. In this section we shall look at a limited range of test material which is intended to assess the learner's writing skills at different levels of language development. You will again find it useful to skim through the appropriate section in *Useful classroom techniques* (pages 67 ff). We shall begin at the sentence stage and ignore the earlier writing of letters and words. Sentence construction involves choice of vocabulary and the use of grammatical patterns, or, to put it the other way round, *chain* and *choice*. Thus, an elementary test in sentence writing is the arrangement of grammatical structures into a correct sequence. Coloured cards can be used to represent the four basic structures (see page 148) and can be manipulated to build up sentences. This is the kind of test which inevitably comes out right in the end; errors are made but never recorded. Learners write the constructed sentence in their books only when correctly assembled.

Example 39 (Please refer to the drawings on page 66.) Put the cards into their right order:

is carrying

Mr Smith

in his right hand

a black umbrella

Many teachers may prefer to use single words on cards rather than structures. Mackay, Thompson and Schaub in their book *Breakthrough to literacy* (Teacher's manual) Longman, advocate the use of cards as sentence builders.

At a later stage clauses have to be joined together to form longer sentences and those sentences have to relate to others within the paragraph. Again, cards could be used initially, and there is a great deal to be said for allowing learners to play with language patterns, make mistakes and correct them. In this case, the cards are clauses or sentences but the joining words are separate.

Example 40   because   although   they went for a walk

              it was raining a little

              they were tired of sitting in the house

Note that there is no single correct answer to this test and note also that there is a problem with capitals and punctuation.

You may well think that this is much more a grammar activity than a test of writing. Nevertheless, the appropriate use of *cohesion* is very definitely an important writing skill. Here is another cohesion test, but without the use of cards as an intermediate stage:

Example 41   Put these sentences into their right order:

        Gradually many of these creatures became extinct.
        Millions of years ago huge monsters roamed the earth.
        There it was easier for them to move their huge bodies.
        Some learned, however, to live in the sea.

In this example, cohesion depends on words which refer back to something in the previous sentence. We shall deal with them in an activity at the end of the section.

Completion exercises are also writing tests, especially if they are of the open-ended type. Please refer again to the drawings on page 66 for the following example:

Example 42   Mr Smith is carrying an umbrella because ...

All the different guided composition exercises are also writing tests and provide the teacher with a great deal of information on progress. The *framework essay* is a good example of guided composition. The following example has been taken from *The Edinburgh course in applied linguistics*, volume 4, *Testing and experimental methods*, Eds J.P.B. Allen and Alan Davies, O.U.P. 1977:

Example 43   Here is the outline of a story. Use the outline in order to write the story for yourself. The outline contains about 60 words; your story should contain about 200 words.

Going home from school – friend suggests take an unusual route – see smoke coming from upstairs window of house – hear children scream – run off to phone Fire Brigade – difficult to find house again – no smoke now and Fire Brigade find house empty – mystery of fire and missing children – Fire Brigade chief cross – but dog barking leads to kidnapper and child – mystery solved.

Another very useful test of writing ability is the dialogue, and this too can be attempted at different stages of guided composition. Students usually enjoy dialogue writing because they end up with something that is usable, something that can be appreciated by the whole class. We shall draw attention to just two types of dialogue writing. The first example illustrates the use of cohesive devices and context clues; it is just one half of a telephone conversation.

Example 44   Jane is talking to Peter. Write down what you think he is saying to her.

Peter: ......
Jane: Yes, it's me. Thanks for ringing. How are you?
Peter: ......
Jane: Oh, that's bad luck. How did it happen?
Peter: ......
Jane: Well, I hope you'll be on your feet again soon. Is it still very painful?
Peter: ......
Jane: She's fine. I've got a message for you from her, but of course she didn't know about your accident when she gave it to me. She wants you to meet her at Sally's party on Saturday. Will you be able to?
Peter: ......
Jane: Well, do be careful, and don't move about too much. By the way, what are your holiday plans?
Peter: ......
Jane: How marvellous! I've always wanted to go there. Do you speak the language at all?
Peter: ......
Jane: I don't think it will matter very much because so many people there speak English. I'm sure you'll enjoy yourself.
Peter: ......
Jane: I haven't made any yet, but Helen and I will probably go somewhere together.
Peter: ......
Jane: I'm sure we will. (doorbell rings) That's the door. I must go. Get better soon and don't forget Helen's message.
Peter: ......
Jane: Bye, Peter.

Example 45   Rewrite this passage as a dialogue:

One day I had to see my boss about getting some time off. I walked into the office and asked his secretary if I could have a word with Mr Smith. She invited me to sit down for a moment, telephoned the boss and asked if he could see me. She was told to let me go in right away, so in I went and wished Mr Smith a good morning. He replied politely enough and asked what he could do for me. I told him that ...

This type of writing test is very useful for making explicit some of the language just hinted at in indirect speech. Students have to supply the actual words used by the boss when he replied 'politely enough'.

We shall end this short section on writing skills by mentioning punctuation, and suggesting a modified revival of the traditional test. This, of course, was to give students an unpunctuated passage and require them to put in appropriate marks. What we suggest here is that such a test should be linked to listening. Students listen to an interesting fragment of language, then listen a second time while following it in the transcript provided and putting in suitable punctuation marks in the places indicated. It is difficult to illustrate this type of test because of its dependence on listening skills, but the first part of the students' transcript might be as follows:

Example 46   Listen very carefully and put in suitable punctuation marks whenever you see this sign *. Remember that some capital letters will be needed.

Bill * who had never travelled by air before * was amazed * he had never seen so much activity * have you got your passport ready * asked his daughter * suddenly appearing in front of him * ...

Such a test must obviously be done in small fragments and the teacher may well be tempted to exaggerate intonation patterns just a little.

Points for discussion

1 In this section we have ignored the very basic stage of writing just letters and words. Discuss the value of activities requiring learners to change a phrase written in capital letters into one written in small letters. For example, changing POST OFFICE into *post office*.

2 To what extent does the activity illustrated by Example 39 make use of the mentalist theory of language learning?

3 The *Breakthrough to literacy* project makes use of individual word-cards as sentence builders, although it also has separate cards for grammatical endings. Does a structure-based system have any advantages over it? What are its disadvantages?

4 The framework essay type of test makes use of a kind of 'grammatical shorthand'. The subject is often omitted and verbs are left in their non-finite forms or dispensed with. How would you justify the use of forms such as 'difficult to find house' and 'Fire Brigade chief cross'? Is there an alternative?

5 Comment on the punctuation test. What advantages does it have over the traditional kind of test that ignores phonology?

Activities

1 Refer again to the pictures on page 66. Write a similar paragraph for Mr Thomas indicating the structures you would use and their colour-coding.

2 Prepare a set of jumbled sentences based on Example 41 and underline the cohesive words.

3 Design a framework essay type of writing test. Use about 30 words in your outline but decide whether you are going to use 'grammatical shorthand'.

4 Turn to Example 44 and pencil in what Peter could be saying. Why is it essential to read the whole thing before attempting to pencil in?

5 Prepare a short punctuation test along the lines of Example 46 but make sure you include a clue for an exclamation mark.

Reading assignment

J.B. Heaton, *Writing English language tests,* Longman 1975, pages 127-151.
J. Haycraft, *An introduction to English language teaching,* Longman 1978, pages 118-123.

D Tests of oral skills

Most of us would probably agree that the oral skills are the most important ones, yet they are the most difficult to test. It is easy enough to get an impression, and probably a fairly accurate one, from just listening to our students talk, but it is very hard to make an accurate assessment. As teachers of English we have all come across fluent speakers who communicate effectively without ever shifting tense or worrying about agreement. We have also come across other students who are so intent on accuracy that their speech is full of hesitation, false starts and self-correction. How do we compare them? The problem simply does not arise in their written work as we place their compositions side by side on our desk.

Oral tests are difficult to administer and their scoring is highly subjective. Nevertheless, we shall examine and discuss a range of oral activities having an obvious test element in them. Almost without exception, these tests will involve the teacher in a one-to-one situation with the student taking the test.

Listen and Repeat This is the simplest type of oral test but it relies quite heavily on listening skills. After all, a student can only repeat satisfactorily what he has first heard accurately. The examiner too needs a sharp ear.

Example 47   Now, listen very carefully to the words I'm going to say and then repeat them. If you haven't heard properly, you can ask me to say some of the words again. Are you ready?

'interesting'   'sentence'   'photography'

Example 48   The examiner introduces the test in the same way but points out that he is going to say a complete sentence.

'I'd like you to take some of them to the library.'

Stress and Intonation After a little warm-up activity involving some more listening and repeating – but listening to and repeating the same sentence with different stress patterns – the student is asked to stress the word emphasized by the examiner.

Example 49   *Jane's* aunt gave her a new dress for Christmas.

Students can be asked to convert statements into questions, or ordinary statements into expressions of surprise, but without lexical or grammatical changes. Again, a warm-up is necessary.

Example 50   The shop's closed. – The shop's closed?

Example 51   She spent £50 on a new dress. – She spent £50 on a new dress!

Questions

1 What phonological features would interest you in the three words of example 47?

2 Which other words might be used for main stress in example 48?

Reading Aloud Many oral tests contain a reading aloud element. The value of reading aloud as a separate skill is doubtful, but it is useful as a test of pronunciation and general fluency. In the classroom, pupils are frequently called upon to read dialogues and a flat dull reading will make it a much less enjoyable activity. It is surprising how often words in italics are ignored. It is important that the examiner should know exactly what he is listening for; overall impression will still be important, but it is advisable to focus on specific pre-selected features in the text. For a very useful example of the examiner's copy of a reading test complete with features to be assessed, refer to page 85 of *Writing English language tests*.

Using Pictures As we wish to examine a number of communicative tests later, we shall end this section by commenting briefly on the use of pictures in oral testing. There are numerous sets of pictures available, from large wall-charts to small cue cards, and they can all be used by the language teacher as material for testing oral skills. We have found the *Telltales* picture cards very useful because of the very wide range of activities illustrated (D. and J. Gahagan, *Telltales*, Evans 1975. There is a teacher's handbook and four sets of picture cards.) Chapter 3 discusses a number of different visual aids, including magazine pictures. In an informal test situation the teacher will give the student a picture to look at for a few minutes and will then invite him to talk about it. He will thus end up with a general impression of the student's oral ability. In a more formal setting the teacher can proceed in the same way initially, but give the candidate a set time and record what is said. He can then count the total number of words spoken and also the total number of errors. A set of three or four pictures illustrating an action sequence can often be more rewarding than a single picture. In the latter, there is a great temptation for the candidate to embark on a dull labelling activity: 'In the picture I can see three children and two ladies. And I can see some houses, some trees and some...' The type of picture will to a large extent determine the sort of language likely to be used, but we shall postpone any criticisms of picture material until we come to the next set of discussion questions. We shall also postpone commenting on those pictures which require the candidate to enter into a dialogue with the examiner.

We can, however, just draw attention to one other test similar to the picture monologue. Students can be asked to prepare brief talks on topics of interest and then hold forth for about two minutes. If recorded, the talks can be assessed as outlined above, but it should be remembered that this is a most demanding test.

We may, in passing, note the usefulness of recording what a student has to say without interruption for errors, and then dealing with them during play-back. Dealt with in this way, errors can often be corrected by the student himself.

Points for discussion

1 We said at the beginning of this section that oral skills are the most important. Is this necessarily true? Can you think of situations where other skills should take priority?

2 Can you think of oral test situations where the examiner is not dealing with individual students?

3 What would you be specifically testing if you used tests of the type illustrated by examples 47 and 48?

4 How much reading aloud do your students do? Have we been a little hard on this activity? Can you justify a certain amount of reading aloud?

5 How would you deal with the folowing problem: A student in your class successfully repeats the word *sentence* as /ˈsentəns/ in a test illustrated by example 47, but persists in saying /ˈsentens/ in a less controlled situation.

6 What are the disadvantages of the type of test outlined under '*Using Pictures*'?

Activities

1 Design a small pronunciation test based on (a) minimal pairs and (b) sentences containing sounds that your students find difficult.

2 Write down five sentences that your students could convert from neutral statements into expressions of surprise, shock, incredulity, etc.

3 Examine the following dialogue and note some of the features you would wish to give attention to if you were using it as a reading aloud test. Note them under *Examiner's Notes* and underline them in the text. The first sentence has been done for you.

TEXT	EXAMINER'S NOTES
A: John says he wants to go to New York for a holiday this year. Peter was there last year with his brother, who lives in Canada now.	/sez/ /t/ linking 'r'
B: Well, I've been there a few times and I've found it just too hectic. When's he going?	
A: July .... I think.	
B: Oh, not July! It'll be terribly hot and sticky there.	

Comment on the use of dialogue material for this test.

4 An interesting test of intonation is one that attempts to link different patterns to contrasting language functions.

Say 'Open the window' to make it sound like:
(a) a request   (If you wouldn't mind.)
(b) a query   (Are you really sure?)
(c) a command   (Do it!)

5 For this activity, please refer to the picture in example 3 on page 87. A student, in his second year of English, had this to say when invited to talk about the picture.

> I can see in the picture ... one house. A girl is taking some apples from the tree. The car is stopping ... one he man is walking out. He is a thin. I think he is angry man because a girl is taking his four apples. A girl's bicycle is in the picture too ... it is under the sun. There are many smokes coming from the ... chi ... chim... from the one house. I think it is that man's house.

Comment on what was said under the three headings of content, grammar and vocabulary. What evidence is there of developing linguistic maturity?

Global tests

We have spent some time examining a range of discrete item tests and other more general tests linked to specific language skills. We found that a number of the latter began to move towards global testing in that they made more comprehensive demands on the learner. A completely global test might be one which required the student to write a report on something rather controversial, such as the need for a new airport. But the report would be based on listening to a brief talk, subsequent discussion, on note-taking and on reading. The marking of the final piece of writing would, however, be subjective. We shall confine our discussion to two global tests that can be marked objectively, namely, dictation and cloze.

A Dictation

Dictation has already been mentioned a couple of times. On pages 76 and 79 we suggest a few classroom techniques and earlier in this section we draw attention to what Donn Byrne (*Teaching oral English*, pages 17 – 19) has to say. But the use of dictation has always been controversial, possibly because it is so easy for a teacher to use it badly. The worst kind of dictation test is when students have to try to write down a dull and unfamiliar passage and then be insulted by having one mark deducted for each mistake. If the wretched passage is still more right than wrong, how can anyone end up getting 6 out of 20?

Dictation was widely used in language tests and examinations of a traditional nature; students studied a text in class and then had to 'learn their lesson' at home before being given a dictation test on it.

Lado (R. Lado *Language testing*, Longman 1961) was very critical of this kind of testing for the following reasons:

1 It does not test word order since this is given.
2 It does not test vocabulary since all the words are given.
3 It does not test real listening comprehension since so many of the words can be identified by context.

However, there has been a reassessment of the value of dictation. Oller (J. Oller *Dictation as a device for testing foreign language proficiency*, in ELTJ, 25, 3) claims that dictation involves making lexical sense out of what is in effect just a stream of noise. The learner has to process the sounds and use all his experience of the language to do so; he draws upon a number of different linguistic systems. Viewed in this light, language perception is an active process. John Haycraft (*An introduction to English language teaching*, Longman 1978) agrees with this reassessment of dictation and also feels that it should be brought in out of the cold after its dismissal by Lado and the audio-lingual teachers. He says that 'dictations are valuable, like written substitution tables, as a bridge between spoken and written English, helping students to consolidate written structures, idiom and vocabulary, which can already be pronounced correctly, and are also a useful test of listening comprehension.' Haycraft, however, feels that material for dictation should be that which is useful and *likely* to be dictated – a point that we shall be returning to at the end of this section. A current criticism of the dictation test is that it is essentially a test of language competence rather than performance, of the speaker's knowledge of language rather than of his ability to use it. At this stage you might like to read again what we said about competence and performance on page 133. Keith Morrow (in C.J. Brumfit and K. Johnson (eds) *The communicative approach to language teaching*, O.U.P. 1979) says of dictation that it does not give 'any convincing proof of the candidate's ability to actually use the language, to translate the competence (or lack of it) which he is demonstrating into actual performance in ordinary situations i.e. actually using the language to read, write, speak or listen in ways and contexts which correspond to real life.'

B Cloze tests

A cloze test (a term taken from Gestalt psychology) is based on a passage from which every n^{th} word has been deleted. It is again a global test which requires perceptive and productive skills and an underlying knowledge of lexical and grammatical systems since both content words and structural words have to be provided. The student does not rely just on linguistic clues, of course; he relies also on semantic clues and on what he believes to be appropriate in a particular context. The following fragment illustrates these clues:

Example 52   Jack got on to his pals and ... them all that the cash would be ... hard to find.

Let us examine the clues. The clue to the first deletion must surely be grammatical – the past tense of another verb, a reporting verb. There are a number of lexical choices, such as 'told', 'informed', 'showed', etc. The first verb is an idiomatic and colloquial phrasal verb, and the nouns 'Jack' and 'pals' suggest a fairly informal style. Therefore, 'told' is the most likely choice so far. Can you think of a more informal choice that would also satisfy the sentence pattern? The clue to the second deletion is largely lexical; we need a word that will qualify 'hard', an adverb. Again, the small context that we have suggests an informal word. It rules out such words as 'singularly' or 'remarkably', or it appears to rule them out, without much more evidence of the writer's style or attitude. 'Pretty' as an informal adverb might be a reasonable choice – or an even more colloquially intensive word!

The nth word in the test usually varies from 5th to 10th and it is usually the case that the closer the deletions come in a text, the more difficult the test. However, the nature of the text is very relevant; some texts have a very high degree of *lexical density* or, in other words, have little *redundancy*. They are more concentrated, with more words carrying significant meaning. A text taken from a book on Nuclear Physics is likely to have much less redundancy than one taken from a simple narrative passage.

Although cloze tests were first used to measure reading difficulty in the first language, they are now widely used in TEFL because of their global nature. The average test contains about 40 deletions, and the marking can be purely objective by insisting on the exact word from the text, or it can be subjective by accepting what the examiner believes to be a reasonable alternative.

Discussion points

1 To what extent is it true to say that most teachers use dictation simply as a means of testing spelling?

2 List those language activities which appear to lend themselves to dictation.

3 Why should students be encouraged to read through the whole text quickly before attempting to deal with individual deletions in a cloze test?

4 How would you wish to complete the following sentence:
   'It is always advantageous to provide a "lead-in": thus no deletions should be made in the first few sentences so that the testee has a chance to .... '?
   (J.B.Heaton, *Writing English language tests,* page 123, Longman 1975)

5 Discuss the advantages and disadvantages of the 'exact word' and 'reasonable alternative' approaches to marking.

Activities

1 The following passages are a text for dictation (taken from John Dent, *David and Marianne* (page 10), Longman Structural Readers, Stage 3) and one pupil's response to it. The original passage (on the left) has oblique strokes to indicate the teacher's dictation units.

Mark the passage on the right, give it a score out of ten and comment on the mistakes. The pupil has been learning English for three years.

Marianne went out to the same valley/ every evening that week./ The weather was fine and warm/ and the sea was quiet./ When the sun went down/ the sky was full/ of lovely colours./ David came every evening./ They walked beside the sea hand in hand./ Night fell and the moon came up,/ but it was still warm./ Sometimes they talked/ but often they were quiet./ They looked at the moon and the stars,/ and they listened/ to the quiet sounds of the sea.	Marianne went out to Sun Valley evry evening in the week. The whether was finding warm and the sea was quite. When the sun when down the sky was fall and loved the colours. David came evry evening. They worked by the sealand in hand. Nightfell and the moon came up, but it was still worm. Sometime they talk but often there quite. They luck the moon and the stars, and they listen too the quite songs of the sea.

2 Attempt the following cloze test. (From *David and Marianne,* page 19)

She was wearing trousers ... a man's coat. She ... her bag, with twenty ... her paintings. She also ... her month's money from ... factory. It was not ... much, but that did ... matter. She was going ... Malapa. She was going ... sell her paintings and ... David. She did not ... his address, but she ... the name of the ... company in Malapa. She ... not take a train. ... hadn't enough money. She ... through the town. It ... full of cars, shops ... people. At last she ... to the main road ... Malapa. She stood by ... road and tried to ... a car or a ... . But it was very ... .

Which are the three most difficult words to place and which the three easiest? Why?

Compare your version with others in the group.

List the reasonable alternatives that you would accept for the first deletion.

3 Compare the following passages in relation to lexical density or redundancy:

(a) The first task for the writer of the vocabulary test is to determine the degree to which he wishes to concentrate on testing the students' active or passive vocabulary.
(J.B.Heaton: *Writing English language tests*)

(b) If it's all the same with you then, we might as well think about going over there as soon as we can after about ten o'clock or so.

Before ending this section on global tests, it may be useful to look at two modified versions of cloze and at an intrusion test.

The arbitrary deletion of every 5th or 7th word, whether it be a fairly predictable grammatical word or an unlikely content word, can sometimes be rather unrewarding. In a sentence such as, 'Should he put it on the table, he asked himself', there is not a great deal to be gained from deleting the preposition, but the deletion of the modal raises interesting possibilities. On the other hand, a cloze test containing 40 – 50 deletions is almost certain to cover a useful range of items. It will also retain its objectivity.

Thus, one type of modified cloze test is the deletion of selected words. Another type uses the multiple-choice format; where words have been deleted, the student is required to make a choice from a frame of four items, one of which is the exact word.

Activity

Use this passage for modified cloze tests as indicated:

Every evening, David and Marianne met in the same valley by the sea. David came on his motor-cycle. A road passed near the valley, and a path went down from the road to the beach. Marianne came on foot, along a different path beside the sea. Marianne did not tell her father that she was meeting David. But Paul, the boy next door, was watching her. He was angry with her because she did not want to marry him. He noticed that now she always went the same way. Often she did not take her paints and brushes with her.

1 Choose from five to eight selected deletions. List them and give brief reasons for their selection.

2 Decide on an nth choice and fit each into a multiple-choice frame of four.

3 Is there any justification for having a 'lead-in' of one or two sentences before introducing deletions?

4 To what extent do the modifications to cloze move it away from the concept of a global test?

C Intrusion tests

The intrusion test is certainly related to redundancy but is based on additions rather than deletions. We shall allow it to speak for itself.

In this now test the learner has and to delete those words which sentence do not belong to the text. It same can be used as a test bright of reading speed, a on test of word order and a test table of these the use of articles. Sometimes the although additional words are from another yet language. Do you and get the point?

Testing communication

Let us begin this section by looking at some fragments of dialogue taking place in different situations.

Situation 1
The office of the manager's secretary. She is dealing with a visitor who has an appointment with her boss.

Visitor: I have an appointment with Mr Smith at ten o'clock.
Secretary: (a) All visitors are required to remain in this office initially. You are allowed to sit down because Mr Smith may keep you waiting a while.
(b) Please do be sitting here. I'm not thinking that you'll have to be waiting too long. All right?
(c) Oh, please sit down. I'm sure Mr Smith won't keep you waiting long.

Situation 2
A village shop
Customer: Have you got a tube of toothpaste?
Shopkeeper: (a) Yes.
(b) What kind would you like? They're on the shelf there.

Situation 3
A living room. An elderly aunt, no longer in very good health, is visiting her niece.
Aunt: Is it just a little colder today?
Niece: (a) It's exactly two degrees lower.
(b) I'll put the fire on. I should have done so earlier but I'm afraid I forgot. I am sorry.

Points for discussion and Activities

Situation 1 1 How do the three responses compare with regard to (a) grammar, (b) vocabulary, (c) friendliness and (d) appropriateness?

2 Taking all the above factors into consideration, give each response a score out of 5. What additional information would you ideally like to have?

Situation 2 3 What is the function of the question? Is the customer requesting information about stock or is he making it clear that he wants to buy something?

4 We would classify the question grammatically as being of the *yes/no* type. Such questions have been severely criticized in traditional teacher-training programmes. Why?
Does the criticism often reveal a preoccupation with form rather than meaning?

Situation 3 5 What do you think the aunt actually meant by her question? Rephrase it so that it is direct and explicit.

6 Rewrite the situation and change the speakers so that response (a) is appropriate.

With the exception of response 1(b), all the responses are grammatically acceptable. That is, they all show evidence of linguistic competence. But 1(b) shows evidence of another kind of competence; the secretary has been a little carried away by the *progressive aspect* of her verbs and has made obvious errors, but what she says is surely very appropriate and socially acceptable. She displays evidence of some *communicative competence*. This communicative competence does not replace linguistic competence, it rather takes it a stage further so that it also covers the language-user's ability to respond to and use well-formed sentences *appropriately*. This extended competence allows the user to recognize the *value* of an utterance, as exemplified by the niece in response 3(b).

We are indebted to Widdowson (H.G. Widdowson, *Teaching language as communication* O.U.P. 1978) for the 'toothpaste' example and also for our reference to the 'value' of an utterance. It would be helpful at this stage if you were to read again our quotations from the same book in Chapter 5, page 160. You could also refer again to Chapter 6, pages 198-205, and Chapter 8, especially pages 249-253, before returning to communicative testing.

The reading that you have already done, and your own examination and use of course books related to functional English, will have made it abundantly clear that the teaching of English as communication, and often communication for specific purposes, is taking over more and more from more traditional approaches. Is this equally true of testing? Are we now concerned about assessing our students' ability to perform in the language, to handle the notorious unpredictability of real communication, to appreciate the 'value' of utterances and to be sensitive to stylistic differences? Keith Morrow (K. Morrow, *Techniques of evaluation for a notional syllabus*, Royal Society of Arts – mimeo, 1977) feels that testing is lagging behind:

Increasingly language teaching is becoming concerned with *communication* and its objectives are being reassessed in those terms; language testing, however, has still by and large failed to develop techniques for measuring effectively the use which is made of language in a communicative situation, preferring procedures which relate to the candidate's knowledge of and ability to manipulate the grammatical and phonological systems of a language.

Having thus criticized the lack of progress in communicative testing techniques, he goes a considerable way towards remedying the situation. He shows that tests can be devised to enable learners to manipulate language functions, to identify utterances as belonging to a certain function of language on account of their appropriateness.

Morrow recognizes nine elements as belonging to the total communicative situation. We shall look at just four of them – *setting*, *topic*, *function* and *status* – as set out in one of his tests, and make use of the material as an activity.

Activity

Example 53

1 *Setting*

'The manager will see you now, sir.'

Where might you hear this? Put a tick by any of the following expressions you might hear in the same place.

(a) Stop talking.
(b) Would you care to take a seat?
(c) I'm afraid he's not in at the moment.
(d) Look, I've told you before. Don't do that.

2 *Topic*

Look at these comments. In some of them the speaker is talking about a train journey he has just made. Put a tick next to the ones which refer to this.

(a) ... and we took off on time, despite the fog in New York.
(b) So by the time we got there we were running over half an hour late.
(c) The guard was very helpful. He found us a seat in the non-smoker.
(d) The trouble was we got a puncture, so that held us up.

3 *Function*

Look at these two columns. Join appropriate sentences from each together to make one utterance.

I'm sorry but it just isn't good enough.	I can't thank you enough.
I really do appreciate what you've done.	Is this the way to the town centre?
I'm not sure if I like it or not.	It should have been here yesterday.
It really was fantastic.	What do *you* think?
Excuse me, please.	I enjoyed every minute of it.

4 *Status*

Is the speaker in 1 (Setting) treating you:

(a) as a friend?
(b) as somebody very important?
(c) as an equal?
(d) as somebody who is less important than he is?

Morrow goes on to deal with the problem that faces all test designers
when they are unable to be present in person to explain the
instructions. This is the problem of the *metalanguage*, the language
used to explain the language activity. He says:

> It may plausibly be argued that the instructions and distractors to
> a number of the questions in the samples (above) involve language
> much more complex than that which forms the point of the
> questions. The optimum solution would be to use the native
> language of the candidate for instructions, but in the present
> context this is unlikely to be feasible.

We feel that a very important observation is being made here. The
metalanguage of instruction can at times be so complex that there is
the suspicion that the students who are able to comprehend it
adequately do not, in fact, need the activity.

Point for discussion

Discuss the problem within your group and comment on the use of
the learners' first language.

In a number of places so far we have just ventured across the border
from *usage* to *use*. In example 25, for instance, we noted that *warriors*
was perfectly acceptable as a grammatical choice, but inappropriate
in the company of the word *tanks*. It is not normally used with a
word relating to modern warfare; in other words, *warrior* does not
normally *collocate* with *tank*. We have also noted contrasts of
formality within sets of words such as: residence, house, place;
encounter, meet, bump into. The use of a good dictionary is
essential here, and we shall make this one of our later activities. It is
obviously difficult to make choices of appropriateness without
sufficient background information, without some of Morrow's
elements of the communicative situation. Therefore, a communicative
test which makes use of a developing text has advantages over one
which makes do with individual sentences. The following fragment
of a test attempts to give the candidate helpful background
information and a realistic situation:

Example 54   Mrs Cox is a school inspector interviewing Tom
Brown for a more senior school appointment. Her
language is politely formal, but Tom has to make a
series of communicative choices. Taking the situation
into account, and their respective roles within it,
indicate which choices you think our hero should be
making. As all the responses are possible, give them
marks out of 3. Give your first choice 3 marks, and
so on.

Mrs Cox:	Good morning, Mr Brown. Please sit down.
Tom:	Good morning, Mrs Cox. Thank you.
	Good day to you madam. You are most kind.
	'Morning. Thanks a lot.
Mrs Cox:	I have your application form here in front of me, but I'd like to ask you a few questions about your experience.
Tom:	Why not? Just go ahead.
	Please don't hesitate; I shall be most pleased to answer them.
	(No linguistic response – smiles nervously)
Mrs Cox:	I believe you do some EFL teaching in the evening?
Tom:	That's right. I teach two lots, a group of kids and a bunch of older characters.
	Indeed, you are quite correct. I have accepted responsibility for two groups at rather different levels of ability.
	Yes, and I'm finding it very interesting. I teach two evenings a week at the institute, an elementary class on Tuesdays and a fairly advanced class on Thursdays.
Mrs Cox:	Which level do you prefer?
Tom:	Well, it's all the same, isn't it?
	I find the advanced group more challenging, and feel it's more useful experience for me at the moment.
	It is my sincere and true belief that the elementary group is in greater need of my endeavours.

Points for discussion

1 How would you label the three choices? If one is about right or fairly appropriate, what are the others?

2 What impression would you say Tom would be likely to make on the inspector if he consistently used (a) your first choice (b) your second choice and (c) your third choice?

3 What are some of the *formal* characteristics of your third choices?

4 Can you think of communicative situations in which your second and third choices would be appropriate?

5 One of Tom's choices is to say nothing – linguistically a zero response. How can such a response be justified?

Activity

Extend the dialogue test to cover two more exchanges and then a final exchange where Mrs Cox indicates that the interview is over.

Competence and performance

We have already established that communicative competence is linguistic competence plus an understanding of the appropriate use of language in its various contexts. The speaker, or writer, who has adequate communicative competence as an extension of linguistic competence is still liable to make mistakes in performance, but they will be *mistakes, lapses* or *social gaffes* and not *errors*. Do we, then, need to test how our students apply their communicative competence, how they perform in real situations? Should we be testing communicative performance rather than competence? Our examples have concentrated very heavily on the testing of competence, on the understanding of language, and not on performance. However, some of the oral tests were related to performance, but we made the point that they are difficult to administer and assess. In practice, teachers will probably have to rely on a battery of activities, rather than tests, but make a point of building up individual profiles for students based on an informal and subjective type of continuous assessment. Teachers must also reject the traditional belief that answers are either right or wrong. Even in multiple choice tests of grammar, the entirely-right or entirely-wrong dichotomy is often suspect. The consensus of opinion as far as communicative performance is concerned is that some form of qualitative assessment is more practical than a quantitative one. Morrow (K. Morrow, *Communicative language testing: revolution or evolution?* in C. J. Brumfit and K. Johnson, *The communicative approach to language teaching,* O.U.P. 1979) says,

> The concept of pass:fail loses much of its force; every candidate can be assessed in terms of what he can do. Of course some will be able to do more than others, and it may be decided for administrative reasons that a certain level of proficiency is necessary for the awarding of a particular certificate.

A Performance tests

The best type of performance is one that is essentially a communication task. The candidate must listen to instructions (or read them), use his language resources to obtain information and communicate this information accurately in order to achieve a successful outcome to the task.

Example 55   Teacher gives following instructions to student:

'Go to the head teacher and ask him politely if he wants our class to join the others in the hall. If he does, ask him what time we should go there.'

Question

Is this a fair test of communicative ability? What are the main disadvantages?

Activity

Design three similar tests at different levels. How would you attempt to assess the outcome?

Towards the end of the section on *Oral testing* we said that we would postpone any discussion of oral tests that involved a dialogue with the examiner. The reason for this of course was that it would allow us to examine such dialogues as examples of communicative texts. Morrow, in his *Techniques of evaluation for a notional syllabus*, outlines a number of tests that require the candidate to enter into a dialogue with the examiner. We shall summarize some of them below along a cline from structured to free.

B Interaction participation tests

1 *Structured*
   The candidate and examiner read a dialogue together but the former is not given time to prepare his part – he has to respond spontaneously.

2 *Semi-structured*
   The candidate is given a dialogue, or a dialogue format, with his own part missing. He is given a certain amount of time to study the material to enable him to anticipate some of the examiner's responses. An example of this kind of test is our example 44 which is the incomplete telephone conversation. That, however, was a writing test, although it is to be hoped that it would later be used as material for an oral activity. The test outlined here is essentially one of spontaneous oral production.

3 *Semi-free*
   A much freer kind of role-playing is required here. The candidate can be told in advance what the topic is going to be, or he can be told that he will be required to use a specified language function in relation to a topic to be given only at the beginning of the test.

   Example 56 When candidate 1 begins his test, candidate 2 is informed that his language function is that of *inducement*. (This is one of the communicative functions of language classified by Wilkins in *Notional syllabuses*, O.U.P. 1976.)

When it is his turn for the test, the examiner says to candidate 2:

'I'm going to talk to you about the town where you live. I want you to persuade me that it's a good place for a week's holiday. I'll sometimes disagree with what you say and ask you to explain things to me. Although you must be truthful about the place, your main concern is to get me to come as a visitor. Do you understand what you have to do? ... Right, let's start.'

4 *Free*

This involves a completely unprepared and unpredictable exchange between examiner and candidate. Many long-established oral tests of this kind are used in first, second and foreign language situations. It is the easiest oral test to administer badly. The type of question asked is crucially important; although some initial questions may begin 'Tell me something about ... ', other more productive questions are more likely to begin 'Why is it that ... ?' The examiner must either have considerable experience and be able to rely adequately on total impression, or be given some kind of assessment formula.

Points for discussion

1 Is the structured test anything more than a test of reading aloud?

2 Taking Example 44 as the model, is such a semi-structured test of communicative performance a fair one? What other factors may be involved?

3 How would you overcome the metalanguage problem here? Would it mean very much to your students to be told that they had to use language in its function of 'inducement'?

4 All tests and examinations tend to put students into stress situations, but in written tests such stress may be hidden and overcome. What about oral tests? Is the shy, and certainly nervous, candidate at a real disadvantage, or is the ability to respond quickly to the linguistically unpredictable truly part of communicative performance?

5 Some tests allow the candidate to be himself, others require him to enter into some form of role-play with the examiner. Discuss the implications of this.

Activity

Plan a semi-free test by selecting a language function and then indicating quite clearly what you would say to the candidate. Also, write down your first question.

Further reading
J. Revell, *Teaching techniques for communicative English*, Macmillan 1979. (Although this is not specifically on testing, it contains a wealth of good ideas for communicative activities.)

Point for discussion

We have ended this chapter with a section on communicative testing. Does it really merit its own section? Is there truly a difference between this type of test and the more meaningful tests of separate language skills?

Summary

We have examined a fairly wide range of language tests, emphasizing the informal teacher-produced variety. For this reason most of them are also language activities which place students in those situations where deliberate linguistic choices have to be made – lexical, grammatical and communicative. We believe that the provision of meaningful contexts for this choice-making process, and subsequent discussion, is one of the chief justifications for informal tests. Language *is* learnt and developed by thinking, being unsure, making mistakes and discussing the options.

We have taken a practical approach to testing throughout this section and, consequently, rather neglected such issues as classification of tests, criteria for tests and the scoring of tests. Indicated reading from the following books, books that we have already referred to, will cover these areas in some detail.

1 Chapter 10, *Assessment and examinations*, from *Teaching English as a foreign language* by Broughton and others. You will find the whole book very relevant and chapter 10 very readable and informative as a general overview of the topic.
2 Chapters 1, 9 and 10 from Heaton's book. Chapter 10 gives a fairly non-technical outline of the interpretation of test scores. This is a very useful book throughout but rather traditional in its approach concentrating, as it does, on the separate skills.
3 Chapters 2 and 3 by Elisabeth Ingram and Alan Davies from volume 4 of the *Edinburgh course in applied linguistics* make more demanding reading but are well worth wrestling with. Chapter 11 in volume 3 is also very useful.

Bibliography

Writing English language tests, J.B. Heaton (Longman)

Teaching oral English, Donn Byrne (Longman)

Techniques in applied linguistics, vol 3 in the *Edinburgh course in applied linguistics*, J.P.B. Allen & S. Pit Corder (eds) (O.U.P.)

Listening and comprehending, M.H. Combe Martin (Macmillan)

Breakthrough to literacy Teacher's manual, Mackay, Thompson & Schaub (Longman)

Testing and experimental methods, vol 4 in the *Edinburgh course in applied linguistics*, J.P.B. Allen & A. Davies (O.U.P.)

An introduction to English language teaching, J. Haycraft (Longman)

Telltales, D. & J. Gahagan (Evans)

Language testing, R. Lado (Longman)

Dictation as a device for testing foreign language proficiency, J. Oller in ELTJ Vol.25, No3

The communicative approach to language teaching, C.J. Brumfit and K. Johnson (eds) (O.U.P.)

David and Marianne, J. Dent, Longman Structural Readers Stage 3

Teaching language as communication, H.G. Widdowson (O.U.P.)

Techniques of evaluation for a notional syllabus, K. Morrow (R.S.A. mimeo)

Notional syllabuses, D.A. Wilkins (O.U.P.)

Teaching techniques for communicative English, Revell (Macmillan)

Teaching English as a foreign language, G. Broughton *et al.* (Routledge)

10 Special techniques for problem classes

In Chapter 5 we dealt with the preparation and planning of both structural and lexical material for what could loosely be termed an 'average' class, that is to say around 25-30 pupils, at the same level of attainment but with normal differences in intellectual ability or in ability to learn a foreign language. However, we are well aware that many classes around the world do not fall into the category of 'average'. There are classes composed entirely of 'weak' learners, who may be generally low in intellectual ability or in ability to learn a foreign language; there are very large classes of maybe 45-60 pupils; and there are mixed ability, or even multi-level, classes where the differences between the 'top' and the 'bottom' may be very great indeed. The aim of this chapter is to suggest some techniques and activities that may help the teacher cope with any of the above mentioned difficult circumstances.

Dealing with weak classes

Initial discussion

Working in pairs or small groups draw up a list of the weaknesses and difficulties found in weak learners. Compare your list with that of another pair or group.

Now read the following text.

Raphael Gefen in his article *Teaching English to less-able learners* (ELTJ XXXV No.2 Jan. 1981) lists four types of learner – the very able, the able, the less able and the unable. This section has in mind the type of class that is composed entirely of less able learners (for example the bottom stream in a system that maintains streaming).

(The unable, unfortunately, are a lost cause and should ideally have the opportunity of opting out of the foreign language lesson to do extra work in another subject.) Faced with such a class the teacher obviously has problems, and much of what has been written so far in this book may possibly not seem applicable to teaching a class of less able learners, or may not be applicable without a degree of modification of techniques and activities. The aim of this section is to suggest ways of modification rather than abandonment of principles.

If we look at a typical less able learner, we will generally find that his greatest weakness lies in the productive skills of speaking and writing rather than in the mainly receptive skills of listening and reading. When he speaks, he rarely does so of his own free will; he may not willingly join in the choral repetition or the drilling; he will not assimilate the structure being taught and transfer it to his own use; he does not generalize from the rule or pattern that is established in order to be able to use the language creatively; he never experiments with the language, never attempts to produce something that he has not yet been taught (as the able or very able learner will); he always falls back into his mother tongue even when a very simple foreign language utterance could be used. In short, he is afraid of using the foreign language. On the rare occasions that he does, his speech is full of errors. When he writes, he takes advantage of the time available for thought in order to translate mentally and consequently his written production is no more than a string of foreign language items tied together by the grammatical system of his mother tongue. Even when listening or reading he pesters the teacher for translation of new items.

To cope with a class composed entirely of such learners, it is suggested that the following three principles could form the basis of a system of modification of techniques and activities mentioned in previous chapters.

A Limitation of aims and objectives.
B Simplification of material.
C Tighter control over learner production.

A Limitation of aims and objectives

As the less able learner has the greatest difficulty in the productive skills it is suggested that work concentrating on receptive skills may be more desirable. In other words understanding rather than using the language would become an overall course objective. In extreme cases, it may be necessary to confine the learner to a passive understanding only, but, ideally, even in these difficult circumstances, some limited form of production is, of course, desirable. We could be accused of giving up the struggle if we 'leave our learners speechless'. However, this section will concentrate on techniques for exploiting reading and listening material for passive understanding mainly – with some development into very limited guided production. This implies that the teacher has to find ways of checking understanding that do not involve production of the language by the learner, or at the most only some form of very limited production. To do this the teacher has to plan his questions on the material (reading or listening) very carefully, as the normal question and answer exchange procedure (see Donn Byrne *Teaching oral English* pages 45-53) may involve the learner in production that is too 'difficult' for him. There are, of course, certain types of questions that do not require production of the language at all, such as multiple choice questions. However, these seem to belong more to the realm of testing than teaching, and furthermore, the production of good multiple choice questions is a difficult and time-consuming activity for the already overworked teacher, and indeed may be virtually impossible at a very elementary level. This type of question also tends to be more suitable for eliciting gist meaning rather than for detailed work on a text or dialogue. There are alternatives that still do not involve production in the foreign language.

1 Question and answer in the mother tongue.

2 Question in the foreign language answer in the mother tongue.

3 Completion of a table of information from reading or listening.

Example:

Mr and Mrs Brown live at number two Rainbow Street. They have two children. Mr Brown has a car and Mrs Brown has a bicycle. They have a TV set and a fridge, but they do not have a washing-machine.

Mr and Mrs Black live at number four. They do not have any children. Both Mr and Mrs Black have cars so they do not need a bicycle. They have a fridge and a washing-machine, but they do not have a TV set. They do not like television.

Mr and Mrs Green live at number three. They have six children. Neither of them has a car. Mr Green has an old bicycle. They are a poor family. They have a very old TV set, but they have neither a fridge nor a washing-machine.

Name of family	Brown	Black	Green
House no.	2	4	3
Children	2	0	6
Car	yes	yes	no
Bicycle	yes	no	yes
TV set	yes	no	yes
Fridge	yes	yes	no
Washing-machine	no	yes	no

Activities

1 The table has been completed as a pupil should complete it. Write a set of instructions for the exercise, in English.

2 You would probably need to give the instructions in the mother tongue. So now translate your instructions.

3 Select a suitable text from the textbook that you are using and produce a table of information for completion by your pupils. Or alternatively write your own text.

4 How could the above table be used for guided oral or written production, assuming that you do not think it desirable to leave your pupils at the stage of passive understanding only? Write a model sentence and indicate the type of guidance you would give the class. Now do the same for activity 3.

So we have seen that whereas question types 1 and 2 involve production in the mother tongue, question type 3 could be exploited for developing passive understanding only or could be used as the basis for controlled oral or written production. However, we appreciate that the production of such material by the teacher may not always be possible. The time and materials may not be available: the texts in the prescribed textbook may not be suitable for exploitation in this way. So the teacher may feel he has to attempt a more orthodox question and answer exchange. However, as was pointed out earlier, this may involve the less able learner in a task that is too demanding for him. To overcome this the teacher would need to exercise great control and patience and plan and use his questions in a strictly graded order, so that initial production is at a minimum.

Activity

Grade the following types of questions according to 'difficulty', that is to say, start with the question type that involves the learner in the 'easiest' answer and continue up to the question type that requires the most production on the part of the learner.

(a) False statements for correction
(b) What + main verb
(c) Alternative questions
(d) What + DO
(e) Yes/No questions
(f) Other WH questions – Who? When? Where?

Then compare your answer with the example below.

An example question and answer exchange for weak learners.

Sentence from text: Ian is watering the flowers.
T: Is Ian watering the flowers?
S: Yes (he is).
T: Is he watering the trees?
S: No (he isn't).
T: Is he watering the flowers or the trees?
S: The flowers.
T: Who is watering the flowers?
S: Ian (is).
T: What is Ian watering?
S: The flowers.
T: Ian is watering the trees.
S: No – the flowers.

At this stage the learner may be encouraged to attempt to produce the entire sentence either by contradicting the false statement or possibly from the question, 'What is Ian doing?' However, for very weak learners this question may be better avoided as it could prompt a learner to begin 'Ian is doing ....' Even when contradicting the false statement the following may result:

Ian is water the flowers.
or Ian watering the flowers.
or Ian water the flowers.

At this point the teacher could attempt to correct by the backchaining technique:

T: flowers
S: flowers
T: the flowers
S: the flowers
T: watering the flowers
S: watering the flowers
T: is watering the flowers
S: is watering the flowers
T: Ian is watering the flowers.
S: Ian is watering the flowers.

However, with the less able learners it may not be psychologically desirable to indulge in such correction as they need all the encouragement and motivation possible. The teacher should possibly be satisfied with the erroneous production and merely repeat the pupil's words in the correct form. For these learners 'fluency is more important than accuracy' (Raphael Gefen). Thus the limitation of aims (mainly passive understanding, and limited, even inaccurate production) may be one way of achieving at least something with 'weak' classes.

B   Simplification of material for presentation of a new structure

In the previous section we saw that certain techniques and activities
involving question and answer based on a text could be employed to
limit the learners to passive understanding only or at the most to
very limited production of the language. This section attempts to
suggest how a similar aim could be achieved by the simplification of
material for presentation of a new structure. It seems that here there
are two options open to the teacher.

1   An initial presentation lesson for understanding only

For 'weak' learners the understanding of the form and meaning of a
new structure will take more time to achieve than with more able
learners, and the presentation stage, instead of being the initial stage
of a lesson, could well be the entire first lesson on a new structure.
'At this step the children do not speak the present continuous form,
but only hear it and respond to it.' (*Argonauts English Course* Lee &
Koullis First Year Teacher's Book page 81.) This can be achieved by
careful exploitation of the classroom situation, and by very
controlled questioning (similar to the graded questioning on a text
that was outlined in the previous section) that will require short
responses only as opposed to a full sentence containing the structure
being taught.

'Start, perhaps, with drawing. Say, for instance, "Draw a house on the board, Peter." As he does so, ask "What's he drawing?" and give the answer yourself "a house". Get other pupils to draw other things. There could be several children drawing at the same time. Ask e.g. "What's Barbara drawing? What are Philip and Vassos drawing?" Short answers such as "houses" or "a fat man" are appropriate, long answers unnecessary here.' (page 81)

The teacher must now be careful not to undo the work so far done on the structure by transferring too quickly to an elicitation of sentences containing the structure. Gradual building up to this is vital for weak learners. The teacher needs to prepare a series of very carefully graded steps. The next stage would be to replace the main verb in the question by 'doing' and again limit the learner's response to a short answer which this time will be *partial production* of the structure. 'Get a pupil to point to something, perhaps the door. "What's he doing? He's pointing to the door." ' (*ibid.* page 82)

It is suggested the weak learners could be limited to the response 'pointing to the door' at this stage as this does not involve *full production* of the form of the structure, where errors may occur (e.g. He/She confusion) and in this way they are slowly guided towards full production of the structure, and as the structure builds so will confidence in handling it. So with this mode of presentation over a number of lessons the weak learner is carefully led from a common lexical item that he knows – 'a house' to 'drawing a house' to 'He's drawing a house.'

Activities

1 The example used has again been the present continuous tense. This is because it seems to demonstrate clearly the principles involved. Of course other structures, other tenses of the verb, can be presented in the same way. Make a list of structures that you think could be exploited in this way, by classroom demonstration, and write out a plan for one of them. Be careful to grade your questions appropriately!

2 The classroom situation has been the one exploited for this simplified approach to the presentation of a new structure. This is because it is easy for the teacher to introduce the visual element to consolidate the meaning that is so essential for weak learners, and physical activity in the classroom would slow down the speed at which examples are used, thus allowing time for further consolidation in the mind, as weak learners tend to think more slowly than more able learners. The classroom situation also allows the weak learner to work with a familar environment, for which he probably has confident knowledge of the lexical set, as textbooks based on this approach recycle classroom vocabulary regularly. 'This is a *pen*.' 'There's a *pen* on the desk.' 'He's holding a *pen*,' etc. However, it is not the only possibility. Make a list of other situations that could be exploited in the same way. What aids would you need? Write out a plan based on one of these situations.

2   Presenting a new structure with one verb only

Activity

Look at the following extracts from a textbook presentation of the present continuous tense. What do you notice about the material?

1 – Hi, David.
  – Hello, Joe. I'm going to the park.
  – I'm going home. See you later.
  – OK. Bye.

  – I'm going to the station.
  – Where?
  – To the station.

  – I'm going to the park, and then home.
  – Where?
  – To the park, and then home.

  Sue is going to the station.
  James is going to the park.
  Sally is going home, Meg is going to the square.
  Andrew is going to the station.
  Jenny is going to the park.
  (*Signpost* Book 1 Austen, Evans & Peters, Nelson, page 12)

2 (In the dark)
  – Hugh, where's the fuse-box?
  – I don't know. I'm looking for it.
  – Hugh, where's the mains switch?
  – I don't know. Bill's looking for it.
  – Hugh, I'm looking for the front door. Where is it?
  – Near the stairs.
  – Hugh, where are the stairs?
  – I don't know. I'm looking for them.
  – Bill, where's the ladder?
  – I don't know. I'm looking for it.
  – Hugh, where are the fuses?
  – I don't know. Helen's looking for them.
  – Bill, where's Hugh?
  – I don't know. I'm looking for him.
  (*Signpost* Book 1 page 18)

Discuss your conclusions with another teacher and then suggest a possible title for the following part on the simplification of material. In what way was the above material simplified?

Referring to less able pupils Raphael Gefen says 'much of the grammar for these pupils can be taught in the form of lexical items rather than generalizable rules' (*ibid*), and just as we do not overload any learner with too many lexical items in one lesson, so we may not wish to overload the weak learner with too many verbs in our initial presentation lesson on a tense of a verb, otherwise he may feel the structure itself is difficult and so lose any motivation or encouragement to learn it. If we examine carefully the material above we see that the stress does seem to be on lexical items . Extract 1 has a lexical set based on the theme of places – park, home, station, square, and extract 2 has a set of 'things electrical' – fuse-box, mains, switch, fuses. The verbs used, only one in each case, are also semantically linked – 'going' with places, and 'looking for' with the things needed when a fuse has blown and we are in 'in the dark'. 'The stress is on vocabulary rather than grammar ... what little grammar is taught should be inductive in approach, very limited in quantity, and fully integrated with the reading material.' (Raphael Gefen) In the material quoted this would certainly seem to be the case, and in listening to and reading these dialogue exchanges the learner could assimilate the examples of the present continuous tense as lexical items.

However, without such material and and possibly without the ingenuity to create such fictional situations, the teacher may feel that this approach is difficult to set up and handle. Nevertheless, it is possible to find examples within a common everyday situation that limit the material to exploitation of one verb only, so that the structure (in this case the present continuous tense) is presented and practised as a series of lexical items. 'Wear' is one such verb. The teacher may present 'He's/She's wearing' by reference to a series of magazine cut-outs from a fashion magazine, and then set up a controlled practice drill by reference to the pupils in his class. Or the reverse procedure may be applied, especially if the pupils are all wearing the same school uniform, which would not give rise to enough variety for a practice drill! In either case there would be intensive practice of the form and meaning of the structure using one verb only and limited lexical sets of colour adjectives and items of clothing.

But 'in my experience the method must involve a variety of activities in any one lesson, the extensive use of visual aids, and emphasis on audio-lingual activities in general and on mimicry memorization drills in particular (as long as they are meaningful, relevant and not too drawn out).' (Raphael Gefen) This approach to the problem of teaching weak classes would seem to contradict the idea of simplification of material so far proposed. How long could one practise the use of 'wear' without making the drill too drawn out? Certainly we could not limit the content of a whole lesson to this. But we could limit the content to a handful of verbs and present and practise *one at a time*. In this way the normal procedure of presentation, controlled practice, free practice ('production') would be abandoned in favour of *a series of mini-lessons within the overall lesson.* E.g.:

1 Presentation of 'He's/She's wearing' (classroom situation)
2 Practice of 'He's/She's wearing' (magazine cut-outs)
3 Presentation of 'He's/She's holding' (classroom situation)
4 Practice of 'He's/She's holding' (visuals of people holding various things)

Of course this procedure is not the only possibility. The exploitation of the classroom situation and the visuals could be reversed. The lesson could concentrate on the third person singular only or other persons could be brought in. Flexibility is there and only the teacher can judge what is the right content and procedure for his class.

Activities

1 Continue the above simplified lesson plan. Find two other verbs that could be exploited in the same way and write out your presentation material and your practice drills.

2 For some very weak learners a drill that is only oral may prove difficult and they may need some form of written support. This could be in the form of a substitution table on the blackboard to accompany the drill. So now write out your drills from exercise 1 in the form of substitution tables.

C Tighter control over learner production

Finally, as was implied by the previous section, a structure lesson with a class of weak learners would possibly be limited only to presentation and controlled practice. Any free practice or production would possibly come out of the type of activity mentioned in *Section A* based on a reading text. One way of control has already been mentioned – a written substitution table to act as a support for one of the 'easier' types of drill, such as a simple substitution drill or a progressive substitution drill. (Intensive repetition of the model sentences would, of course, have been necessary first, in the form of a listen and repeat drill.)

Another possible technique, based on a short dialogue, is slowly to 'phase out' the dialogue. Stage 1 would consist of repetition leading to virtual memorization, then gradually words would be erased so that learners reproduce lines from the dialogue based on the skeleton that remains, until maybe only one-word cues remain.

Activities

1 Look at the following dialogue, and decide how you would 'phase out' the model. Which words would you erase from the blackboard first? Underline them and write the number 1 next to them. Do the same for the second, third etc. erasings.

Tim is miserable. He's got a splitting headache, terrible toothache, and a very bad cold.

Father: Tim, you must take a couple of aspirins.
Mother: And you must lie down for a while.
Father: You must arrange an appointment with the dentist.
Mother: And you must brush your teeth more often.
Father: You must take something for your cold.
Mother: And you mustn't go out tonight. You must stay in bed.

Tim: Oh, parents!

(adapted from *Structures in context*, N. Sikiotis, Longman page 31)
Compare your results with those of another teacher.

2 Make a list of the techniques and activities suitable for weak learners that you have mentioned in this chapter. Can you add any others of your own?

3 An overall lesson may be based on a text as a starting point, for the development of passive understanding initially and then for development into structure work. Write out a plan for such a lesson based on the following text. Try to incorporate techniques that have been mentioned in this chapter.

A fashion show
Caroline is wearing a short skirt and a blouse. The skirt is blue and the blouse is red. She is carrying a blue handbag and she is wearing blue shoes. Marlene is wearing a long skirt and a jacket. The skirt is black and the jacket is white. She is carrying a black handbag and she is wearing white shoes.

Recommended further reading
1 *Teaching English to less-able learners*, Raphael Gefen ELTJ XXXV No.2 Jan.1981.
2 *Teaching learners of various ability levels*, Mary Finocchiaro ELTJ XXXIII No.1 October 1978.

Dealing with large classes

In the introduction to this chapter we suggested that classes of over 45 learners would demand special teaching techniques and would present the teacher with numerous problems. Many of you may disagree with this very arbitrary lower limit to what might be designated a large class, and we appreciate that it is impossible to give any kind of realistic and meaningful definition. A class of thirty in a restricted space may present the teacher with many more problems of management and organization than a class of fifty in a large and well appointed classroom. Lack of adequate space may well have a more damaging effect on teaching style than just additional numbers.

Activity

Attempt your own definition of a large class in relation to your own average teaching situation and compare it with other definitions proposed by other members of your group. Consider also the teaching level.

Although we cannot state with any certainty that some teaching techniques are possible and others not in a large class, we can think in terms of what is likely to be encouraged or discouraged.

Activity

Indicate with a tick below those language skills and teaching techniques which you believe to be encouraged or discouraged by what is, according to your definition above, a large class.

	Encouraged	Discouraged
Listening comprehension		
Dictation		
Language songs		
Reading aloud		
Reading comprehension		
Chorus work		
Mechanical drills		
Role-play		
Group-work		
Pair-work		
Using a wall picture		
Language games		
Written exercises		
Oral composition		
Written composition		
Grammar exercises		
Dramatization		
Lecturing		

The main problem is really very obvious; the individual learner is in serious danger of being denied sufficient time for speech and, consequently, of spending a great deal of time listening to teacher talk. A secondary problem, related to this lack of time, is that there is the great danger that the learners and their teachers lose the sense of community. It is less easy for the teacher to remember names so that the lesson tends to become somewhat impersonal. Only the most skilful of teachers can maintain a good rapport within a very large classroom; learning can become boring and over-formal; the friendly chat (in English we hope) at the beginning of the lesson is less appealing and the flashes of humour less likely. In other words, the teacher is encouraged to use 'transmission' type of teaching and to adopt a lecturing role.

What then can the teacher do with his class of fifty students? We believe that there is very little he can do which has not been already discussed; that is, there is no *separate* methodology for the handling of large classes. What we propose is first the recognition of the dangers already outlined and then a more careful selection of appropriate teaching techniques and strategies. With the latter in mind, we shall discuss several approaches and suggest some accompanying activities.

A Teaching room

The ideal teaching room is large enough to accommodate all the students' desks (or tables and chairs) and allow sufficient extra space for such activities as dramatization and role-play. It is not a square or rectangle in shape, but has instead a more irregular outline with alcoves to serve as quiet areas or group areas.

Activities

1 Draw a diagram showing the floor plan of such a room.

2 Indicate how you would use such a space for a class of fifty during a single period.

You may prefer to leave these activities until you have finished this particular section.

B Pair-work

It is tempting to dismiss pair-work as impracticable with such a large class, but remember that the additional noise is much more obvious to the teacher than to the pairs themselves; they will not be aware of any great increase in noise and will be able to continue with their exchanges in the usual way.

However, there are other considerations (such as the class next door perhaps) and it might be useful then to restrict pair-work to half the class at any one time.

C Class sections

Where possible, modify the class organization rather than the teaching method. It is often very helpful to have two established sections in the classroom so that the teacher can direct his attention to just one of them from time to time. Chorus work might have to be restricted to a section activity. We are, of course, getting closer and closer to group-work, which makes such heavy demands on the teacher's organizational ability.

Activity

Outline a lesson plan which would make use of such a class division and allow the usual oral and writing activities.

D Group-work

There is a tendency for the EFL teacher to be much more dominant in his teaching style than is the case with his counterpart who teaches English as a first language. For the latter, group-work, as opposed to the class lesson, has been the order of the day for some years now, and we may have a great deal to learn from this more flexible approach.

Question

A great deal of group-work is linked to the so-called discovery method of learning. Groups work on small projects using a variety of source material, and the teacher's role is largely that of provider and organizer of material. To what extent can this method be used in EFL teaching?

If groups are set up, they should look like groups; they should not be set up by simply isolating different rows. Students should be grouped together around a table and should form the structure of a group with their own leader. The leaders should be the most competent in the class and should be able to form a demonstration group with the teacher whenever necessary.

Question

Bearing in mind that a large class is almost certain to contain a number of ability levels, do you think the group should be streamed accordingly, or should they be of mixed ability? If the group is of mixed ability, do the members necessarily have to work on the same material and at the same level?

We have already pointed out that group-work makes heavy demands on the teacher as organizer, especially if material has to be prepared at different levels. It would be intolerable if a language teacher had a succession of such large classes to contend with. Whereas he appreciates that weaker learners will require more of his time, that mixed-ability classes will require additional planning and that resources must often be less than adequate, he may feel with some justification that very large classes are an administrative convenience at the expense of the learners' progress and his own professionalism. That is, there is the danger that strategies, such as group-work, will not be effectively attempted because of an underlying belief that the situation ought not to exist.

Activities

1 Here is one possible model for the organization of group-work within a class of 56 at an intermediate level:

A LISTENING COMPRE-HENSION USING TAPE-RECORDER JUNCTION BOX IF AVAILABLE	**B** READING COMPREHENSION (LOWER LEVEL)
C READING COMPREHENSION (HIGHER LEVEL)	**D** WRITING ACTIVITY (HIGHER LEVEL)
E LANGUAGE GAME (e.g. taken from: D. Byrne *It's your turn* Modern English Publications 1980)	**F** WRITING ACTIVITY (LOWER LEVEL)

G ORAL ACTIVITY DIALOGUE (In alcove or 'quiet corner' if available)

Group A
Select a suitable passage for the listening comprehension and devise an exercise based on it which will require the group to write down the main verbs in a list and then fill in blanks around them in order to produce meaningful sentences.
What is the main disadvantage in having a group of eight learners working with a tape-recorder?

Group B
Select a suitable passage and design a multiple-choice test to assess simple understanding of the passage.

Group C
Using the same text as for Group B, write five open-ended comprehension questions.

Group D
Outline three writing activities which would be appreciably more difficult than the activities for Group F.

Group E
Choose an appropriate language board-game and outline your objectives.

Group F
Give an example of a paragraph-writing exercise based on a guided composition technique.

Group G
Write a brief dialogue for this oral activity, indicate how you would use it and what the follow-up would be.

2 How would you deal with (a) individuals who finish early and (b) groups that finish early?

3 If you were organizing this type of group activity, how would you use your time during the lesson?

4 Indicate the role of the group leader in each activity.

Group-work is a fragmenting influence in the class; it causes a certain loss of the sense of community already referred to. There must be ample time for handling the class as a single unit and groups must be allowed to interact one with the other. There will be times when one group will perform for the whole class – Group G might well act out their dialogue for the whole class at some stage. It will be vitally important for the teacher to learn and use the pupils' names, and this may necessitate the initial use of name cards.

E Team teaching

If the problem causing large classes is lack of accommodation rather than lack of staff, working closely with a colleague may be a useful approach. Two teachers working together can demonstrate language functions very effectively and can then share the normal teaching responsibilities. Again, the size and shape of the teaching room is of considerable importance.

Activity

One model for team teaching with a large class is for one teacher to present the new material to the whole class, then both teachers to work with a section each and for the second teacher to do a general conclusion for the whole class again.

Using this model, or any other, outline a lesson plan, simply indicating the teachers' roles and the work to be undertaken by the two sections.

R.S.A. Certificate for Overseas Teachers of English – examination question.

A class of 60 secondary school students is a large teaching unit. Describe activities which you have found effective in breaking up the whole class.

Dealing with mixed ability classes

All teachers will surely admit that very weak classes and very large classes pose serious problems and make language learning and teaching arduous and frustrating. But what about mixed ability classes? Should they be included in our list of problems requiring special techniques and expertise? Perhaps you feel that the mixed ability class is the norm and, therefore, already covered in Chapters 2 and 4. We must then define what we mean by *mixed ability* here, and to do so we shall return to Gefen's classification of learners. For our present purposes, a mixed ability class is one that contains within it students from at least *three* of his categories of *very able*, *able*, *less able* and *unable*. Although the very able will undoubtedly make excellent progress come what may, and the unable group, with equal certainty, make little or no headway, the fate of the larger middle groups will depend a great deal on the teacher's ability as an organizer.

Question

Comment on Gefen's classification. To what extent do you accept it? What, in particular, is your reaction to the label given to the fourth category? Does it perhaps owe as much to the demands of euphony as to reality?

Whatever your response to the question, we shall retain the classification, but with a degree of caution. With this very wide ability-range the traditional class lesson is a non-starter; all the basic ingredients for group-work are present in the situation. Indeed, the groups themselves would appear to have been already formed. It would be very tempting to set up four groups to coincide with the four levels; the very able students would form the elite 'express' group and would forge ahead, the unable group could do some useful copying and colouring and the middle groups could get on with some solid work and have a great deal of teacher attention. Tempting it may be, but is it just a little too tidy? Should we not explore other more flexible grouping arrangements and take other factors into consideration? The following activity will give you an opportunity to experiment with a number of theoretical group formations.

Activity

Suggest grouping arrangements as specified below for this class of 26 students of very mixed ability. They are all aged from 13 to 14 and you are given a certain amount of information about them.

A	Girl	Excellent all round – Not very popular
B	Girl	Very able – Great extrovert and well liked
C	Boy	Very able – Shy and stammers a little
D	Boy	Very able
E	Girl	Very able but rather quiet
F	Boy	Able – Very popular and a fine athlete
G	Girl	Able but with rather poor spelling
H	Girl	Able
I	Boy	Good when motivated, otherwise tends to be lazy
J	Boy	Quite good but very disruptive at times
K	Girl	Fair
L	Boy	Fair – Badly behaved and a bad influence on 'J'
M	Boy	Fair – Keen but makes many mistakes – A bad listener
N	Girl	Rather weak and very shy
O	Girl	Less able and shows little interest
P	Girl	Less able – Her constant companion is 'O'
Q	Girl	Less able – Absent a great deal
R	Boy	Less able – Claims that English is of no use to him – Fair in other subjects
S	Boy	Less able – A bully and a very disruptive influence
T	Boy	Very weak but appears to be interested – Very keen on fishing
U	Boy	Very weak but interested – Had a long absence from school following a serious accident
V	Girl	Very weak – Not interested
W	Boy	Unable – Very much under the influence of 'S'
X	Girl	Unable – Causes many problems because of bad behaviour
Y	Boy	Unable – Should be in a special school
Z	Boy	Unable – Very low intellect – A reading age of about 7 in his first language

1 Indicate the composition of four groups at different levels of ability and appoint group leaders.

2 Comment briefly on your placing of 'T', 'U', 'M', and 'F'.

3 Make up a remedial group and then place the other students into three groups of mixed ability.

4 What criteria did you use for setting up the mixed ability groups?

5 What are the advantages and disadvantages of setting up a remedial group?

6 Are there certain activities that would allow you to dispense with groups and have the whole class involved?

7 Would you want to change the composition of the groups for different language activities?

8 Draw a classroom plan showing the composition of four mixed ability groups. Indicate group leaders and comment briefly on the placing of 'L', 'S', 'W', 'X', and 'Y'.

When we examine the advantages and disadvantages of one kind of grouping over another we are really concerned with streaming as opposed to non-streaming. Where there is streaming within the class, groups can work with material which is appropriate to their level and can do so by means of useful discussion. Where there is no streaming, where, for instance, 'B' is sitting next to 'C', the former can certainly be of enormous assistance to the latter, but what kind of dialogue is 'B' going to have at her own level? We must not isolate a good student from the stimulating conversation of her peers. It may be useful to think of mixed ability grouping in terms of pairs rather than individuals. Consider the following group:

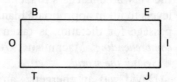

Such a group has certain advantages. 'B' is still in a position to help motivate 'O' and can talk across the table to 'T'. She can also work at her own level with 'E' and possibly be a good influence on 'J'. Of course, it is unlikely that the other three groups will work out quite as nicely as this one.

Thus, we have seen that the teacher's first task is to organize groups that are either representative of different ability levels, or mixed so that each is a small cross-section of the class as a whole. Whichever approach is adopted, individual students will require material and presentation which is at their level. It was suggested in the section on weak classes that the less able learners have rather more trouble with the production of language than with its reception. If this is true, then the *initial* presentation of new material, or the general introduction to the lesson, can be done with the whole class. If, for instance, a picture is to be used (such as one of the Donn Byrne and Douglas Hall wall pictures, Longman 1975), the whole class can join together in its first reaction to the picture. It is fairly easy to grade questions at this stage – 'What is the little boy doing?' contrasting with 'Why do you think the shop assistant looks worried?'. Later activities related to the same picture will need to be graded in a much less 'off the cuff' style, and it is at this stage that group-work becomes something of a problem for the busy teacher. Teacher-produced material is very demanding on time and energy and it will not be possible to cater in this way for each lesson. It is necessary to have a wide choice of books and visuals, especially graded readers, and it is very necessary for the teacher in this situation to be given adequate time for preparation and good facilities for duplicating.

We shall devote the remainder of this section to an overview of some graded material and techniques for using it. We shall also implement our 'escape clause' and consider just three ability levels, freely admitting that those learners designated 'unable' cannot possibly be given normal foreign-language activities. You may, of course, disagree and such disagreement may very understandably stem from your prior rejection of the label itself.

A Dictation

The value of this activity has been noted a number of times already. It is flexible enough to be used in a mixed ability situation, allowing the very able learners to tackle the entire passage and the other two levels to fill in appropriate blanks in their own copies. The following passage for dictation is taken from Combe Martin, *Listening and comprehending*, Macmillan 1970:

Seeing the world

David was an energetic, ambitious young man / who lived in a remote village in Yorkshire / where there was little for him to do to earn a living. / He ran errands for the local farmers,/ delivered newspapers for the village shop / and helped his parents who ran a small, picturesque hotel./ One morning he announced he was going to leave home and see the world./ His father was very upset / and reminded him that the money he had saved would not last very long./ But David insisted,/ telling his parents that they need not worry / as he was sure he would be able to manage.

Level A (very able)

Lexically, this is quite a difficult passage and is certain to be a challenge even at this level. These students should do it as a straightforward dictation first and then use it for follow-up activities.

Level B (able)
This level could do a partial dictation. Certain structural words and content words would be missing from their copies of the dictated passage and they would have to be put in.

Level C (less able)
In this case, students would have the complete passage in front of them, but there would be multiple-choice frames within the text and they would indicate the word, or phrase, which they thought they had heard.

Activity

Redesign the above passage so that it can be used for Levels B and C as outlined.

Questions

How would you organize the three groups for this activity? Would you keep them as mixed groups or not? Could they be mixed for correcting the passage, bearing in mind that level C has all the answers?

B Reading comprehension

We shall make use of the same passage to illustrate levels of comprehension and ways of encouraging members of the group to help each other. In using the same passage, however, we must be aware of the danger that the material itself could be too difficult for the third level, but this is an area where the group can help itself.

Although the passage has a number of difficult words in it, and the opening sentence has a fairly complex grammatical structure, it is not too difficult from the point of view of content and concepts. Young people are interested in reading about other young people with a sense of adventure and a desire to leave home.

Before giving out work cards to the groups the teacher could introduce the material as follows:

1 Class discussion of the general theme. The passage goes on to describe David's problems in London before he eventually met a friend who helped him to get a job on board a cargo ship.
2 Dealing with difficult vocabulary by making the fullest possible use of the very able students. It may be necessary to use some first-language equivalents at this stage.

3 Group discussion based on a few very general questions put on the board by the teacher. Again, the more able students will assist the weaker ones.

(a) What kind of person was David? (Group leaders will *not* accept 'an energetic, ambitious young man'.)

(b) Why didn't he have any proper work?

(c) Why was his father worried?

(d) If you were David's friend what advice would you give him?

4 Use of work cards at appropriate level. Although firmly based on an understanding of the passage, the questions would encourage a variety of different activities.

5 Follow-up work and more extended writing.

Sample work cards

WORK CARD A

1 What sort of activity is suggested by the phrase *ran errands*?

2 Why do you think the writer uses the word *announced* rather than *said*?

3 Suggest the actual words David might have used when he made his announcement.

4 Do you think they would have been any different if the writer had used *said*?

5 Describe the father's attitude.

6 To what extent do you think David's decision was inevitable?

7 Work with a partner and write a short dialogue between David and his father. Be prepared to act it later.

WORK CARD B

1 Suggest three errands that David might run for the local farmers.

2 Guess David's age and give your reasons.

3 How do you think David made contact with the local farmers?

4 Give another phrase with about the same meaning as *see the world*.

5 Why did David have very little money?

6 What do you think David's actual words were when he insisted that he wanted to leave home?

7 Complete the following dialogue between David's parents:

Mother:	You look upset, dear. Is anything wrong?
Father:	David has just told me ....
Mother:	Oh no. .... him not to go?
Father:	I've ... but ... determined ....
Mother:	Let me ....
Father:	I don't think ....

WORK CARD C

1 David did not have a proper job because he was lazy.   TRUE ☐
                                                           FALSE ☐

2 Energetic means
   (a) lively
   (b) unhappy
   (c) selfish
   (d) quiet

3 David was an ambitious young man. What was one of his ambitions?

4 David delivered newspapers for the village shop.
This sentence means
   (a) He brought the newspapers to the shop.
   (b) He was the shopkeeper.
   (c) He worked for the shopkeeper.
   (d) He read many newspapers.

5 Did David have a lot of money?
Answer: Yes, he did because ....
   or   No, he didn't because ....

6 What was David's father's work? What was his mother's work?

7 Complete this conversation between David and his father:

   David: Dad, there's something I want to tell you.
   Father: Yes, what ... it?
   David: You know that I ... find any ... here.
   Father: Well, you ... for the local farmers and you ... the newspapers.
   David: I mean ... work. So, I'm ... home. My ambition is ...
   Father: But you ... money for that. ... with us for another year.
   David: No, Dad, I ... go. I ... stay.

Activities

1 Specify three follow-up activities and indicate how you would present them at two or three levels.

2 Choose a suitable passage and prepare two sets of work cards at Levels A and C (very able and less able).

3 Outline a 40-minute lesson plan for a mixed ability class. Indicate clearly which elements will be for the whole class and which for the groups. Use only two levels (you may have 5 or 6 groups of course) if you think it is more realistic for your situation.

Question

How would you deal with individuals and groups that finish early when you are still busy giving attention to others?

Follow-up suggestion

You might consider using a pop record at this stage. A record by Cat Stevens, *Father and Son*, has very appropriate lyrics. The words are sung very clearly and most students will enjoy the music. You will think of various ways of using the material.

C Writing

Weaker students have many problems when it comes to writing. In oral work they can often stumble through and come up with an adequate response after suitable prompting, but errors in written work are semi-permanent and can be very demoralizing. These students should be given writing activities that preclude serious error; there must be adequate control and guidance so that a measure of confidence can be gained. We have already discussed various stages of guided composition, from the use of simple structure cards for sentence building, through some of the more enlightened substitution tables to the framework essay. We shall not do more than reiterate the crucial importance of adequate support, and use our comprehension passage again as a brief illustration. A follow-up activity to it might be letter writing or a telephone dialogue. The three ability levels could be asked to write the sort of letter David might send his parents after a couple of weeks looking for work in London. The A level could discuss together how David could be reasonably truthful about his plight and yet minimize parental concern. Level B would write a fairly straightforward letter following discussion with the teacher; they might be given a few ideas. Level C would do the letter as a completion exercise. At least one letter from each group would be read out to the whole class.

Cloze exercises lend themselves quite well to multi-level work. Again the same passage can be used if well chosen. Level A could tackle an exercise with each 7th word deleted, level B could have every 10th word deleted (or the teacher could delete selected words) and level C could make use of a modified cloze exercise and be given multiple choice frames. On the other hand, if multiple choice items are not used the teacher can save considerable time by duplicating the same passage for all students and deleting appropriate words for each group by covering them with sticky paper or cutting them out with a razor blade.

Activity

Use the comprehension passage again and indicate clearly how you would use it at two or three different levels. Note that if you use each seventh word for deletion, one of them will be *picturesque*. Is there a case here for just a little bit of cheating?

D Drama

This is a blanket term that covers a wide range of oral activities that have an element of creativity present. If students are using a simple dialogue that they have written themselves the creativity is obvious, but even if they are reading someone else's lines, with at least one other person listening and watching, they are being creative. Dialogues and small plays are very useful indeed in mixed-ability situations because major and minor roles are so natural. Also lines can be learnt and rehearsed to give confidence to the weaker speakers. At the other end of the scale, able students can improvize and project their own personalities. The different levels can, of course, be mixed; as long as the more able student ends with the right cue for the less able to come in and read his part, he can improvise all he wants. Let us look at an example, a fairly simple one with just two characters. A rather pompous lady is complaining to a shop assistant about a pair of shoes she bought the previous week. For our star performers we shall return to our mock class, giving the pompous lady's part (Mrs Cross) to 'B', who should do it great justice, and the assistant's part (Mr Heel) to 'R'.

Mr Heel:	Can I help you, madam?
Mrs Cross:	You certainly can. Do you recognize these?
Mr Heel:	Well, they're a pair of lady's shoes.
Mrs Cross:	And what about this?
Mr Heel:	It's a broken heel. How did it happen?
Mrs Cross:	How did it happen indeed! I bought them here last week and wore them for the first time when ... husband tried to repair them ... brought them back, shop closed ... must have been faulty ... should be given money back ... *What are you going to do?*
Mr Heel:	Were they the right size for you?
Mrs Cross:	Of course they were ... I want to *see the manager*.
Mr Heel:	I'm afraid he's out.

Activity

Either finish this dialogue or write your own along similar lines.

In this brief section on mixed ability classes we have examined criteria for setting up groups, ways of presenting new material to the class as a whole and techniques for providing appropriate activities to coincide with levels of ability.

We have said nothing about teacher attitude, but it can be the decisive factor in a mixed ability situation. Where there is a sense of community within the classroom and a genuine desire to help, there can be real progress at all levels. If we have to use emotive labels and terms, then *disability* may be much more meaningful and productive than *inability*. At least, it suggests the need for help.

Bibliography

Dealing with weak classes
Teaching English to less-able learners, R. Gefen in ELTJ Vol.37, No.2
Teaching oral English, Donn Byrne (Longman)
Argonauts English course Teacher's Book 1, W.R. Lee & L. Koullis (O.U.P.)
Signpost Book 1, E. Austen *et al.* (Nelson)
Structures in context, N. Sikiotis (Longman)
Teaching learners of various ability levels, Mary Finocchario in ELTJ Vol.33, No.1.

Dealing with large classes
It's your turn, Donn Byrne (Modern English Publications)

Dealing with mixed ability classes
Teaching English to less-able learners, R. Gefen in ELTJ Vol 37 No 2
Wall pictures for language practice, D. Byrne & D. Hall (Longman)
Listening and comprehending, M.H. Combe Martin (Macmillan)

Appendix

Practical suggestions on lesson planning

The authors feel very strongly that the planning of a lesson is a highly personal undertaking: only the teacher knows what he can do and what his students are like. We feel, therefore, that it is dangerous and wrong to prescribe what form a lesson should take. This is something that only the teacher can decide.

However, since many teachers ask for help in lesson planning, the following suggestions have been set out in the form of a checklist. These suggestions are based on experience gained by watching many lessons ranging from 'highly impressive' to 'poor', taught by non-native speaking teachers of English, and by discussing the lessons with the teachers afterwards.

Aim: What is to be taught?

1 Decide on the main teaching point. This may be a new structure (pattern). If so, isolate the *use* (or uses) to be focused on. (See Chapter 5.) Or it may be a particular function expressed by more than one form. (See Chapter 8.) In either case, list the forms that are to be included. Alternatively, you might decide to make your main teaching point the teaching of a particular skill (reading, writing, listening, or some other activity). In this case, there may not be any major new language items to be included, but remember that the lesson should still have some focal point or main aim, and that there should be an attempt to balance the different types of activity included in the lesson. (For suggestions here, see Chapter 2.)

2 Which stage of practice is to be attempted with the patterns isolated above (if patterns are to be part of the main teaching point)? (Controlled, freer, completely free?) This will determine the types of activity to be included. (See Chapter 6 or Chapter 2 here.)

3 Choose a suitable situation or situations for the activities you have in mind. (See Chapter 5.) If the situation is already

determined by your textbook, think of ways of setting or introducing this situation.

4 What new *lexical* items (or lexical sets) fit in with this (these) situation(s)? (See Chapter 5.)

5 What *phonological* problems or teaching points should be included? (See Chapter 7.)

Activities: What are you going to do in the lesson?

1 Plan the stages to be followed in introducing and practising your main teaching point(s), bearing in mind what you have decided in 'Aims'.

2 Calculate the timing of these stages. Is there too much for your lesson? Is there time left over?

3 If the former, simplify your aims – make them less ambitious. If the latter, what extra activity could be fitted in? (Do you need a warm-up activity at the beginning? Could you add a brief activity at the end – a song or a game, for example?)

4 At this stage consider: Has your rough plan got a reasonable balance of activities? Different skills (reading, writing, speaking, etc. in the right proportion)? Variations of pace to suit the students' levels of concentration, tiredness at each stage of the lesson? If not, make suitable changes.

5 Finalize your rough plan and the timing of each stage. Write this out.

Aids: What aids are you going to use?
(See Chapter 3.)

1 Which are likely to be most effective?
2 Are they varied or attractive enough?
3 Are you making full use of them?
4 Do not forget that the blackboard is an aid. Plan your blackboard work in detail.
5 List the aids beside each stage planned so far.

Anticipated difficulties: What could go wrong?

1 Try to guess which errors are mostly likely to occur. Why will these occur? Work out alternative strategies to sort these out. (See Chapter 4.)

2 If you have a 'difficult' class, you should look at Chapter 10 before planning your aims and plan a special lesson for your group.

3 If there are likely to be serious phonological difficulties, work out some strategies for dealing with these briefly or include a suitable phonological practice activity. (See Chapter 7.)

4 Bear in mind that no lesson, however carefully prepared, works out exactly as planned. Flexibility in carrying out a plan is one of the signs of a good teacher. There is a danger in *overplanning* your lesson. To some extent you must rely on your experience and instincts to do the right thing when the unexpected occurs.

Now write out your plan in full, stating the aims at the top. Try to make it brief, clear and easy to follow while you are teaching.

General view: Is the lesson going to be a success?

Finally consider these general questions before committing yourself to teaching the lesson:

1 Are the students going to learn something in this lesson? (One hopes that this coincides with the stated aims above!)
2 Are they going to enjoy the lesson? Is it likely to be fun, varied and satisfying?
3 Does the lesson as a whole have a sense of coherence and purpose?
4 Does the lesson connect up with what went before? Is it building on previous learning?
5 Does the lesson lead the way to useful activities in later lessons? Is it opening up new areas of knowledge and practice?

Epilogue

During the last fifty years, for reasons which are not completely clear, English has emerged as the most sought-after language for foreign learners throughout the world. As the demand for effective English teaching has increased, the critical awareness of both teacher and taught has heightened. At the same time, the commercial value of English tuition as a commodity has initiated competition for more effective methods and materials; and, as a consequence, more money has been funnelled into research and development.

Independently of these pragmatic moves, important break-throughs in academic disciplines concerned with the nature of language and language learning have pushed EFL into exploring new paths. The last fifteen years have seen developments that will be viewed in retrospect as a turning point in language teaching methodology.

It is not surprising, therefore, that the present mood in language teaching is one of restlessness and continuous movement. Nothing could be healthier for a profession. And in no other profession would one find so many young, critical and enthusiastic practitioners.

But because of this constant search for new directions in ELT, the teacher owes it to his profession to keep abreast of developments. The only way to do this is to read the articles and books that come out; and to attend local, national and international conferences.

The teacher who has read patiently through the chapters in this book will realize that the authors have been concerned above all that teachers should think for themselves and never accept any idea on trust. The wealth of scientific expertise and practical experience which we have inherited constitutes a technology. But it is a technology developed in the classroom, as well as from abstract theories about language and education. The teacher must make his own contribution by critically examining each new technique or method and by having the courage to voice his criticisms. Furthermore, he must experiment with each new technique that is suggested and develop some of his own. The teacher who settles for a certain repertoire of techniques and does not continually strive to expand it, will find his teaching becoming mechanical and lifeless. His students will sense this and lose enthusiasm for learning.

Teaching languages (and perhaps all teaching) should be regarded as a never-ending experiment for both teacher and students, with both parties intensely interested in the outcome.

Finally, there is the simple fact that a teacher in a class is a human among humans. No sophisticated techniques, nor libraries of books on methodology, will help the teacher who fails to understand that students *do* have problems learning languages and that it is his responsibility to try to solve these problems. Only by mentally putting himself in their place will he achieve insight into his own effectiveness as a teacher. And, in the process, he will find that he has generated the right kind of atmosphere for happy and productive language learning.

Cyprus, May 1981

Glossary

(Items appear in alphabetical order.)

approach   An *approach* to language teaching involves commitment to a particular theory about language or learning.

appropriacy   Choosing the most suitable of a number of nearly synonymous expressions for the occasion in question. The appropriate choice depends on factors such as the relationship between speakers, the topic under discussion and other circumstances of the interaction.

aspiration   In English, initial **voiceless** plosives (/p//t//k/) are *aspirated*. *Aspiration* as much as **voicing** distinguishes these sounds from /b//d//g/.

audio-lingual approach   Based directly on **behaviourist learning theory**, this **approach** assumes that language learning can be broken down into a series of individual habits, which can be formed (**habit formation**) by **reinforcement** of correct **response**. In practice, this **approach** gives rise to **methods** consisting largely of repetition and **pattern** drilling. The **approach** also places emphasis on the ordering of the skills – listening, speaking, reading, writing – and the need for maximum **error prevention**.

authentic material   Samples of language that are real, not produced specially for language teaching. These could be written or recorded on tape.

backchaining   Teaching pronunciation of a **pattern** by getting students to repeat successively longer portions of it, starting with the last part and extending backwards to the beginning. This technique eliminates the distortion caused by attempting to chain it forwards.

behaviourism   Unlike **mentalists**, *behaviourists* restrict themselves to studying only the externals of speech behaviour. Their analysis of language **use** is therefore entirely in terms of **stimulus** and **response**. (See **behaviourist learning theory**.) For *behaviourists*, ability to perform in the language is represented as the possession of a set of habits which enable a speaker to respond correctly to any given **stimulus**.

behaviourist learning theory   The theory that human and animal learning is a process of **habit formation**. A highly complex learning task can, according to this theory, be learned by being broken down into small habits. These are formed when correct and incorrect **responses** are rewarded or punished, respectively. Language is regarded by the **behaviourists** as a complex network of habits.

chain and choice   Two axes of language most easily pictured as:

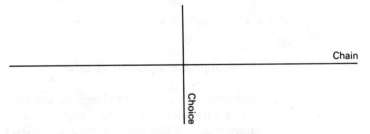

although this picture is sometimes misleading.

The horizontal axis represents the syntactic linking of words and phrases, and parts of words which are grammatically important (such as the plural *-s*), as they are strung together. **Errors** in the *chain* of language are those such as word order, lack of agreement, incompatible tense-adverbial and tense-tense combinations. **Errors** in the *choice* axis are incorrect choices of word or phrase in a given 'slot' in the sentence.

cloze test   A test where every n^{th} (5th, 6th, or 7th, etc.) word is removed from a passage. The student has to fill in the resulting blanks.

cohesion   The linking of sentences into logical sequence, especially in a written text, often aided by the use of linking and sequence expressions, such as *therefore, next, finally, on the other hand,* etc.

collocate   To be found together with. Especially used for **lexical items**. One **lexical item** can be said to *collocate* or not with another.

communicative approach   The *communicative approach* to language teaching takes as its starting point the **use** or communicative purpose of language. This **approach** therefore strongly advocates careful attention to **use** rather than merely **form/meaning**. It would also favour **functional-notional** organization of teaching materials. It might tend to support a 'deep-end' approach to **presentation** of new language, in which students are first to cope with the communication task as best as possible before being given the new, necessary **forms**.

competence   Knowledge of the grammatical and other rules of a language which enable a speaker to use and understand it. By definition a native speaker has perfect *competence*. (See **performance**.)

correction test   A test which asks the student to correct errors.

cue   The device used by the teacher (or another student) to elicit a **response** from a student while drilling. *Cues* may be verbal, visual, numerical, mimed or sound effects.

dialogue frame   A skeleton dialogue with slots in it where new words or phrases may be inserted. In its most controlled form, the *dialogue frame* is an extended four- or six-line **substitution drill**. In its freest form, it is highly open-ended and may result in a fairly genuine S – S conversation.

direct method   A **method** consisting of bombarding the student with samples of the target language, spoken by a native speaker, and encouraging him to imitate, respond and gradually participate as a speaker. It made the assumption that older students should learn in the same way as a child learns his mother tongue.

discrete   See **specific**.

distractors   The incorrect choices in a **multiple choice test item**.

eclectic approach   An **approach** which adopts any technique or procedure, so long as it can be shown that it results in successful learning.

error   As opposed to **mistake**, imperfect production caused by genuine lack of knowledge about the language (**competence**).

error prevention   The principle that students learn better by having correct **responses** rewarded, than by having incorrect **responses** punished. According to this principle, strong measures should be taken to ensure that each step is well within reach of the student, so that he has a very high chance of making a correct **response**.

extensive reading   Reading in quantity for information or enjoyment, without bothering to focus on every unknown **item** which occurs.

flashcards   Small pieces of card with pictures or words on them, used as teaching aids.

form   The actual words (written) or sounds (spoken) used to express something in language, as opposed to **meaning** or **use**. *Form* is often synonymous with structure.

four-phase drill   A language laboratory drill consisting of the following four phases: (1) Taped **stimulus**; (2) Student's **response**; (3) Taped correct **response** (= **reinforcement**); (4) Student's repetition of correct taped **response**.

free practice   In completely *free practice*, the teacher does not speak, interfere or attempt to control student production at all. Practice varies in the extent to which it is *free*. *Free practice* is sometimes called 'production'.

function   The *function* of a structure is the communicative purpose of that structure on a particular occasion – what the speaker is trying to do through language. For example, '*Have you read this book?*' may be present perfect interrogative in **form** but the speaker may be using it to make a *suggestion*, to suggest that the listener read the book. *Suggesting* is the *function* of the structure here. The **use** of a **form** can often be expressed in terms of *functions*.

global questions Comprehension questions requiring general understanding of the passage as a whole.

global test As opposed to **specific** or **discrete** tests, this is a test of the student's all-round knowledge of the language, and his language skills.

graded questions Questions on a comprehension passage, ranging from easy to difficult, in that order.

grading Putting language **items** in course materials into the best arrangement to maximize learning.

grammar-translation method The traditional deductive **method** of language teaching, based on classical studies of dead languages, which consisted of giving rules, **paradigms** and vocabulary and getting the students to apply this new knowledge to translation (to and from L_1) and to grammatical analysis.

group-work Independent work carried out simultaneously by groups of three or more students on a task or tasks.

habit formation The process of building up a habit by reinforcing behaviour when it occurs.

information gap The principle that two (or more) students engaged in a practice activity do not share exactly the same information. If the task is correctly set, the students must pool their information and are thus forced to communicate through English. The *information gap* is therefore an important element in many communicative practice tasks.

intensive reading Reading a passage in depth for complete comprehension and/or analysis.

intonation The rise and fall in pitch which accompanies an utterance. The phenomenon is related to sentence **stress**. Different *intonation* and sentence **stress** patterns can entirely change the **meaning** of an utterance.

intrusion test A test in which the student has to strike out words which should clearly *not* be included in a passage.

item A language *item* is a teaching point. A distinction is made between **structural, lexical** and **phonological** *items*.

key The correct choice in a **multiple choice test item**.

key questions The questions that the teacher uses to draw attention to the **meaning** or the **use** of the structure, to check whether the students have understood the **meaning** and/or the **use**.

L_1 First language; mother tongue.

L_1 **interference** The effect of mother tongue on a student's production of the L_2, causing errors through analogy with L_1.

L_2 Target language – the foreign language (often but not always the second language) being learnt.

lexical density   The opposite of **redundancy**. This occurs when the sense of the passage is highly dependent on the meanings of most of the words contained in it.

lexical item   A piece of vocabulary to be taught. Not only the **meanings** of new words, but also phrases, idioms, etc. *Lexis* = vocabulary.

lexical set   A group of words that have something in common, for example are related in **meaning** or belong to the same **situation**, subject matter etc. A word family.

lockstep   The traditional system of class management where the teacher is in control of every interaction and where only one interaction takes place at a time.

meaning   The conventional or literal *meaning* of a particular **form**: for example, that past tense **form** *means* past time. The purpose of traditional grammar books is to explain **form** and **meaning**. (Compare **use**.)

meaningful drill   A drill which cannot be performed correctly without an understanding of the meaning of what is said.

mechanical drill   A drill which requires students to produce correct examples of the language without needing to think about the meaning of the sentences (etc.) they produce, e.g. simple repetition or meaningless substitution.

mentalism   The *mentalist* view of language learning and use accepts the fact that speakers make conscious choices when they speak. Their use of language reflects their thoughts, which may be entirely original or unpredictable. Language use is therefore potentially creative. For *mentalists* ability to perform in the language results from knowledge of facts about (the rules of) the language. (See **competence**.)

metalanguage   Language used for talking about language, e.g. the grammatical terms, *noun*, *verb*, etc.

method   A language teaching *method* is a set of techniques or procedures. These usually follow a systematic scheme. Unlike an **approach**, a *method* need not be tied to any particular theory about language or learning, but may simply be claimed as successful in practice.

mistake   As opposed to **error**, a slip of the tongue etc. which the student can self-correct when challenged, because it is not caused by lack of knowledge (**competence**). A *mistake* is sometimes referred to as a '**performance error**'.

mixed ability classes   Classes containing a mixture of good, average and bad students, either in terms of their initial level in the language or in terms of their ability to learn a foreign language or study at all.

model sentence   See **pattern**.

multiple choice test   A test in which students have to answer by choosing one of a number of alternative answers (see **stem**, **options**, **key**, **distractors**).

notions   Concepts such as time, space, quantity, motion and all ideas related to these. E.g. for time, we have: point of time, duration, frequency, time relations, etc.

nucleus   The stressed syllable in an utterance, upon which the change of tune occurs.

OHP   Overhead projector – a device for projecting writing or pictures horizontally placed on transparent acetate sheets on to an overhead wall screen.

objective tests   Tests, such as **multiple choice tests**, which have the advantage that the marking does not depend on the subjective judgement of the marker, as a **test item** can be clearly marked 'right' or 'wrong'.

open-ended test item   A **test item**, such as sentence completion, which does not force any particular choice on students, as a **multiple choice item** does, but leaves it open to their imagination.

options   The alternative possibilities to choose from in a **multiple choice test item**.

overgeneralization   The tendency to apply a rule which has been learned beyond the extent to which it applies. E.g. if a student learns that the past tense in English is formed by adding -*ed*, he may overgeneralize, producing **errors** such as **goed*, **must worked*.

pair-work   Independent work by pairs of students working simultaneously on a task or practice activity. Often an extension of ordinary controlled practice or drilling, with more opportunity for students to talk, hence higher **STT**.

paradigm   A list of related grammatical **forms** to be learnt by heart, e.g. *take – took – taken*.

pattern   A **model sentence**, etc., which exemplifies a **structural item**. *Pattern practice* or *pattern drilling* is controlled practice in producing sentences which are modified versions (analogues) of a given *pattern*.

performance   What a speaker actually does when performing in a language, as opposed to what he knows of the language (**competence**).

Native speakers make lots of **mistakes**, even though their **competence** is perfect. *Performance* is therefore an imperfect realization of **competence**.

personalization   Extending practice based on a fictional **situation** into that based on the students' own knowledge, opinions, experience or personal lives.

phonological item   A teaching point concerned with the pronunciation of the language. This could be the contrast between two sounds, **intonation** patterns or phenomena such as word or sentence **stress**.

plausible reconstruction   An attempt to guess what the student was trying to write or say. An *implausible reconstruction* is a bad guess.

presentation   The process of introducing a new language **item** for the first time (including its **meaning**).

pre-teaching   Isolating a language **item** about to come up in a text and teaching this first.

realia   Real objects brought into class for teaching purposes.

realistic drill   A drill which is disguised to resemble a natural conversational exchange.

redundancy   Languages are said to be *redundant* in that not every grammatical, lexical or phonological feature is essential for the meaning to be conveyed clearly. Semantic aspects such as past time are invariably represented by more than one feature (e.g. an adverbial, *last week*, and a past tense, *went*). It is seldom therefore that a single linguistic **item** is crucial from the point of view of meaning. This has important implications for the teaching of comprehension skills, both listening and reading.

reinforcement   *Positive reinforcement* is reward; *negative reinforcement*, punishment. When **responses** to **stimuli** are consistently *reinforced*, a habit is formed (**habit formation**).

response   The behaviour observed to result in the presence of a **stimulus**.

STT   *Student Talking Time*, the amount of time in a class spent by the students talking.

selection   Choosing what **items** or aspects of language are to be included in language course materials.

situation   The (often non-linguistic) context in which language **items** occur. Usually a *situation* is established to make the **meaning** (or **usage**) of an **item** clear. Note that it is possible to establish a non-linguistic *situation* through words (e.g. by describing it verbally).

situational drill   A drill in which the **cue** is a **situation** to which the student must respond. Although it is still quite controlled it elicits a 'free' **response** from the student. A good drill for practising the **use** as opposed to the **form** of a structure.

sound linking   The phenomenon which occurs at the boundary between words, where sounds from one word meet sounds from the next, resulting in changes of sound quality, omission and addition of sounds.

specific   A *specific* **test item** focuses only on *one* teaching point at a time (= **discrete**).

specific questions   Comprehension questions testing understanding of **specific** details of a passage.

stem   The basic frame of the sentence containing the **multiple choice** which students have to choose between.

stimulus   The **cue** or signal which releases a bit of behaviour or a habit. A *stimulus* may be verbal, visual or presented through any of the other senses.

stress   Greater muscular effort expended on the articulation of parts of a word or sentence, giving an auditory impression of emphasis.

structural item   A grammatical teaching point. These are most often introduced in the form of **patterns**.

structural-situational method   A **method** consisting of drilling structural **patterns** within **situations** which ensure that drills are always **meaningful**.

substitution drill   The type of **pattern** practice where students are required to produce new sentences (etc.) by substituting new elements for parts of the **pattern** and modifying the sentence as necessary. Usually one element (one variable) is required to be changed at a time.

TTT   *Teacher Talking Time*, the amount of time in a class spent by the teacher talking.

task-oriented work   Activities where students are set a clear task to complete, as opposed to a practice activity, where students go on practising until told to stop.

team teaching   Two or more teachers working together as a team to teach a class (or classes).

test item   One single 'question' in a test (which may not of course be a *question*).

transfer   *Positive transfer* is the beneficial effect of having similarities between L_1 and L_2. *Negative transfer* (**L_1 interference**) is the bad effect of mother tongue on a student's production, causing **errors**.

usage   Refers to examples of language that are correct grammatically and have **meaning**, but which have no communicative value; in other words there is no reason why these examples should be produced, except as examples of **form** and **meaning**.

use   The way in which a speaker uses a particular language **form** to communicate on a particular occasion. The *use* of a **form** may be described in terms of its **function** or communicative purpose.

voicing   *Voiced* sounds are accompanied by vibration of the vocal cords in the larynx, as produced in all vowel sounds or when singing. Examples of *voiced* consonants are /b//z//g/. The vocal cords do not resonate during the production of *voiceless* sounds. Corresponding *voiceless* consonants are /p//s//k/.

weak forms   The phenomenon of changed vowel values in parts of certain common words when they are *not* stressed. E.g.: /wəz/ for /wɒz/, *was*.

work card or worksheet   A card or sheet of paper containing a task or tasks for a group, pair or individual to complete. May be prepared by the teacher or sometimes available commercially.

Index